THE GOALSCORERS

By the same author

100 Years of the F.A. Cup – The official Centenary History (Heinemann)

The Football Managers (Eyre Methuen)

Tony Pawson

THE GOALSCORERS

from Bloomer to Keegan

with a Foreword by the
Chairman of the Football Association
Professor Sir Harold Thompson

Cassell
London

CASSELL & CO. LTD.
35 Red Lion Square, London WC1R 4SG
and at Sydney, Auckland, Toronto, Johannesburg,
an affiliate of
Macmillan Publishing Co., Inc.,
New York.

Copyright © Tony Pawson 1978

All rights reserved. No part of this publication
may be reproduced, stored in a retrieval system,
or transmitted, in any form or by any means,
electronic, mechanical, photocopying, recording or
otherwise, without the prior permission of
Cassell & Co. Ltd.

First published 1978

ISBN 0 304 29855 7

Printed in Great Britain by
The Camelot Press Ltd, Southampton

Foreword

by Professor Sir Harold Thompson
Chairman of the Football Association

I am glad that Tony Pawson has written about goals and I wish his book success. In present English football they have become a scarce commodity, and unless the supply increases soon the malaise will get worse.

Many spectacular goals stay in my memory. One was a shot by that outstandingly promising wing half-back Duncan Edwards, killed tragically in the Manchester United air disaster. Playing at Wembley some twenty-five years ago he hit a half-volley at a distance of some thirty-five yards and left the goalkeeper helpless as the ball swerved away like a rocket into the top corner of the net. Another was when Bobby Charlton, gathering the ball some forty yards from his opponents' goal, sailed like some proud Spanish galleon through a fleet of players, finally to slash the ball with deadly skill left-footed along the ground to the far corner of the goal.

There were happy days too when Stanley Matthews, after outwitting all defenders, took the ball to the bye-line and switched it back on to the instep of an oncoming forward colleague for him to score a simple, orthodox but beautiful goal.

Yet the goal that I personally enjoyed most was scored by John Tanner at centre-forward in the 1951 Amateur Cup Final when, after tricking his opposing centre-half, he found the field clear, went on, and shot the ball with force and precision inches past the legs of the advancing goalkeeper; so that it rolled on – two or three seconds seemed like eternity – to hit the inside of the post, turn into the net, and make the score 2–0. Then, for the first time, I felt sure that Pegasus had won its first Amateur Cup Final, against the mighty Bishop Auckland.

In those days, when football was mostly played for the enjoyment of all, the Pegasus forward line was usually Tony Pawson, John Dutchman, John Tanner, Donald Carr and Jimmy Potts. As each week we faced another match, I would reflect that if no one else scored this time, Tony Pawson would, even with his head. And he often did.

HAROLD THOMPSON

Preface

Caught in the pressures and excitement of the early games of the 1958 World Cup Finals Danny Blanchflower, Northern Ireland's captain, was taken aback by a Brazilian journalist's comment, 'Brazilian football is too platonic, too devoid of passion. For us the ball is God. The goal does not matter.'

For a man whose world had just been spun violently on its axis by a goal which beat Czechoslovakia, and by the goals which then gave victory to the Argentinians, this was too much to bear. 'As the competition quickens towards the finishing tape even the Brazilians will learn that the ball is not God and the goal matters very much more. Each game becomes more tense and each goal explodes the highly charged atmosphere, changing feelings from joy to despair,' wrote Blanchflower in the *Observer*.

How right he was. Emotion over a goal was soon to lead to at least one Brazilian being carried away – on a stretcher. Poor Vava, after scoring against Russia, was off the field for five minutes, knocked out by the ecstatic embraces of his colleagues.

For today's commentators the goal is 'what the game is all about'. Naturally, then, the goalscorers are the kings of soccer just as the run-makers lord it over the cricket field. And there is this in common with both games that the most effective are not necessarily the most stylish to watch. Boycott's attraction lies mainly in his batting average, and goalscoring records too are sometimes held by the less graceful forwards, like Arthur Rowley.

Tostao scored a crucial goal against England in Rio in 1969 when lying on the ground. Ramsey remarked on it as if England had been unlucky to lose to such a chancy goal. 'What Ramsey does not know,' the Brazilian manager, Saldanha, told journalists, 'is that Tostao scores twenty goals a season sitting on his backside.'

England's hopes of reaching the World Cup semi-final in Mexico in 1970 were also dashed by an unusual goal. Germany's Uwe Seeler appeared to misjudge a deep cross, but the ball bounced off the back of his head to float over Bonetti. That vital equalising goal destroyed the possibility of a repeat of the joyous triumph of 1966 and may have destroyed Ramsey's career as England manager as well. Had it been anyone but Seeler who scored, this would have seemed an outrageous flick in the eye from the fates. But from Sweden to Mexico Seeler had spent a soccer career getting odd parts of his body to make contact with awkward balls which somehow ended in the net.

It is not how you score, but *how many* that matters and the scorers come in all shapes, sizes and styles. The goals count just the same whether it is a thunderous drive from Bobby Charlton, or the ball slid closely and quietly home by Jimmy Greaves.

This is a look at some of those who have had the 'knack'. The gift is so individual that it is hard to pass on, or to coach into a player unless he came out looking for goals as the midwife was still slapping his bottom. And if fewer have that inborn drive today the knack is even more priceless. There is nothing platonic about it. Only those with a passion for scoring can defeat the disciplined caution of the modern game.

Contents

Appendixes

Illustrations

Roll of Honour

Scorers of over 300 Goals in peacetime in English or Scottish League

Arthur Rowley (West Bromwich Albion, Fulham, Leicester, Shrewsbury)	434
Jimmy McGrory (Celtic, Clydebank)	410
Hughie Gallacher (Airdrie, Newcastle, Chelsea, Derby, Notts County, Grimsby, Gateshead)	387
William Dean (Tranmere, Everton, Notts County)	379
Hugh Ferguson (Motherwell, Cardiff, Dundee)	363
Jimmy Greaves (Chelsea, Tottenham, West Ham)	357
Steve Bloomer (Derby, Middlesbrough)	352
George Camsell (Durham City, Middlesbrough)	348
David Halliday (Dundee, Sunderland, Arsenal, Manchester City, Clapton Orient)	336
Vic Watson (West Ham, Southampton)	317
John Atyeo (Bristol City)	315
Joe Smith (Bolton, Stockport)	315
Harry Johnson (Sheffield United, Mansfield)	309
Bob McPhail (Airdrie, Rangers)	307
Harry Bedford (Nottingham Forest, Blackpool, Derby, Newcastle, Sunderland, Bradford, Chesterfield)	306

Five players have scored over 300 goals for one club, McGrory (Celtic) 397, Dean (Everton) 349, Camsell (Middlesbrough) 328, Atyeo (Bristol City) 315, and Watson (West Ham) 306.

Acknowledgements

My grateful appreciation goes to the goalscorers who have made the game such a pleasure to watch and to the odd goalkeeper who has made it such a pleasure to play. My thanks go also to the many players who have given me generously of their time and recollection. Especially I am grateful to Tom Finney, my early mentor in the arts of the game, to Joe Mercer, my former coach in my Pegasus days, and to Danny Blanchflower, with whom I covered the World Cup Finals in 1958 for the *Observer*.

I must also thank Billy Liddell and Eric Houghton, Billy Wright and Bill Slater, Walter Winterbottom and Alan Wade, all of whom gave me valuable advice. I could have been cursing John Arlott, who reeled off a list of important names omitted just as I thought I had finished, but thank him unreservedly since he at once supplied information and anecdotes about each.

For contributions I am grateful to Hugh McIlvanney to whom I devolved the Scottish chapter, and to Basil Easterbrook for his work on penalties. The Newspaper Library at Colindale was most helpful and I am grateful for extracts from the *Observer*, *The Times*, the *Daily Express*, the *Daily Mail*, the *Daily Telegraph* and the *Liverpool Football Echo*.

For converting my illegible writing into clear type my thanks to Marguerite Rogers. For research facilities I am grateful for the use of the F.A.'s extensive library. The following books have provided guidance or extracts:

The Football Annuals (Heinemann)
F.A. Year Books (Heinemann)

Rothmans Football Year Books from 1970/71 (Queen Anne Press)

Captain of Hungary by Ferenc Puskas (Cassell, 1955)

Cliff Bastin Remembers by Brian Glanville (Ettrick, 1953)

Encyclopaedia of Association Football (Purnell, 1972)

Football's All-Time Greats (Marshall Cavendish, 1974)

Jimmy Greaves as told to Clive Taylor (Nicholas Kaye, 1962)

Herbert Chapman on Football (based on *Daily Express* articles) (Garrick, 1934)

One Hundred Years of Scottish Football by John Rafferty (Pan Books, 1973)

Pegasus by Ken Shearwood (Oxford Illustrated Press, 1975)

Soccer: The Great Ones edited by John Arlott (Pelham Books, 1968)

Spurs by Julian Holland (Phoenix Sports Books, 1956)

World Cup by Brian Glanville and Jerry Weinstein (Robert Hale, 1957)

World Cup by John Camkin (Rupert Hart-Davies, 1958)

World Cup '66 by Hugh McIlvanney (Eyre & Spottiswoode, 1966)

World Cup '74: Official FIFA Report

FIFA Technical Study Report (FIFA, 1976)

My grateful thanks also to that knowledgeable collector of football facts, Dick Williamson, who was so helpful in providing statistics and assisting in research.

One

Where Have All the Goals Gone?

Shortly after the war I went with the England Amateur Team on a tour of Sweden. Our first match was against the Gothenburg Alliance – a combined XI from the teams in the area. The Alliance team had recently beaten a visiting First Division side and expected no trouble from amateurs. With rain making conditions difficult, however, we won by the only goal of the game.

At the dinner afterwards there was a series of speeches from our hosts, mainly explaining why we had not really deserved to win. We had won, it seemed, only because we were more used to playing in rain, because their players had been holding back in view of important League games coming up, because the ball had run unkindly for them, because of this, that and the other. Finally our Captain was called on to reply. Charlie Fuller of Bromley was a man of few words. 'I have sat here in amazement listening to you lot saying why you lost,' he said. 'I'll tell you why you lost. We put the ball in the net once and you didn't.'

That is what matters and the players who can do it have always been without price. 'Call them what you like,' said Crystal Palace's Bert Head when asked if he was going to buy 'strikers'. 'I am after the buggers who can score goals.' So was everyone else, but there have been very few of them on show in English football in the Seventies.

In the late Twenties, on my first day at preparatory school, I had the rules explained to me and was then let loose on a football field. There was only one objective in the game – to get the ball through the posts. At that time every schoolboy wanted to be a forward and the heroes we read about so eagerly were those who made or scored the goals: Alex James, Dixie Dean, or Hughie Gallacher. It was still the same in the Forties and Fifties with Finney, Matthews, Lawton, Mortensen,

Greaves, or Lofthouse to capture the imagination. In the mid-Sixties came the switch to defensive thinking, to the back four with its stifling effects on the outnumbered forwards' initiative and on the creative skills of the midfield players left with too few target men to aim at. With a decline in goals schoolboys have looked to other heroes, to Moore or Hunter, Brooking or Bremner, according to temperament.

Once the game becomes too important to lose, the natural developments are defensive. Former Wolves and England centre-half, Bill Slater, who is Head of Birmingham University's Physical Education Department, sees the trend as inevitable: 'I used to feel comfortable when we won one-nil, uneasy if we won four-three. The first was an indication that we had been well in control, but the goal-swapping seemed like a lottery, which you were likely to lose next time. As a professional you have to be concerned with winning and with leaving as little as possible to chance. Inevitably developments aim at eliminating mistakes, at playing it "safe".

'You cannot blame Jack Charlton for his management of a Middlesbrough side which scored only seven goals in their first ten matches in 1976. Their strength was defensive and by exploiting that they got the best possible return for themselves, thirteen points from their seven goals, leaving them third in the First Division. When they tried to play more attractively they started to slide down the table and you cannot expect players to relish that. Year after year it's the sides who give away few goals who win titles, not the ones who score the most.'

The effect of defensive tactics and defensive thinking can be traced in these two accounts of England *v.* Portugal matches, the first in Lisbon in 1947, the second at Wembley in 1974. What a world of difference in mood and method! This was the *Daily Telegraph* account by Frank Coles, when Portugal were annihilated by as good a forward line as has worn the England colours.

Sixty thousand people overflowed the crescent-shaped stadium in Lisbon which cost £300,000 and where everyone had a seat. As many women as men crowded into the arena and multi-coloured sun hats presented an unforgettable scene on this blazingly hot day.

The pitch was Wembley all over again and in ideal conditions England found their true form. Portugal, yards slower, could not hold the English attack in which Matthews was dashingly brilliant in the second half.

Finney supplied the answer to the left-wing problem and

Mortensen's dash transformed the whole line. Though England walked away with the game there were some disturbing features. The French referee, de la Salle, disallowed two perfectly good goals for amazing offside decisions and the rule regarding substitutes needs clarifying. With England four up in half an hour Portugal changed their goalkeeper and right back, though neither was injured. The game was held up while England officials protested in vain.

Never was the value of a quick goal better demonstrated on the Continent. In half a minute Mannion raced through on the right and Lawton headed a picture goal. Portugal never recovered from the shock.

In 12 minutes England were three up through Mortensen and Lawton. Quickly followed the best goal of the match and one of the most spectacular I have seen. Starting in his own half Finney beat four challengers, ran inside and rammed the ball home.

Before the interval Lawton completed his hat-trick from another fine Finney run. Finney was soon in the picture again, beating three men only to hit a post. Within quarter of an hour Mortensen made it six and the next minute Lawton scored his fourth, both from brilliant Matthews runs.

With half an hour to go many thousands of disappointed Portuguese were leaving the ground. A third Matthews masterly movement gave Mortensen the chance to complete a hat-trick and then he ran through from half-way to make it nine. Matthews fittingly completed the rout. The England team was: Swift (Manchester City), Scott (Arsenal), Hardwick (Middlesbrough), Wright (Wolverhampton Wanderers), Franklin (Stoke City), Lowe (Aston Villa), Matthews (Blackpool), Mortensen (Blackpool), Lawton (Chelsea), Mannion (Middlesbrough), Finney (Preston North End).

The Portuguese players were so disgusted with their own performance that they did not show up at the dinner afterwards. The disgust was differently expressed in 1974. Before the match it had been reported that Portugal were so alarmingly inefficient in their friendly against Switzerland that Don Revie had given the TV video-tape recording of the match a 'C' certificate – 'Censored' in case it might make the side over-confident. There was nothing in the 0–0 draw or the crowd's reaction to leave any confidence at all as England started their slide out of the European Nations Cup.

As David Miller recorded in the *Daily Express*:

The sweet music of clicking turnstiles became a discordant handclap last night as 85,000 disillusioned Wembley spectators gave Revie's 'new' England a resounding 'Thumbs down'.

After Portugal had stonewalled their way to a thoroughly dishonourable draw the England team gathered in the centre-circle only to be greeted by the chant 'what a load of rubbish'. The late breakthrough which saved England after an hour against Czechoslovakia never materialised and they were left floundering, frustrated and not a little discredited. The plain unpalatable truth for a crowd that had paid dearly for their tickets – and the truth for English football at large – was that the team was just not good enough.

The control and passing on a difficult pitch was not so good as Portugal's, never mind Holland. Worse still there were those in the team last night who seemed to accept the result as 'just one of those things'.

The reality of English Soccer – often too hasty, often too physical, sometimes tactically naïve – was suddenly revealed to Revie as it had been revealed to Sir Alf Ramsey a little over a year ago.

The writing at least had become more lively while the game had staled.

There is an infinite variety of tactical and technical changes to account for the sad decline. Goalkeeping has progressively improved with goalkeepers dominating the whole penalty area. Their agility is expressed not only in the saves, but in the cutting out of through passes and deep centres. It was a change first given impetus by Sam Bartram of Charlton, that most adventurous of goalkeepers, and it has further reduced the forwards' opportunity near goal. 'Dixie' Dean terrorised goalkeepers with his heading, but so many of the pictures show him nodding the ball home from a few yards out while the 'keeper is rooted to his line. He would not be given that freedom today.

Then there has been the steady reinforcement of the defensive walls. Oddly, that development started just after the end of the last war despite the Germans' demonstration that, in battle at least, the Maginot Line mentality is no match for those with a committed belief in the Blitzkrieg. But it is always easier to think in the static terms of defence than in the fluid, imaginative terms of creative attack.

The Swiss began the move with their 'verrou' system which had a brief vogue and fleeting success as forwards struggled against a defensive network in which the wing-half would mark the winger and the left back be free to act as a second centre-half. But at least the natural centre-half was permitted some of the attacking freedom which had once been his main role.

The Italians refined this with their 'bolt' defences while in Britain we progressed from Herbert Chapman's 'stopper' centre-half to Arsenal's retreating defence, not challenging in midfield, but falling back to form an impenetrable screen some eighteen yards out, to third backs and back fours and even to a sweeper behind the back four. Fewer forwards with less support were taking on more numerous and better organised defences.

Some decline in the forwards' scoring powers was inevitable, but the trend was aggravated in England by the loss of the particular ability which had both characterised and distinguished our forward play – certainty in shooting.

The foreigner might weave his pretty patterns in mid-field, but the English forwards had the sublime knack of putting the ball in the net. They were direct, purposeful and accurate, while the 'clever-clever' Continental players were too elaborate and too hesitant in front of goal. That was an article of faith in the Thirties that was justified in practice. That was the ability which won England two matches against the world's best, confirming the insular sense of superiority. When Spain beat England 4–3 in Madrid in May 1929 the memory of that first defeat by an overseas side was soon erased in a return at Highbury eighteen months later. Seven goals went past Zamora, the nervous goalkeeper billed as the best and most expensive in the world. Zamora could only admire the English finishing as Dean beat him once, while Crooks, Johnson of Everton, and Portsmouth's Smith, each put two past him in England's 7–1 win. The same sure finishing saw England win the 'battle' of Highbury in 1934 against an Italian team, which had won the World Cup a few months before.

Italy came to Highbury on 14 November 1934 as the World Champions. Yet within fifteen minutes they were three goals down and their towering centre-half Monti was out of the match. The ferocity with which they clawed themselves back into the game in the second half brought the game the title of the 'Battle of Highbury'. Incensed by what they regarded as an unfair tackle on Monti, pride injured by the early goals, the Italians played with such passion in the second half that they fought back to 3–2. It needed Arsenal's Wilf Copping, the iron man of English soccer, to contain them. *The Times* account, although partisan, looked soberly at the play and ignored the violence:

Monti, the Italian centre-half, was off the field before the first goal was scored and so, on paper, it looks as though the Italians were unfortunate to lose. Actually they were not. In the first fifteen minutes England scored three goals and not only won the match, but played such brilliant football that the Italians were forced into the parts of mere lookers-on. The English half-backs and forwards were allowed to continue with a smoothness and subtlety which made a difficult game look easy.

In the first minute of the match Drake broke through and was brought down in the penalty area. Brook took the kick and his shot was brilliantly saved by Ceresoli. This failure to take the lead made not the slightest difference to England, who continued to play the ball as if they had no opponents against them, and after eight minutes went ahead, as Britton placed a free-kick in the goal mouth for Brook to head it through. Almost immediately another free-kick was given just outside the penalty area and Brook was given another chance. He shot again with his left foot and this time Ceresoli had no chance of saving.

Monti and Hapgood at this point were both off the field, but Hapgood returned soon after a movement on the right wing had given Drake the chance to hook the ball into the net to give England her third goal.

As half-time approached it became obvious that the England right wing was not so good as it should have been. Bowden was always too willing to part with the ball and Stanley Matthews at outside right had not the pace to beat L. Allemandi. To be three goals down at half-time and to have only ten men to take the field for the second half, that needed courage and faith and the Italians proceeded to display not only good football, but a real fighting spirit.

That was the nearest *The Times* came to saying that the second half was something of a brawl with the Italian centre-forward, Meazza, snatching two goals. When he headed the second past Moss from a free-kick 'the crowd was wildly excited and emotional – anything might happen and the Italian section prayed for an equaliser. The English defence however remained staunch to the end and England's centre-half, Barker of Derby County, who played a brilliant game throughout, can congratulate himself as much on his control of Meazza as on his long constructive passes out to his wings.'

In his autobiography *Cliff Bastin Remembers*, Bastin's player's eye view accords with *The Times*'s that the 'battle' was not quite as violent as legend makes it. He attributed Hapgood's broken nose to his being deliberately elbowed in the face by Ferraris and he regretted the Italians resorting for a time to unfair tactics. This he ascribed to the shock of their being three goals down and to the degrading effect of the large incentives offered by Mussolini for an Italian victory. Bastin added, however, that reports of the game greatly exaggerated the unpleasantness and that he played in many 'dirtier' games, particularly against a rough Swiss side in 1939.

Ted Drake had come in as third choice centre-forward when Frank Tilson of Manchester City and George Hunt of Tottenham cried off. With Male also coming in for the injured Tom Cooper this was almost a home match for Arsenal, who provided seven of the side. And Bastin admitted they owed a lot to Wilf Copping. He quoted Jack Crayston, the other Arsenal wing-half, who was a spectator, as saying, 'If we play Italy again tomorrow there is only one half-back line to put out: Copping, Copping and Copping.'

Again the seven-goal match against Austria's 'Wunderteam', which had dominated Europe for two seasons, turned on England's better finishing. The match was played two years before the 'Battle of Highbury' and how close England came to defeat was recorded in this account in the *Observer* by J. A. H. Catton, the most authoritative football writer of his day:

When the Austrian eleven met England in mid-week officials and enthusiastic players from Holland to Turkey gathered at Chelsea. Even Stephen Bloomer, now in his sixtieth year, had his curiosity aroused and looked on with keen eyes. There has never been a more representative assembly at any game. This was a test of the relative capacity of England and Austria, the most formidable of any continental country. England just won, but the victory was far from convincing. . . .

Some express the opinion that England did not acquit themselves as they can. There is a football proverb that teams play as well as opponents permit. Even on this basis the Englishman must admit that the margin of supremacy was trifling when conditions did not favour the Austrians. They are not accustomed to good turf, to a sticky surface and to the bleakness of a December day in our island. They were soon two goals in arrear yet were merely beaten by 4–3. In two goals the Austrians were unfortunate though such experience is inevitable in manly and moving games with quick changes.

The old game, forwards advancing in a line, with the support of all the half-backs, was used once more. Not for years has such smooth combination been seen in this country. The Austrians could give each other the ball with the accuracy of a Bloomer passing to a Bassett. They always knew where each man was in position and positional play is 60 per cent of the art of football.

Again had the old country a centre-forward like Sindelar? In Vienna he is called 'Der Papierene', the man of paper. He is so light, with spindle shanks and narrow shoulders, that it would seem as if he could be blown aside. He has the elasticity that deceives. With perfect control of the ball – this was a common characteristic of the team – he served the wings with old-fashioned passes of the sweeping type. A dribbler full of wonderful footcraft, he was 'up' for the centres and quite busy among the defenders. He is not a crack shot, but the goal he got was due to close command of the ball at his toe and sure touch in placing.

The best goal-getter is usually Schall, the inside left. Small and sturdy, he is another to have power over the ball. He is known as the 'Freispieler' of the side, with his fellows trying to manœuvre so that Schall is free and unmarked. He is looked to as a man to shoot the goals, just as Dean of Everton was when he first appeared.

The Austrians scorned all modern crazes such as 'third back' and the W formation. Though beaten they took the honours of the game by their quality. Only constant practice can produce such combination and deft control. Most certainly ball practice is quite a minor part of a footballer's training in England and team work is supposed to grow as naturally as wild flowers. What fallacies are these! Skill in any game is the reward of constant striving.

One natural talent, carefully nurtured, still kept England in command, however: the strength and precision of their shooting. Appropriately, the decisive goal which checked the Austrian recovery was blasted home by Eric Houghton, the Aston Villa winger with a shot as powerful as Liddell's or Lorimer's. His free-kick glanced home off a defender who was 'left rubbing his head for some minutes'.

It was accurate shooting by Jimmy Hampson, the Blackpool centre-forward, which gave England their two-goal lead at half-time despite the efforts of goalkeeper Hiden, 'a tall fellow all arms and legs who would come striding out to the edge of his area'. But it was the speedy wingers Zischek and Vogl whose counter-attacks might have given Austria the game with better shooting in the middle. Zischek scored twice and prompted *The Times* to comment severely on our team, 'Most of the players are now too old for such matches and cannot keep pace with these faster, younger players.' Not until 1953 did the Continental game finally shatter the myth that England were still 'masters' and they 'pupils'. Puskas and his 'magical Magyars' gave the finest display of football ever seen at Wembley as England suffered her first home defeat from an overseas side.

1953 was the year the F.A. celebrated its ninetieth anniversary and the country found it had lost its football mastery. In two high-scoring games the rest of Europe showed they had overtaken us in skills, even those we had regarded as peculiarly English. The first of the celebration showpieces was a game against a FIFA eleven with the best of Europe's players, excluding the Hungarians, the Olympic champions, who would play us a few weeks later. This was the hint of the deluge to come.

Derek Ufton came into the side against FIFA, the only time he was capped for England and the first time he met the withdrawn centre-forward just becoming fashionable on the Continent. It was a puzzling experience which Ufton recalls. 'There was no chance in the two days of preparation to get to know how the rest played or wanted you to react. Odd little things also made me feel ill at ease. The only other new cap was Albert Quixall, the young wonder boy of the moment, who inevitably attracted all the attention. He was an outstanding player, and the fair-haired forward always seems to catch the eye on the field. So he was regarded as something special.

'At Charlton we were always serious and reserved on our way to a match and I felt out of place with everyone singing and joking on the ride to Wembley. The Press had told us they had watched FIFA training and that they were tubby and unfit, due to be beaten 5–1 at least. That seemed comforting in prospect, but made it the more worrying when, unexpectedly, they began to walk over us.

'Our Manager, Walter Winterbottom, had sensibly told me there was no time to try and change my style and I would have to play as I did with my club. That outstanding Swedish centre-forward Gunar Nordahl was the man I had to mark and I followed him when he went deep, because at Charlton I was trained to stay with the centre-forward. When Nordahl found I was containing him he began to play the ball back to his Austrian wing-half, Oczwirk, who instantly chipped the ball over my head. That meant we had no cover. Billy Wright and Jimmy Dickinson were attacking wing-halves, so it was up to the full backs. Alf Ramsey appreciated the danger and covered across, but Bill Eckersley, trained by his club in zonal marking, stayed wide on his wing no matter what his winger did. So the dangerous Boniperto stole into the centre and helped himself to goals, leaving us 3–2 down at half-time. In the dressing room I heard Eckersley saying loudly, "I'm not taking the blame for this bloody centre-half", which hardly helped my confidence. Walter came over and discussed it. We agreed it was not working out and I had better stay back and let Nordahl go. He created much panic in midfield, but we were better with the centre sealed.'

Only Zeman's poor goalkeeping and a dubious last-minute penalty, stroked home by Ramsey with impressive calm, let England get away with a 4–4 draw. That was only the preliminary oppressive roll of thunder before the team were struck by the lightning of the Hungarians. After the match Ufton was praised for a self-sacrificing performance and promised another game by the manager. But the unpredictable selection committee left him out of the next home international and of the match against Hungary. And it was Harry Johnston of Blackpool who had to face the deep-set wiles of Hidegkuti and be even more baffled by them.

Tom Finney was injured for that match, his place taken by George Robb of Tottenham, who had been my opposite winger in the England amateur team the year before. With a courtesy seat in the press box Finney was amused to be told by many of the pressmen, 'It will be the old story. We saw these Hungarians held to a draw in Sweden recently. They are clever enough in midfield, but we will win as usual because we can take our chances and they won't.' Finney, and those of us who watched them kicking in before the game, were less certain. For the Hungarians not only juggled the ball on thigh, boot or head with a subtlety not seen at Wembley before, but their practice shooting was fierce and true as the shots seared past Grosics. Perhaps in play it would all be different. One minute was all that was needed to show they would hit as hard in the match as in the shadow boxing before it. As Johnston still searched for the man to mark, Hidegkuti came gliding in from deep to arrow the ball past Merrick.

That Hungarian forward line still rates as the most graceful and deadly that any country has fielded, since comparisons can be made. Czibor and Budai were fast, tricky wingers ready to cut in and shoot. More often their precise centres were invitingly placed in front of Kocsis, the sharpest and surest of finishers with head or boot. There was Hidegkuti to confuse the defenders, prompt the central attacks and steal up unnoticed to finish off the sweeping moves. As if that was not enough for any one team to have at any one time, there was the 'galloping major', Puskas himself, the finest forward of his day. And behind there was the forceful member of parliament and goalscoring wing-half,

Bozsik. There was also the dead ball specialist, Lantos, who was to score one of the seven goals with which the Hungarians chastised us in the return match in Budapest. There his driven free kick sped so swiftly through the wall that Billy Wright was mystified how it got through until the pictures showed the ball sliding past Ivor Broadis' turned back.

At Wembley it was Puskas who mystified Wright with as good a goal as has been scored there. As Wright raced into the tackle Puskas rolled the ball back under the sole of his boot and wheeled to hit an instant shot that was bulging the net before Merrick moved.

Puskas' Hungarians were a blend of exciting players, with chance bringing all that talent together for a few seasons of glory, just as in the Seventies Cruyff's Netherlands team was a sudden, brief flowering. For the ninety minutes at Wembley, Hungary had the challenge of facing another team ready to attack, of outmatching the formidable Matthews, Mortensen and Sewell. England's contribution had its magic too. There was Sewell's run and precise shot, a characteristic flourish from Mortensen dashing through to score yet another courageous goal, and Ramsey stroking home a penalty with typical composure after Robb had been brought down. That was enough to let the crowd enjoy, without humiliation, the wonder of seeing a Continental team whose finishing was as swift and sure as the lancing approach play which left England's defenders breathless and bemused. This was unrivalled entertainment, the flourish and style of the scoring as important as the goals, which gave Hungary their 6–3 win.

Two

The Link Man

Herbert Chapman stands as the watershed between the modern game and a different concept of football. With Charles Buchan's assistance he devised the system of the 'stopper' centre-half, or third back game, which dried the flood of goals after forwards had run riot following the change in the offside law. The 1925 alteration made it necessary for the player to have only two, instead of three, opponents between him and the goal, when the pass was made, and the new freedom soon allowed Newcastle to put seven goals past the Arsenal 'keeper. That was seven too many for Chapman, who introduced his new defensive tactics and acquired 'policeman' Herbert Roberts to take opposing centre-forwards in charge. They had never been close marked before and the effect was devastating. Here is Chapman's account in his book, *Herbert Chapman on Football*, published in 1934, of a conversation with an outstanding centre-forward of the day:

> One day, through the open door of the Arsenal dressing-room I watched Jimmy Dunne pacing up and down, obviously deep in thought. His hands were pushed into his trouser pockets, his head was bowed, and his brow puckered.
> 'What's the trouble, Jimmy?' I asked.
> 'I was thinking about the match with Chelsea,' he said. 'As I sat in the stand (he was unable to play, owing to an injured ankle) I was sorry for George Mills. I've had some. I've played against Herbert Roberts, and he keeps you so closely in his grip that you feel that you have no chance at all. I was also wondering what the crowd thought about it all and whether they had any sympathy for Mills who is a really fine centre-forward. They would if they only spent five minutes

out there. And I was wondering if there was any way of beating Roberts and other centre-halves who play in his style. I know all about the theory of centre-forward play and how I should get into the open spaces, but there are none when Roberts is up against you.'

Those who follow football regularly must, I think, sympathise with the modern centre-forward, who is cribbed and confined as never before.

Chapman inevitably had considered the methods of defeating his own ploy and this was his conclusion:

There is hope for a player who faces his problem boldly and searches earnestly for the solution. Gurney, the Sunderland centre-forward, is supposed to have discovered the way to beat the 'stopper' in the centre-half position and he carries out a movement which is undoubtedly most effective. Sunderland have cultivated the practice of sending a long pass down one of the wings. Usually it is on the right flank, and it may be made by the wing half, the inside right or the outside forward. Immediately Gurney goes out to collect the ball and the opposing centre-half, whose job is to cover him, follows. But Gurney has obtained the essential few yards' start and it is his object to pick up the ball and instantly swing it back into the middle. At the same time, in anticipation of this cross pass, Gallacher, the inside left, and Connor, the wing man, as well, have raced up and in all probability whoever gets the ball has to face only one back. In the circumstances he has a great opportunity to meet the ball on the run and deliver a telling shot first time.

The 'two for three' change in the offside law had given forwards a brief period of freedom and free-scoring before the defensive walls began to close in on them again. But the extra goals were paid for in sweat and toil and the benefits soon disappeared as new methods were devised to shackle the goalscorers. Better systems, higher work rate, was the response then as it has been to the developments of modern times. This was Chapman's assessment of its effect on the style of play and of how fundamentally the game was changed through managers adapting to the new law.

Even if the modern game be not harder, it is very much more exacting. This has come about swiftly since the alteration of the offside law. The object of this was largely to reduce the number of stoppages and to please the onlooker, but I sometimes wonder whether it would have been made if it had been realised how the structure of the game as well as the play was to be changed. Clubs would, I think, have pondered longer over it if it could have been foreseen how managerial difficulties were to be increased. Having been educated on different lines I doubt very much whether the public would today be satisfied with the old football with all its precision and deliberate accuracy. It does not fit modern tendencies. It would be out of tune with the bustle and excitement of everyday life. Spectators want a fast-moving spectacle, rapier-like attacks that have the spirit of adventure and ever more goals. The heavier the scoring the more appealing is the match.

But I should do an injustice to the old-timers if I did not believe that they would have been able to accommodate themselves to modern requirements. Their natural ability would have ensured this, but they would have had to alter their whole mode of life. They would find that the game now carries far greater responsibilities than they used to bear and they would have to tackle it far more thoroughly and, to succeed, make many personal and social sacrifices. They would discover, too, that the play made greater demands on them. They would have to keep much fitter; otherwise instead of being 'ninety-minutes men' they would fade out very quickly.

As Chapman stood in the bridging position between old and new he is the ideal guide to select the best of the past and the pick of the early thirties:

> I set down this team of old players to amuse myself in comparing them with the chief players of today.
>
> Hardy (Aston Villa); Crompton (Blackburn Rovers); Pennington (W.B.A.); Warren (Derby); Roberts (Manchester United); Needham (Sheffield United); Simpson (Blackburn Rovers); Bloomer (Derby); Shepherd (Newcastle); Holley (Sunderland); Spikesley (Sheffield Wednesday).
>
> This is truly a wonderful array of the richest talent and it goes a long way to convince one that football has lost its personalities. Some of these men have, in my judgement, never been equalled. . . .
>
> But suppose I were selecting the ideal team in modern conditions? If I were looking for a goalkeeper I do not think I could find one more suitable than a quick and daring Rugby full-back, who could kick strongly with both feet and catch a ball with the certainty of the

fieldsman in the slips. He would also require to be tall, somewhere about six feet, so that when the ball came over from the wings he would be able to punch it out, and by use of his hands beat the Hodgsons and the Deans with their heads.

The game today demands that a back should be speedy, quick in turning, so that he may go back to recover and clever enough in ball play to be able to work his way out of a tight corner.

It used to be thought that the centre-half was the key man of a team. Today I think there are four key men, the two wing-halves and the two inside forwards. The centre-half may still play an important part in a constructive sense, but under the altered conditions the wing men have more scope as schemers and it is on this account that such players as Strange, Bob John, Campbell, and Jimmy McMullan are so valuable. . . .

Coming to the forwards, we find a notable change in the play of the wing men. In their case, pace is more than ever important. They should make ground quickly and now that the danger of being jockeyed into offside positions is less, they have far greater opportunities than the old players possessed. Their duties, too, have changed in the sense that whereas it used to be thought that their main job was to get the ball across to make chances for the insides, they now have exceptional scoring opportunities themselves. But they must break away from the old idea that their place is on the line. They should always be ready to move inside, not only when they have the ball themselves, but whenever there is a likelihood of it coming over from the opposite wing. In these circumstances it follows that they should, as we say, have two feet and be able to shoot like a Hooper with both. Another wing player who has been quick to grasp his scoring opportunities is Davis of Bradford.

Give me a Strange and a McMullan in the wing-half positions, Jack and James as the inside forwards, and a Dean as the centre, and I should think I was getting very near to my ideal. Add two fast, scoring outside players and the plan would be as complete as I could ever expect to make it.

Chapman might have named a couple of fast, scoring wingers. He had two of the best at Arsenal in 'Boy' Bastin and Joe Hulme.

Three

Striking Wingers

'Boy' Bastin and Joe Hulme remain one of the best wing pairings of any age. They were a nice balance of opposites, Hulme with his burning speed, Bastin with his ice-cold finishing. Joe Hulme was a real flier, aptly named 'The Express'. He was a natural games player, equally good at cricket and football. The wing indeed seemed to suit many of Arsenal's bi-sporting personalities. The more ponderous Denis Compton was later to be a formidable influence on Arsenal's left wing in their Cup win of 1950, while the wiry Arthur Milton was also to represent England in both sports.

Hulme and Bastin between them scored 53 of Arsenal's 118 goals in 1932–3. Of that great haul Bastin had 33. He was a jackal of the penalty area so precise in his shooting that as he closed in others would wheel away in anticipation of his scoring shot. This is Catton's description of a typical goal. 'Lambert steered it to Bastin, the mere boy, who was at outside left. Bastin was challenged and tackled, but with rare self-possession in a player so young and so fresh to big matches he trapped the ball and shot it into the net with his left foot.'

No wonder Chapman commented on him, 'I have never known a youth with the same stability as Bastin. Temperamentally he is like a block of ice, untouched by excitement. In his first two Cup Finals you might have thought he was about to take part in some Combination match. Watch him run in to seize a scoring chance and you are sure he will never fail through over-eagerness, which is the fault of so many forwards.'

Bastin was only seventeen when Chapman signed him from Exeter City. His coolness was at once apparent. Far from being overawed by the great man he showed more concern about being late for a tennis match and it took all Chapman's considerable persuasive powers to get him to Arsenal. He had his first game as an inside right with Hulme scoring the only goal in a 1–1 draw at Everton. Then it was reserve football until Chapman brought him back as a left-winger. It was typical that Chapman should not only see this was his best position, but make the youngster believe he would soon be the best winger in England. Christmas 1929 was the first time Bastin played on the wing and it was from there he scored most of his 150 goals for Arsenal. That remains a club record with John Radford, the next highest scorer, still 39 behind when he moved on to West Ham.

Before he was twenty Bastin had his share of all the game's major honours. In 1930 he had a vital part in the Cup Final win over Huddersfield. On the coach to Wembley he and James worked a free-kick move, then executed it so precisely that James scored from his return pass. That goal was the turning-point of Arsenal's 2–0 win and made Bastin the youngest player to get a Cup-winner's medal. Next season Bastin had 28 of the 127 goals which gave Arsenal the championship, seven points clear of Aston Villa but one goal short of their 128, which is still the First Division record. In November 1931 he gained his first cap against Wales, but so closely did Arsenal team-mate, Charlie Jones, mark him that it was two years before he was given another chance. In all, he had 21 caps and scored twelve goals for England. His international career ended in style with a successful tour in Europe and a brilliant display in the 6–3 defeat of Germany in Hitler's Berlin in 1938.

Before that match the officials had a difficult decision after being requested to ensure the team gave the Nazi salute, as a courtesy gesture, when the German national anthem was played. The F.A. Secretary agreed to do so, after consulting the players, in order to preserve the atmosphere of a great sporting occasion. The England team then gave so thrilling an exhibition of attacking play that there was tumultuous applause even from the Germans.

Hulme had none of Bastin's coolness and consistency. The nerveless Bastin, whose slight deafness seemed to insulate him from the roar of the crowd, recognised the difference in his more jovial and extrovert partner. 'Joey Hulme was one of the best outside rights I have known,' he wrote. 'Yet he could also be one of the worst. His nervousness sometimes made him play far, far below his normal form.' Hulme could have his off-days all right, but he could also win matches on his own with his dazzling speed and adroit ball control. He excelled also in hitting accurate centres when in full stride. Both he and Bastin were given every chance to shine with wee Alex James sending the passes where they wanted them. And the little man was sensitive enough to recognise if one was having an off-day, and switch the ball to the other.

Hulme was already an experienced player when he came to Arsenal from Blackburn Rovers in 1926, and he scored 108 goals in his 333 games for the Gunners. In 1938 he was transferred to Huddersfield in time to play for them in the fifth Wembley Cup Final of his career. 'The other side have objected that I am playing on my home ground,' he joked. There was no need to object. Mutch's penalty in the last minute of extra time gave Preston a 1–0 victory, and deprived Hulme of his ideal exit line.

For me the two who best meet Chapman's requirement of fast, scoring wingers were Tom Finney and Billy Liddell. Finney, the natural left-foot player, preferred the right wing, and a similar instinct for goals had the right-footed Liddell playing on the left. Both trained themselves so that each foot was strong and flexible, but there was more power and accuracy as they cut in to shoot for the far post with the natural foot.

In his young days Liddell always aimed to squeeze the ball between goalkeeper and near post. But after a schoolboy international against Ireland in 1936 he pondered a journalist's comment, 'Liddell would be a better player if he aimed his shots for the far post. It is easier to score there.' Liddell soon appreciated there were other advantages than a wider angle at which to aim. If he sliced his shot the goalkeeper might still palm it out to another forward or it might go straight to the other winger closing in at the far post. So it was there that Liddell thundered his shots in future.

It was Liddell's headmaster who taught him as a youngster to run with that characteristic crouch, leaning slightly forward over the ball. 'I wince now when I watch Steve Heighway careering down the wing for Liverpool, standing straight and tall. If you lean forward you are well balanced to meet any challenge. Stand straight and you will be jolted and jarred or sent flying by the hard tacklers. It's difficult to last long that way.'

Liddell lasted 23 seasons with Liverpool, playing more matches for the club than any other footballer, until Ian Callaghan passed his total.

The style Liddell learnt with Lochgelly Violet needed little change for First Division football. Strong and fast-running, he would bore in on goal. Matthews might feint to go inside then flick the ball over the tackler's lunging leg to go past on the outside, but Billy Liddell would do the opposite. Forceful in everything he did, Liddell could hit a ball with ferocious power. His centres were usually hard driven and whenever he did go down the touchline there was always a forward running in to meet that low raking cross to the far post.

Liddell was an accurate hitter of a dead ball and many of his goals came from free kicks or penalties. Only once did he miss a penalty for Liverpool and ironically it was saved by a back, Alf Sherwood, deputising for an injured goalkeeper. There was irony too in his record for Scotland. The master penalty taker took only two for them and missed both.

As with all his play, Liddell went for the simple and straightforward. He hit his penalty kicks so hard with his right foot that the goalkeeper had no chance, even if told where he was aiming.

Constant practice, constant observation of good players, and Matt Busby were the formative influences on his career. Busby was the man who brought him to Liverpool, passing on to the club a tip from his golfing partner, Alec Herd. It was Matt who coached him on the field. It was Matt who pressed for his inclusion with Scotland. And for Liddell Busby was the model footballer.

'Busby was a remarkable player himself. I have never seen anyone who could pass better. He sent the ball to you early, ruled to the exact inch where you hoped it would be.'

The first time Liddell was invited to play for Scotland the game was abandoned because of the severe weather – a fact which could not be mentioned in wartime papers, to the mystification of many who looked for a result. To keep fit Liddell asked to play in a reserve match. His manager warned him against it, saying he feared injury. The premonition was only too correct. Liddell ended in hospital after challenging for a cross and thumping the back of his head on the frozen ground as he fell.

But he played in the high-scoring war-time International at Hampden, the 5–4 defeat of England in a gala game of great forwards. By the end of the war he was well enough established to be in the Great Britain XI which beat the Rest of Europe 6–1.

Billy Steel was the forceful inside forward for whom he made openings in that game, lying deeper than usual to fit in with Steel's style as second front runner.

Liddell scored 214 league goals in his career and was so much a team in himself that his club was often referred to as 'Liddellpool'. Yet throughout those 23 seasons he remained a part-timer. His father had impressed on him the need to have a career outside football and in this too Liddell has always been a success. He remains a familiar figure on Merseyside, Accountant for Liverpool University Students Union since

1962, Justice of the Peace, and still hero-worshipped along with the Callaghans and Clemences. In a city more concerned with living out the present than romanticising the past he is instantly recognised as one of their footballing greats, although not part of their period of greatness. There was indeed one First Division Championship to celebrate in his time, but there was also a brief period of Second Division football until Shankly took the Club to the heights, just as Liddell was retiring.

As a part-timer Liddell trained intensively for three or four weeks before the season. During it he could spare only two evenings a week. He recalls, 'The routine was mainly lapping and fitness training in the gymnasium with plenty of work with a skipping rope. Heading tennis was a popular game and we would also have some ball practice – but not much until we started imitating the Continentals in the fifties. Having reached peak fitness at the start of the season I did not find it a handicap being a part-timer. In fact, it was probably easier to stay fit without getting stale.'

To his natural skills and strength Liddell added the total commitment that was to remain a Liverpool characteristic. He had absorbed Busby's chivalrous attitude to the game, playing it very hard, but very straight. There were occasional disillusionments:

'Before one of my first International matches I shared a room with another Scottish player. He told me that he would only be playing for himself, aiming to score goals and catch the selectors' eyes: "All I am concerned with is adding to my own transfer value. I am not interested in any team play."'

For the 1950 Cup Final Liddell was the man Arsenal feared and he was the one they double-marked. Watching that match I can recall wincing as Forbes chopped him down time and again with ruthless expertise. Liddell took it calmly. 'Perhaps I was naïve then. All I was concerned with was to make the maximum effort to play my best and that was how I assumed other professionals would play. I accepted hard knocks and I gave them too, going fairly for the ball. Once against England at Wembley I knocked out Wilf. Mannion when I was back covering on the edge of our area. That was a clash of heads as we both went for the same ball. We all accepted that type of accidental injury as part of the game. But you didn't expect anyone to set about you in the way I was savaged that afternoon. Joe Mercer has told me since that they were instructed to keep me quiet. They were a bit crude in how they did it.' They were, indeed. That was the one blemish on the fine precision of Arsenal's play, with two goals by Lewis giving them the Cup, which always eluded Liddell. It was not the Arsenal tackling he blames for missing it. 'The Manager told us the side he would be playing, but the Directors over-ruled him and chose another. The leaving out of Bob Paisley was a mistake and, even more, the exclusion of Balmer at back.'

The back Liddell most enjoyed playing against was Alf Ramsey, with whom he had many International tussles.

'When Alf won the ball he always tried to use it effectively, rather than clear it quickly. That gave you the chance to chase and try and win it back.'

The man Liddell did not enjoy marking himself was Stanley Matthews. 'I was always told to chase after him and try and tackle him on the *inside*. That meant the wing-half could catch him as he went *outside* as always. But as soon as he won possession the half always hit a long ball straight back up the wing and shouted "Where the hell are you?" as I cantered breathless after it.'

Stanley Matthews was the most striking winger of his day, but he was indeed platonic about goals. For him they were an after-thought. Ball control was his passion, destroying defenders his pleasure. 'I aim to dominate them, to destroy them psychologically so that they are left without confidence or ability,' was his declared intent so often fulfilled.

He never did a better demolition job than in the International against Belgium in 1946. It was Finney, Lawton and Mortensen who scored the five goals, Matthews who had the Belgians writhing and their crowd roaring with delight. An even first half had given the strong Belgian team hopes of a first-ever victory against England. Then came the decisive moment.

Matthews trapped a ball in midfield near the touchline and hovered provokingly over it. Three tacklers moved in on him in line ready to cover each other no matter which way he darted. A feint to the left sent one speeding past, a sway to the right had another sliding by over the touchline, then a double shuffle had the third sprawling, his legs twisted as he tried to follow. And the master *still* had not touched the ball.

Thereafter he did as he liked, cutting the ball back to Finney and Lawton hovering in the penalty area. The Belgian centre-half played the game in an elegant pair of gloves, but finally decided it was time to take them off against Matthews. His scything tackle missed as the winger skipped nimbly over the flailing leg. In desperation the Belgian twisted to seize the back of his pants, pulling them down round his knees. Hobbled as he was Matthews still slid a pass to Carter who laid the ball through for the unmarked Lawton to hit home.

Whoever scored the goals it was Matthews whom both teams

clapped as he loped back to the centre, Matthews whose name the crowd chanted to send it echoing over Brussels.

Walter Winterbottom once made his training point to the England players by putting large bibs round their necks, protruding so far that they could not see their feet or the ball at their toes. Shown on television it made such an impression on one former forward of great distinction, Billy Walker, that he nearly threw his shoe through the set in disgust at such antics. But the impression that it made, and was meant to make, on the players was that at their level of skill they had no need to look down at the ball when dribbling or short-passing. They could do that by touch and instinct as confidently as a blind man walks his own room. And Matthews, despite that crouched, shuffling run, always had his eyes up darting over the field, searching, judging, memorising. It seemed sometimes that he had eyes in the back of his head as well, for he had that extra-sensory perception given only to a few players.

That sense kept him playing First Division football longer than anyone else. Stanley Matthews was born on 1 February 1915 and had his last League game for Stoke on 6 February 1965. He is the only man to have played First Division football when over fifty. The oldest man ever to play in the English Football League was a goalkeeper, the late Neil McBain, who was born in November 1894 and turned out, aged 52, in a Third Division North match at Hartlepool in March 1947. McBain was managing New Brighton at the time and saved his side from being short, but he can hardly claim to challenge Matthews for durability and fitness. No one can do that. He seemed only to mature with age so that he took part ineffectually in the 'Battle of Highbury' against the Italians in 1934 and was a significant force in England's 4–1 win against Denmark on 15 May 1957. That was his last cap but the year before, Matthews, aged 41, had played a major part in England's only defeat of Brazil. That memorable occasion at Wembley lacked nothing in goals or incident.

With only two minutes gone Tommy Taylor had twice broken through, shooting once over the bar and once into the net after Matthews and Haynes had made the opening. Soon Matthews caught the Brazilians off balance again, slipping the ball through his marker's legs then sending Hall away to start the move which ended with left-winger Grainger scoring a simple goal in the fifth minute of his first International.

Brazil fought back to 2–2 in the second half with goals from Paulhino and Didi, the 'cobra', who was given few chances to strike by his shadower, Ronnie Clayton.

Then an indirect free kick, awarded in the penalty area for obstruction on Taylor, brought a colourful Brazilian protest. When Haynes was at last able to take it, right-half Zozimo palmed the ball down and a penalty was awarded just as Atyeo was sweeping his shot into the net. That was the last Atyeo saw of the ball for some time. Alvaro and Santos walked off the field with it, while the rest of their side made theatrical appeals to the French referee, Guigue, to reconsider his unpopular verdict. The confusion confounded Atyeo. When order was restored his penalty was hit straight enough for Gylmar to save before being smothered by fervent Brazilian embraces. When the kissing had stopped, the crying started again as Matthews' curving centre was headed back by Atyeo and in by Tommy Taylor. Zozimo and Gylmar then staged a repeat performance, Zozimo handling again and the goalkeeper diving to save Roger Byrne's too softly taken penalty.

With a few minutes left Matthews, just back from changing his boot, went weaving down the line again and Grainger met his centre at the far post to head home the killing goal.

Bob Pennington of the *Daily Express* had this to say of Matthews after the match:

Two Matthews-made goals smashed Brazil in this second half although he was slipping and slithering on the rain-drenched Wembley turf almost without studs.

He had changed his boots at half-time as the studs had not been equal to the strain of the 'slow, quick-quick, slow flash' as he shuffled and darted down the wing. He was still having trouble with his boots when he swung over the perfect centre that led to the third goal. And a few minutes later he signalled the trainer's bench and walked off the field. 'The old man wants a rest,' said the cynics, but all Stan wanted was yet another right boot and a full set of studs. Their light weight had not been equal to the rain-soaked turf and soon Matthews was sliding on his back again when three more studs went missing as he evaded Santos' tackle.

Yet six minutes from time Matthews pounced on a pass from Geoff Hall and ran twenty yards to clip across the precise centre which Colin Grainger headed into the net.

In his last game, against Denmark, Matthews was appropriately paired again with Tom Finney. Their partnership was reminiscent of Scotland's best, Morton and Jackson. Alan Morton, the 'wee blue devil', the 'man who cannot be stopped', had all the trickery of

Matthews with the long striding, hard-shooting Jackson as good a finisher as Finney. Morton's special centre, the floated cross which 'hung' behind the defence, gave Jackson his goals when the 'Wembley Wizards' destroyed England 5–1 in 1928. Two years later England fielded a pair of goalscoring wingers, Sammy Crooks of Derby County and Ellis Rimmer of Sheffield Wednesday who, on the day, left Morton and Jackson standing and did as thorough a job in destroying the defence. James Catton's account for the *Observer* caught the mood of excitement.

'The victories of England over Scotland have been so rare during the last decade that the 5–2 win at Wembley roused a crowd of 80,000 to a pitch of enthusiasm that has not been seen South of the Tweed since that memorable match on a slimy surface at Sheffield in 1920 when England triumphed 5–4.'

A touch by David Jack to Vic Watson made the first goal for the West Ham centre-forward. Thereafter it was the two wingers who made the game a nightmare for Harkness in the Scottish goal, not the last of their 'keepers to be unnerved at Wembley.

'Outside right Crooks, playing right up to Law, the left-back, took the ball from the Chelsea man and, running to the goal-line placed a timely centre with such care that Watson headed the ball into the net. Again, Crooks had a raid and with another choice centre enabled Rimmer to head a third goal. Surprise succeeded surprise for Crooks again did just as he pleased against faltering defenders and Jack, the English captain, shot them the fourth following a corner kick. These three goals were obtained in four minutes and the riddling of the Scottish defence recalled the course of events in the first half of the match in 1892 – when the "old crocks" as they were styled put in four goals in about twenty minutes.'

After Fleming, playing in place of the injured Gallacher, had scored two for Scotland, prompted by Morton's clever play, Rimmer raced clear to shoot home on the run.

Catton's final comment underlined that it was wing play which won the match. 'Although Watson and Rimmer's two goals against Scotland are so rare a feat that only G. Wall, R. Kelly, and Dean have done so in thirty years, it is impossible to resist the conclusion that Crooks, as plucky as clever, was the forward of the match.'

Denis Howell had to adjudicate on many matters as Minister of Sport and has the right background to referee a football controversy. He has no doubt about the best pair of scoring wingers, or indeed forwards, whom he has seen. Eric Houghton and Frank Broome are a choice with which many of the older Aston Villa supporters would agree.

'Houghton was said to be one-footed, but there is a goal of his which haunts me now. He drove the ball left-footed against the post and when it bounded straight back to him 20 yards away he hit it home just as hard with the right.

'Broome was the speed and precision paired with the power. He was always dangerous when he cut in because he aimed so accurately for the far post instead of trying the improbable near post shot, which obsesses so many modern forwards.'

Eric Houghton was the master kicker of a dead ball. For Villa he scored 55 penalties and a further 26 goals from free kicks. He was a striking winger of awesome power. Like that other fierce hitter of a ball, little Johnny Hancocks of Wolves, he scored 10 or more goals from the wing in ten successive seasons of top-class football.

Houghton is remembered as a left-footed player, who was a left-wing specialist. His left was indeed his *stronger* foot, but his *natural* one was the right. So determined was Houghton to become a two-footed player that he worked endlessly on his left, wearing a boot on that, a tennis shoe on the other. Ceaseless practice made so perfect that he is recalled as one of the hardest left-foot kickers of all time. For penalties, however, Houghton favoured the right. 'You need to hit a penalty firmly, but accuracy is more important than power. And for accuracy I was more comfortable using my natural foot. With all dead ball kicking if I wanted precision I used the right, if power then I hit it with the left.'

Eric Houghton's experience spans most of football's history. As a young player he was coached by one of the great players of the early days when Villa dominated English football. As a player he was outstanding for club and country. As a Villa Manager and Director he has been a part of all the phases of post-war soccer, of all his club's past vicissitudes and present excitement. He is an ideal commentator on goalscoring, for he was brought up to believe that this was all that really mattered in the game.

'There are welcome signs that sanity and goals are coming back into the English game. Goals are all-important and you make them by swift attacks using the whole width of the field. We didn't mind opponents scoring three, so long as we scored four – and that is the best attitude to make the game enjoyable for spectators and players alike.

'Simple ideas are usually best in football. John Devey was my guide when I started at Villa. He had been their Captain when they did the double in 1897, scoring the decisive goal against Everton in that fluctuating Final. He had also been a County cricketer, as I was to be myself. "Keep it simple," he would say. "Never try to beat a man if there is a good pass you can make. The pass is so much easier and quicker, so why gamble?"

'Jimmy Hogan, that expert coach who was so revered on the Continent, had the same theme. "Use common sense all the time. Shoot for the far post because it gives you the best chance. Find the strengths of your other forwards and play them the ball as *they* like it, not as *you* think they *ought* to like it."'

There was strength enough for Houghton to find at Villa. He himself scored 30 goals from the wing in that season of 128 goals. And at one time there were three international centre-forwards competing for the positions inside him: Pongo Waring, George Brown, and Dai Astley, who scored more goals for Wales than any other pre-war player. And at the start there was the great Billy Walker, so poised and clever on his feet, so good with his head.

'For Billy I used to *drive* my centres over, ignoring the fashionable lob into the middle. And I didn't hit them low like they do today, but raked them across just beneath the bar. Walker was a tall man and coming in on my crosses he got up so high he reached the ones the defenders couldn't. Then he hit them powerfully down past the 'keeper or flicked them delicately wide of him. He knew instinctively where the 'keeper was without breaking the golden rule of heading, "Keep your eye on the ball."

'John Devey taught me always to look for the man well placed for the pass rather than run head down along the wing. So I was very aware of centre-forwards who made it easy for me. Jimmy Hampson was one in the England side. The Blackpool man was only five feet eight inches tall and depended on skill. He was fast and elusive, with a fine positional sense, always moving into space. When you wanted him you could always find him free. And with his perfect balance he was a very efficient finisher.

'George Brown, who had been in Huddersfield's team when they had three successive League championships, was another like him. He played inside mostly at Villa, because there was such competition for the centre-forward position and he had enough craft to play anywhere.

'Pongo Waring was a thrusting centre in the tradition of the day, a broad, forceful six-footer like William Dean and Gordon Hodgson, who was usually right inside for Liverpool. With that type of forward you could play the ball in front for them to burst through the middle, particularly on the muddy days. Or you could hit it high in front of their foreheads, for they were all wonderful headers of a ball whether lobbed or driven.

'Muddy grounds were more frequent when I was playing. Better pitches – better weather too, I think – have reduced the number of those days in which goalscorers revelled. Control was so much easier in the mud than it is now with firm grounds and light balls. These light balls can be made to swerve more than our heavy old T balls. But with lighter boots there is no way you can hit the modern ball as hard as we hit the old, wearing those thick boots with reinforced toe-caps.

'There are fewer two-footed players today and they don't practise scoring as much as we used to. At Villa we always had one whole morning a week practising instant volleys and half-volleys or shooting under pressure.

'Goalscoring is in part instinct, but it improves with practice. There are some essentials which few seem to master. Balance is vital. Billy Walker used to tell me, "Never rush the actual shot. You must be balanced and confident when you hit the ball. So take the time you need to feel right."'

The goalscorer must be balanced, but he must try to catch the goalkeeper unaware.

'That was why we also concentrated on instant first-time shooting. To be effective with it you must have practised until you are sure of hitting the target. Jimmy Greaves is the supreme example of the finisher always well-balanced. That is also the exciting quality in Andy Gray, and why he has been such an instant success at Aston Villa.

'Finally, the scorer should always be able to beat the goalkeeper when through on his own. To the spectator that looks easy, but it can be the most difficult shot of all – *if* you shoot. Goalkeeping is about angles, so he is going to come out fast and let you see very little of the goal. If he leaves space behind, it is best to go round him. Frankie Broome was the expert at it. He would dummy one way, slide past the other, and hardly ever tried to beat the goalkeeper with a shot in this situation, unlike so many present players. Broome was the fastest man I played with or against. He was like a dog who's been chained all night, then sees a rabbit as his lead is slipped.'

Those on the left were a hard-hitting lot. Houghton's closest rivals for power in kicking were four other left-wingers, Eric Brook, Cliff Bastin, Fletcher of Brentford and George ('Jud') Harrison.

Their characteristics might change, but there remained a special quality about left-wingers after the last war. Denis Compton, with his eye for a moving ball, was the best volleyer of his or any day. A crashing volley is one of soccer's most thrilling sights, and there is a rarity value in one perfectly struck. With Denis the rarity was when for once he would slice this most awkward of balls to hit true.

On the left there were also the tricky dribblers to challenge even Matthews' control. On the big occasions Newcastle's Bobby Mitchell could be the most baffling of them all. In Wembley Finals the St John Ambulance men had their stretchers ready as soon as his name was on the programme, for first Barnes of Arsenal, then soon afterwards Meadows of Manchester City was twisted to destruction trying to follow his elusive swerve. Gordon Dale of Portsmouth was another whose sleight of foot had the defenders tackling air.

Yet it is as pairs that wingers are most formidable and in the Midlands they might vote for the couple who did so much to make Wolves the power of the Fifties, Mullen and Hancocks.

Little Johnny Hancocks was a scoring winger of an unusual type. Wolves' attacking method depended on the long ball hit wide to the wing and the raking cross often nudged home by the opposite winger. Hancocks stood only five feet four inches on his studs, but he had the kick of a frightened horse. He could send the heaviest mud-soaked ball skimming to the far post, or arrow his shot for goal as he cut in. Hancocks lacked the speed of the flying wingers, or the trickery of a Matthews, but he could pick his way through a packed penalty area like a startled snipe. And above all he was an outstanding kicker of the dead ball. He took penalties the way they should be taken. No question for him of deceiving the goalkeeper with a clever feint; he beat him by sheer speed and precision.

Free kicks, too, Hancocks could hit with such ferocity that goalkeepers, unsighted by their defensive walls, only heard them slap against the net. Bill Slater recalls his most remarkable effort. 'We were close to the League Championship and we needed to beat Huddersfield. Time was running out and we were still level. For once Johnny had missed a sitter and we knew he was desperate to redeem himself. With a few minutes to go we had a free kick nearer the half-way line than the penalty area. As our forwards surged up and the big defenders moved to join them in the area we saw Johnny stalking up to take the kick, face set in grim determination. "You *cannot* score," we yelled at him. "Don't waste it. Lob it over." We were still shouting "Don't waste it" as the ball billowed the netting high in the far corner with the goalkeeper left staring and incredulous.'

After the 1953 Wembley defeat by Puskas' Hungarians it was Wolves who restored England's shattered confidence with an emotional victory over the Honved Club side that was almost the Hungarian National team. With the floodlights glistening on the sticky surface the going was ideal, for Wolves revelled in such conditions like mud-fixated hippos. From two goals down they were lifted by their wingers to a famous victory.

Wingers were prominent again in the first-ever European competition victory for a British Club when West Ham won the Cup Winners Cup in 1965.

Rolf Gonther of the Munich *Abendzeitung* had this to say of West Ham's 2–0 victory over Munich 1860 in the Final.

West Ham never at any time looked like losing this splendid final. But I think Munich gave the crowd a good display of continental football. They tried to outfight West Ham and that was their mistake. They should have tried to match their football. West Ham's wingers – Sissons and Sealey – were undoubtedly the match-winners. And Bobby Moore – oh! how he had that defence organised – was superb. Munich foundered whenever they ran up against him. How I wish the German players could use the ball as well as West Ham.

Sissons twice hit the post and Sealey scored both the goals in the second half after the German goalkeeper, Radenkovic, had kept West Ham at bay in the first. Sealey had scored only three League goals all season and hardly rates as one of the great scoring wingers of any era. But he helped stretch the defence and took his chances.

As the back four moved in, the winger was moved out of the limelight. Ramsey ignored specialist wingers partly because his front runners were all-purpose forwards, partly because he had backs who could overlap in their place, but mainly because there was a dearth of good wingers in English football. The tricky little Bryan Douglas of Blackburn, and Burnley's strong running John Connelly, were not what he wanted, well though Douglas had served England in his thirty-six Internationals. Liverpool offered him the subtlety of Peter Thompson, the direct, disciplined play of Ian Callaghan, but neither fitted easily into his teams. Too much perhaps was expected after Finney and Matthews, and even Terry Paine was given only one game in the World Cup Finals. The success of Ramsey's 'wingless wonders' led Clubs to ignore wing play, which was stifled for a decade. More are giving them their chance again, but the growth has been stunted with few forcing the selectors to take notice. Dave Thomas and Gordon Hill have had their moments of glory, but they were only fringe players in Revie's World

Cup plans, as was Dennis Tueart. We have got used to running down the central alley, rather than working wide to stretch the defence as Ipswich do so well through Clive Woods. 'The longest way round is the quickest way there' was the Army's tactical advice for infantry attacks in the last war. Footballers, too, might do better to filter in from the less well-guarded areas.

The last of the really effective wingers was Terry Paine and he illumined Wembley's first floodlight international with a hat-trick of goals, in November 1963.

Desmond Hackett had this to say in the *Daily Express*:

Jimmy Greaves and Terry Paine, with a highly commendable supporting cast of the best in English football, put the gallant Irish in their humble place at Wembley.

On this historic night, the first floodlit international at Wembley, England matched the brilliance of the arc lights with their many-splendoured play.

Greaves with a control and speed which puts him high among the princes of World football, scored four shining goals. And new boy Terry Paine, so quiet, so modest off the field, positively swaggered through the game, bewildering those who sought to check his three goals. As Greaves and Paine pitifully bemused the great-hearted Irish defence, Bobby Smith became a mighty wrecker with his fine goal. George Eastham, who started ineffectually, developed gradually into a menacing designer of goals. Only Bobby Charlton failed to fit the England victory march – a march so dominant the fans roared criticism when England failed to put more goals past the shot-battered Harry Gregg in the last twenty minutes.

Criticism of eight goals would certainly sound strange today. But the odd reversals of fortune have not changed. Three days later Terry Paine was clapped and cheered on to the field at Southampton in recognition of his outstanding wing play for England. But it was Leeds' left-winger, the tall, tricky Johanneson, who scored an early goal and helped Leeds to easy victory. All Paine achieved was to be booked for dissent. Other names to go in the book in that Second Division clash were Billy Bremner and Norman Hunter. The more football changes the more it stays the same, so perhaps we shall see the wingers back in their glory in the fullness of time. It is too early to write their obituary and invite them to rest in peace. Already the ghosts are walking in English football, with Brian Clough exploiting the skill of wingers like John Robertson to make Nottingham Forest a power in the First Division once more.

Four

The 'English' Centre-forward

The concept of the 'English' centre-forward changed radically after the First World War. In 1905 there is this comment made in the book *Association Football and the Men who made it*: 'One can count on the fingers of one hand the great centre-forwards of the last decade, J. Campbell of Sunderland, J. Goodall of Derby County, R. S. McColl of Glasgow Rangers and G. O. Smith. And the greatest of these is Smith. One day we may probably have to add the name of Vivian Woodward to the list. . . . Never in the history of the game has there been a centre, for consistency over a number of years, who has equalled G. O. Smith. For at least ten years the old Charterhouse boy stood without rival in England.'

Yet by 1912 Woodward had surpassed Smith as goalscorer and as representative of the best in English football. Ivan Sharpe, who was his outside left that year in the United Kingdom Olympic team which won the gold medal, wrote of him: 'No ambassador of sport had a greater influence on the European Continent than Woodward – the man with over sixty caps. No forward has ever seemed to jog through the game in such an effortless way, to create openings with so little subtlety, and score goals with smaller fuss.'

There were as endless arguments about the merits of Smith and Woodward as later over Finney and Matthews. Woodward clearly had more of the talent that mattered – the ability to score goals. While Gilbert Oswald Smith scored 12 in 20 Internationals Vivian Woodward went one better even than Steve Bloomer with 29 goals in 23 full Internationals, a record which stood until Lofthouse broke it almost fifty years later. In addition Woodward had 53 goals in 38 Amateur Internationals, playing in the very first, when Ireland were beaten 2–1 in

Dublin. He also scored five times and won two gold medals in Olympic football.

Whichever was the better of them, jointly Smith and Woodward were the outstanding centres of their age. They were two of a kind, Byronic figures with aristocratic good looks, who assumed a natural command on the field and played with gracious gentility. They were the epitome of the amateur ideal, along with C. B. Fry, who was as unconcerned to be offered the crown of Albania, as to turn out at right back for Southampton in a Cup Final, or face the Australians at Lord's, or set a world record long jump. There was much similarity too in their styles. Of Smith, James Catton commented: 'Rather frail in physique, gentle in manner, and kind in disposition. On the field he was courageous and most unselfish. Anyone could knock him off the ball if he could get contact with him. But he was difficult to find, so elusive was he. His value consisted chiefly in wonderfully accurate passes to either wing.'

C. B. Fry was Smith's Captain in the Oxford XI and had this to say of him: 'What made Smith such a player was his skill in elusive movements, his quickness in seeing how best to bestow his passes, his accuracy and his remarkably penetrative dribbling.' Of his own shooting talent Smith commented, 'I always try for low cross shots because that is where the goalkeeper least likes them.'

Woodward had more of the scorer's instinct and egotism, although he worked well enough with his partners. He also looked too frail for the rough and tumble of the penalty area, yet while Smith confined himself to playing for Old Carthusians and the Corinthians, Woodward took in his elegant stride a season with Spurs and six with Chelsea. He excelled in the 'single-handed dash on goal' and his whole bearing ensured that he was never mistaken for anything but the amateur he remained, even in League football. In Sharpe's view he was 'a quiet, simple, transparently honest sportsman, and that is how he played the game. The only spectacular phase of his football was the way he rose to the ball amid the press of players and headed goals.' Charlie Buchan played against him at his peak and found he 'made the ball do all the work. He seemed to stroll through the game.'

Woodward made a deep impression in the England tour of Hungary, Austria and Bohemia in 1908 and 1909. More than his 15 goals in 7 matches, the manner of his play did much to popularise the game in central Europe. For them he typified the 'English centre-forward'. But soon that phrase would bring a stronger, harder image and signify a more professional approach. The dash for goal and the 'leap amid the press of players' were the only links between the old and new models.

Thereafter English centre-forward play has always been at its best with a powerful, hustling striker to take the goals and create space for others to use. And the 'English' centre has made more deadly the goal-poachers who work in their shadow, like Jimmy Greaves stealing in unnoticed as defenders continued their battle with burly Bobby Smith.

It is a long and distinguished line, often with high skills to add to the brash, brave challenge and the strength in the air. West Ham's Vic Watson, the courageous Ted Drake, the insatiable 'Dixie' Dean, the promising Tommy Taylor, big clumsy Derek Kevan, have all been more typical of the breed.

In the late Seventies, Malcolm Macdonald and Joe Royle still played in this tradition, but the best example of the 'English' style is the Scot, Andy Gray.

There was more choice just after the Second World War. From the same Castle Hall School at Bolton came two of the bulldog breed of 'English' centre-forwards, Tommy Lawton and Nathaniel Lofthouse. Lofthouse modelled himself on the elder man, who was already famous, but he was the one who best expressed the sterling values of the 'English' style. His courage, strength and dash won space and respect wherever he played – if you gave him space you gave him goals.

In the record books it is his International career that made him outstanding, his 30 goals at last beating Woodward's long-standing record. And it was a key International, the game against Austria, regarded as for the unofficial championship of Europe, which won him the nickname 'The Lion of Vienna'.

He settled that game with a typical Lofthouse break, dashing through from the half-way line and never flinching as the goalkeeper collided with him, while he coolly slid home his shot. Yet it was Bolton Wanderers who had the best of him. He joined them as a 15-year-old junior during the war and finished his career with them. Like Billy Wright, or Tom Finney, he was a one-club man at heart, the call to his loyalty enough to prevent any lucrative move elsewhere.

Twice he was on the point of leaving. At 21 he was still working as a miner in the Mosley Common Pit by day and training in the evening when he told Bolton he could do better elsewhere. Fortunately for the Club, Manager Walter Rowley appealed to him to stay and Lofthouse agreed.

The Club were not themselves so accommodating in 1957 when they threatened to dismiss him if he became licensee of the Castle Hotel. Nat charged the management head-on as if this was just another tiresome centre-half in his way.

'Because I haven't been the subject of sensational transfer headlines, don't take me for a mug,' he wrote. And, like so many centre-halves, the Club backed down as he thundered in on them as fair and fearless as on the field. They were wise to do so. He still had a Cup Final to win for them.

That was one of the great emotional Finals as a Manchester United team, cobbled together from helping clubs, rose phoenix-like from the ashes of the Munich air disaster to reach Wembley in 1958. They were willed along by the feverish support of Mancunians, and the fervent sympathy of the rest of the nation. Only Bolton refused to be carried away.

Bolton had already suffered defeat in one such emotional Final when the old master, Matthews, at last achieved his winner's medal five years before. Not for a second time would Lofthouse be the stage prop for another's act of triumph and he made sure of victory with the only two goals of a one-sided game. All eyes were on United at the start but the spotlight settled unwaveringly on Lofthouse. He was fire and ice, blazing through an anxious defence with cold precision. And the decisive goal was a characteristic effort so simple it took Gregg's breath away as Lofthouse bundled ball and goalkeeer over the line.

Off the field controversy raged round the interpretation of Law 12, but this was how the incident appeared to me, writing at the time.

A swift move between Bolton's forwards left Stevens running in to shoot at Gregg. The goalkeeper could only push the ball up and, as he turned to catch it, Lofthouse came crashing in to sweep everything into the net.

No doubt the fairness of the charge was difficult to assess, but Lofthouse seemed to be going for the loose ball rather than the goalkeeper and to be entitled to do so. If it had been regarded purely as a charge on the goalkeeper then surely this must have been given as a foul, since Gregg was not in possession of the ball and was hit in the back. The referee however had no doubts about the validity of the goal and to their credit the United players did not challenge the decision.

Goalkeepers always had to have a wary eye on Lofthouse, but he was fortunate to have this goal allowed.

There is a pleasant little verse which sums up this encounter so soon after Lofthouse had won his argument over being a licensee:

> Harry Gregg just after t' Final
> Went into Nat's for a beer
> Who returned his money and told him
> We don't charge goalkeepers here!

The Cup wasn't all that Lofthouse won for Bolton. In 11 of his first 13 seasons he was leading goalscorer and of the 804 goals Bolton scored in that period Lofthouse claimed almost a third, 252.

Lionheart was a good name for him. He was indispensable to the Club, yet he never once played in every game in a season. Each year the knocks he took kept him out for some of the matches. And it took a lot to keep Lofthouse off a football field.

Early in 1949 in a Cup replay at Villa Park he was injured as he scored the equaliser, the clash with the goalkeeper rupturing a muscle. He was carried off and Manager Bill Ridding described the injury as 'a lump on his thigh bigger than a lemon'. With a minimum of attention he was back on the field and with the injured leg drove in the two hardest shots of a cup-tie that stretched over six hours before it was resolved. The second pushed even him too hard and he collapsed. That was the Lofthouse style – go hard and drive yourself to the limit. Take the injuries without complaint and without holding back. There was a lack of sophistication in his play, but some of the best defences of the time bowed to the storm of his challenge, crude sometimes, but always effective.

Tommy Lawton was a more polished version, a man without a weakness, master of all the arts. He was too much the all-rounder to be the typical English centre-forward, but he had the distinguishing characteristics of the breed – strength, fearlessness, power in the shot, force and precision in heading. Lawton had in addition all the other attributes of athleticism, control, perceptiveness and perfect balance. In these days of utility forwards he would fit smoothly into any tactical plan.

The modern forward has fewer to support him, more and better organised defenders to defeat. It needs the complete player to score goals regularly in the day of the back four. But those with special individual talent, Jimmy Greaves or Bobby Charlton, or Johan Cruyff or Gerd Muller have been able to find a way through the maze. Lawton would have sent the same ripples of apprehension through those well-drilled, well-organised rearguards.

Standing 6 feet tall Lawton was deadly in the air. That was a natural talent in the Everton successor to 'Dixie' Dean who modelled himself on the master and was coached by him in his early days. A natural athlete, Tom had no difficulty in emulating the elastic spring, that certainty in meeting the ball in the centre of the forehead, that disguised deflection which left the centre-half stranded, the inside running clear. Had so much of his career not spanned the war years Lawton could hold all the goalscoring records in League and International. In 48 games for England Lawton scored 46 times, but the wartime and Victory Internationals were not to count. Yet some of them were played against outstanding sides as in the match Scotland won 5–4 at Hampden. When John Snow was told his wickets against the Rest of the World XI did not count in the official Test Records he commented, 'Not count! When I had to bowl against a side with Barlow, Sobers, Pollock, Richards, Lloyd and with Procter coming in at No. 8! These wickets ought to have counted double.' So might Lawton feel about all those wartime goals, wasted so far as the record books go.

Goals came naturally to him from the start with a phenomenal 570 in 3 seasons of school football in Bolton. By the time he was 14 the scouts were swarming to watch and two years later he played his first game for Burnley in the Second Division. It was a quiet début against Doncaster Rovers, but he scored twice in his next match against Swansea Town.

Not until he was 17 could he sign as a professional and four days later he celebrated with a hat-trick against Tottenham. The manner of the goals confirmed him as already commanding all the scoring skills. The first came after only two minutes as he raced through from Brocklebank's pass to leave backs and centre-half trailing before he swept the ball into the net. There was no clever dummy to wrong-foot the goalkeeper, no sliding the ball home with the inside of the foot. Instead it was hit cleanly and explosively with that thrilling assurance which seemed to make goalkeepers superfluous. That was to be the Lawton hall-mark throughout his playing days.

His second was a soaring header as Lawton outjumped the rest to meet a corner. Even at this age he had the special characteristic of the great headers, timing his run to rise above the markers, then appearing to hang at the height of his jump with time to flick the ball where he willed. His third was coolly taken, steered home without fuss as he mastered the over-eagerness that had wasted two other good chances. That showed him too complete a player to stay with Burnley, the unfashionable club that is always developing outstanding footballers for others to exploit.

Everton, searching for a successor to Dean, paid £6,500, a huge fee for a youngster in those days. Lawton had no difficulty in justifying it. There was a natural self-assurance about him and he had none of the self-deprecatory fears of other high-priced players. In both his first two seasons he was top-scorer in the First Division with 28 goals and then the 35 that played a major part in winning Everton the League Championship in 1939.

Of his nine years on Everton's book six were wasted by the war, although his posting to the Army Physical Training Corps allowed him to continue scoring goals.

At the war's end Chelsea, aiming at the stars, went for the best centre-forward in the country and acquired him for £11,500. In 34 matches Lawton scored 26 goals, a Chelsea record then for the First Division, but the club did not score a hit with him. He was soon asking to move on.

Lawton, cool and confident of his own talent, went to the highest bidder and the headlines filled half the page as England's centre-forward went to Third Division Notts County for £20,000.

On the field Lawton was incapable of giving less than whole-hearted endeavour and the investment was quickly repaid. His 31 goals gave Notts County the Championship of Third Division South in 1950. Their gates soared from 9,000 to 35,000, but Lawton's pay was frozen at the maximum of £12 per week in the playing season, £10 out of it, with a possible £2 extra for a win.

'Pay peanuts and you get monkeys' is the current catch-phrase. Yet for that pittance Lawton, like so many of his generation, gave total endeavour, born from the pride and pleasure he took in his performance. He continued to lion it over the field with a dominance rarely matched by today's high-priced performers. At least that is how some of us remember it. Here is Terence Delaney's total recall of the player and his impact in *Soccer: The Great Ones*.

For me that was one of the unforgettable sights – Lawton, with his smooth and certain stride, moving swiftly and watchfully into position, his dark head jutting forward, and then, at precisely the right moment, gathering himself and rising from his toes in a slow and easy leap, clear above the rest; pausing, it seemed, at the top, and suddenly, with a powerful swinging twist of the neck, striking the ball downwards, right off the centre of the forehead, hard into the goal. Or Lawton, his feet wide apart, lounging and prowling, deceptively relaxed, just outside the penalty area, until the man with the ball let it run just a shade too far; then a pounce, two more strides, and the shot

– that incomparable shot, lazily executed apparently, but travelling like a shell, just inside the post, just under the bar. Nothing to be done; the goalkeeper and the backs, still flatfooted, staring at each other with wide-palmed gestures of anger and reproach. Another Lawton goal; in his twenty years of first-class football he scored 500 of them.

The mere presence of Lawton made the best and coolest of defences uneasy. He was skilful, powerful and dangerous, and one of the great pleasures of watching him was that he looked the part. The footballer's strip of the forties – heavy boots, bulging shin-pads, big flapping shorts – already begins to look as old-fashioned as the whiskers of Dr W. G. Grace; but even in this gear, at a glance, here was a man born and built to be a footballer. He was six foot tall, and just under thirteen stone. His black hair was slicked back from a widow's peak, each side of straight centre parting. His forehead was broad, with high temples, his face long and intent. His eyes were dark and sharp, and his nose commanding. He was wide enough in the shoulders, and big enough in the chest, but it was the solid muscular power of his neck and legs that were most characteristic of him, conditioned his style, and made him the greatest of all headers of the ball. Powerful as he was, his actions were balanced and graceful. 'He was the lightest mover,' Alex James said, 'of any big man who ever played football.'

At the peak of his career, Lawton's reputation in this country, and in any country where football was played, was something extraordinary. Admiration, criticism and controversy followed him everywhere, for he was not only a great player; he carried about with him that extra quality, indefinable but instantly recognisable – he was a star. You felt it the moment he came on the field

Lawton's last two international appearances were a neat illustration of just how quickly soccer success can turn sour. In May 1948 he took his usual leading part in one of England's most impressive victories, scoring for the twenty-second time in his 22 full Internationals. Tom Finney recalls that final goal of his England career, a devastating thrust in the 4–0 defeat of Italy. 'Mortensen's first goal from an impossible angle was the one which drew all the praise. Lawton scored the second at a crucial moment when the Italians were threatening to get right on top of us. The pass was rolled to him some twelve yards out and he made it look so simple, hitting the shot left-footed with effortless power. 'The goalkeeper was still poised, knees bent, hands spread before his face, all set to dive when the ball was already in the net. That's how I remember Tommy – so lithe and so athletic he made the difficult look simple.'

His next International should have been simple enough. In September he played against a Danish side which had recently conceded three goals to England's amateurs. With Len Shackleton and Jimmy Hagan as his insides he got no goals and the game was drawn 0–0. Such was the selectors' shock that this was the only International the talented Hagan ever had, and Lawton was never to be chosen again.

Lawton took crowds, clubs and Managers in his stride, making no concessions, no attempt to please. He was still self-sufficient as he moved on to Second Division Brentford. Bill Slater coming into the team as a youngster remembers him as reserved and introverted, professionally competent but, with powers and energy on the wane, no longer the dynamic leader. Yet he still had enough ability to be sought out by Arsenal. He was 34 when they turned to him and had three more good years before he moved as player-Manager to Kettering with success, and back to Notts County with disillusion. It was a sad end as Notts County dismissed him with acrimony in 1958. Football at the top can be a hard and soulless game even for the great. Lawton had never retaliated in the field throughout a career in which he was the target for every type of obstruction. Now he went with the same quiet dignity from a sport not always fit for heroes.

Sadly Lawton's ability on the football field has not been matched by his management of his affairs off it and he has often hovered on the verge of poverty.

In his youth Lawton contributed to the customary whip-round for an old-timer down on his luck and hanging around the entrance to the dressing-room. The unfortunate had been a fine footballer in his day and now had nothing but the past to live for. As they discussed his situation one perceptive young player asked, 'Is that the end? Is that what we all come to?' Since the abolition of the maximum wage only the feckless among the stars need come to that, but Lawton was born out of time with the gifts of a millionaire, the reward of a pauper.

Five

Hot Shots and Cool Creators

English centre-forwards were brought up to be hard men. The English League was physically the hardest in the world as well as the most demanding endurance test. And they were the Uriahs, forever in the forefront of the battle.

None was harder than Bobby Smith. I had the chance to observe this early in his career. In 1953 our amateur team, Pegasus, played against him. This was how the encounter appeared to our centre-half, Ken Shearwood, who wrote in his *Pegasus* book:

We had one set-to in November with the Chelsea reserves in a so-called 'friendly' at Oxford. We had a strong side out and were 4–2 up at half-time. Towards the end of the first half the Chelsea captain, Joe Willemse, marking Tony Pawson, who had already scored twice, got, as they say, well and truly stuck in.

I was marking Bobby Smith, who was to play at centre-forward for Spurs and England. He was physically immensely strong and for high balls down the middle, held me off with a back as broad as a barn door, so that by half-time I had not won a single ball in the air. 'Lie off him a bit,' advised our coach, George Ainsley, 'and come in with a run.'

I did so, soon after the start of the second half, and sailing in high through the air won the ball, but caught Bobby Smith in the small of the back and down he went, all thirteen and a half stone of him.

'Sorry,' I said, and he gave me an old-fashioned look as he got to his feet.

'There's too much bloody sorry in this game, mate, I'm getting stuck in from now on.'

So it was with interest that I saw Bobby Smith create similar havoc against more powerful centre-halves in games where no one was saying sorry.

The most profitable pairing in the early Sixties was between Jimmy Greaves and Bobby Smith, the two working with the deadly co-operation of a Butch Cassidy and the Sundance Kid. Greaves, the gentle humorist, had a special affinity with 'Big Smithy' dating from their Chelsea days. Together they were doubly formidable, the skills of the one enhanced by the strength of the other.

Bobby Smith was often criticised as a clumsy bull of a forward, lacking control. On occasions, however, there was a surprising delicacy in his play. One of the best goals seen at Wembley was scored by Smith in England's 4–2 defeat of Spain in 1960. Bobby cleverly worked clear, drew the goalkeeper and chipped the ball cheekily over his head. It was an impish Greaves-type goal scored by a rogue elephant of a player. Smith indeed had ability enough and success enough to be counted among the outstanding goalscorers, making a vital contribution to Spurs and England's years of triumph.

Form can be ephemeral, however. The 1960–1 season was bitter-sweet for Smith as success turned sour. He had 8 of the 32 goals England scored in only five matches while Greaves hunted even more profitably in the space Smith created. Even so he lost his place to the more delicately balanced strikers like Pointer, or Crawford, or Hitchens. In April 1962 he was recalled just before England's World Cup party for Chile was to be chosen. But it was a disastrous comeback at Hampden with Scotland winning 2–0 and Smith looking too ponderous now to appeal to the selectors. So Hitchens, and Peacock of Middlesbrough, were preferred, and soon Smith was drifting down the Divisions.

So many of the outstanding scorers in English football have been centre-forwards of his type. In the last fifty years there have been another dozen as forceful and as memorable as Bobby Smith. Among those who bulldozed their way to goal with resolute courage and shot with killing power, Vic Watson of West Ham and England was outstanding in the Twenties. Here is a contemporary account of his six goals in an 8–2 defeat of Leeds United in a First Division match in February 1929.

This was a triumph for West Ham's international centre, strong in the legs, broad in the shoulder, quick in his shooting and alert in wit – especially in seeing the next move.

The heavy turf, for the surface was just sludge, suited him. He lay well ahead, got some long passes sent to him, swished the ball to the wing (generally Yews), and then closed in on goal. His sure foot did the rest, Watson has just the build to play well on such a pitch.

A man might get six goals and still be an indifferent performer, but Watson was the moving spirit all the time.

He was a fine header of the ball, following in the tradition of Jack Cock, the first Cornishman to play for England. They said of Watson that when he was in form the ball arrowed into the net from just above his left eyebrow. Yet such was the competition he won only five caps between 1923 and 1930. And yet the forceful Vic Watson is one of only fifteen players to score more than three hundred League goals.

A similar type of player was the Irishman, Jimmy Dunne, whose success with Sheffield United led Chapman to buy him up for Arsenal, the mecca of all the best players of the time. Here is Catton's commentary in the *Observer* of the early demonstration of his prowess in the Sheffield side in 1930.

Little is seen now of Billy Gillespie, but another Irishman has come into the forwards in J. Dunne, who has held the berth against all rivals. He is not a new man, although he only played twice last season.

In September he scored three goals against Leicester City and that success put him on his feet. Yesterday he scored four against the same Midland team – his second set of four in a week as he was also responsible for all four goals against West Ham on New Year's Day.

Two 'fours' within four days in First Division is rare indeed. At once Dunne comes to the fore with an aggregate of 23 goals already. A well-built man, he is both thrustful and sure-footed.

Dunne had 41 goals before the season ended, a Sheffield United record. This big fair-haired man with the short, fast steps continued to score the goals. He had 14 for the Republic of Ireland in 15 games, a record until Don Givens passed it with the aid of 3 goals against Russia and 4 against Turkey in the European Nations Championship 1974–5. The best always attracted Herbert Chapman and he went after Dunne, but when Arsenal did get him he was past his best and made less impact than Jack Lambert.

Lambert was looked on as just a strong finisher who scored the goals that Jack made – or James, or the wingers made. Yet always he kept out the more polished forwards Chapman bought to replace him. He kept his place against Dave Halliday, scorer of 336 goals in a career that took him from Dundee, to Sunderland, to Arsenal, to Manchester City, to Clapton Orient. He kept out Tim Coleman and George Hunt. If a striker has the gift of goals you don't want to examine that gift too closely. The Italian Club, Roma, once had a high-scoring centre who did not look stylish enough to the club President. So they spent more than a million pounds on five replacements, including John Charles, all of whom failed to oust him. Jack Lambert in the same way stayed on at Arsenal, a better player than he was credited with being, except by Bastin, who thrived on his partnership. In his autobiography Bastin rated him higher even than his final successor, Ted Drake, and marvelled that he never had a single International cap.

Ted Drake set the Arsenal record of 42 goals in 1934–5, his first season at Highbury, with the blind courage, the impetuous dash of his play. Yet the cool, analytical Bastin preferred the uncapped Lambert, though recognising that Drake solved the problem left by his departure. 'Ted had terrific speed, great strength, and an immensely powerful shot. A nightmare to any centre-half, he was particularly good at taking advantage of the long ball down the middle. Jack, however, was more of a footballer, did a good deal of wandering and fitted in better with my style. When Ted received the ball, he would charge straight down the middle, taking it, and often the attendant centre-half, with him.' Lambert's misfortune was to have such a wealth of competitors. Even Dixie Dean had only sixteen matches for England, while George Camsell had a mere nine caps, although his record makes him one of the most consistent scorers in the game. Harry Bedford, another forceful centre-forward, only managed to get into England's side for one game against Sweden in 1923 and one against Northern Ireland in 1925. Yet Bedford had a career record of 309 goals for his seven clubs, Nottingham Forest, Blackpool, Derby, Newcastle, Sunderland, Bradford, and Chesterfield.

Ted Drake represented his country only five times in the period from 1935 to 1939. Yet he was at least as good a centre-forward as Bobby Smith, who had three times his number of caps. Ted Drake indeed is one of the immortals, and not just because of his 7 goals in a game. In this most demanding of all positions at that time he had not only high courage, but great sportsmanship and good humour. In the last League match of 1936 he headed a goal which proved his fitness to play in the Cup Final and also ensured the relegation of Aston Villa, the team against whom he had scored 7 earlier that season. Drake thought only of their dejection, not his triumph. Instead of giving today's gladiatorial salute of success Drake wheeled instantly to apologise, genuinely regretful that *his* goal should have relegated a sporting team fighting hard for survival.

Ted's exit from the game was in the grand manner, scoring 4 goals in his last League match against Sunderland before the war ended his playing career.

Without Drake Arsenal were struggling in that first season after the war, bottom of the table in the middle of October. For salvation they turned not to the young thrusters of the day, but to two men of character and experience. Within a fortnight Joe Mercer came from Everton and Ronnie Rooke arrived from Fulham. Mercer was still one of football's brightest stars, but Rooke was rated a 'has-been', even though he had scored so freely for Fulham, and had netted 6 in one cup-tie against Bury. He was in the Drake mould, but at 33 his form was beginning to desert him and he was expecting to drift out of the game. The call to Highbury set the adrenalin flowing as never before, and he restored Arsenal's fortunes as well as his own. Until he came that gifted scorer, Reg Lewis, had no support, having scored 11 of the 15 goals Arsenal had managed.

'You must get goals by hook or by Rooke,' Manager Whittaker told him, and he did that well enough to lift Arsenal to a thirteenth place, which seemed lucky after so disastrous a start. Next season Arsenal ended 7 points clear at the head of the First Division and Rooke was the Division's leading scorer with 33, aided by the skills of little Logie, who had something of the style and stature of Alex James.

Rooke was a craggy, determined player with billiard-table legs, a deeply lined face and the large, crooked nose of a pugilist. He was strong in the air and a certain scorer from close in, since he could hit the ball so hard with so little back-lift. Often he looked to have stumbled past the ball, yet with his body a foot in front he would still reach back and hit it firmly into the net. Joe Mercer recalls his instinct for knocking the ball in somehow, anyhow. 'We had an overwhelming win against Middlesbrough with David Jack in his first season as their Manager. Jack was getting more and more depressed as the goals went in. Then a goalkick hit Rooke on the back of the head and rebounded into the net. To Jack it was the final agony, to Rooke a typical goal.'

For Ronnie Rooke there was a happy ending, but not for the man with the fairy story start, which promised to make him one of the outstanding goalscorers.

The most meteoric centre-forward of them all flamed too briefly across the scene. Derek Dooley was a one-season sensation, the ideal target man for Sheffield Wednesday as his red hair flared above the defenders. And once the ball reached Dooley there was no stopping this 6 ft. 3 ins. man of muscle with the size 12 boots. The net was the target he hit with bewildering frequency, scoring a remarkable 46 goals in only 30 games to take Sheffield Wednesday to the Second Division title in 1952. He did not come into the side until October and yet he had these 46 out of the hundred goals they scored that season. 'Thunderboots' they called him and that expressed the awesome power of his shooting, the powerful bustle of his play.

Scorers do not live by power alone and Dooley had this instinctive feel for the position of goal and goalkeeper, his shots homing for the unguarded spot. He had the fiery courage of Wales's Trevor Ford, the accurate finishing of a Greaves, an elemental force beyond the experience of most defenders. From their own fear they reacted with threats. 'Right, Dooley, you'll get no goals today, lad, or I'll break both your legs' was a sample of the psychological warfare aimed at taming the young phenomenon. And a broken leg was indeed the only thing that stopped him scoring. But it was pure accident. Chasing eagerly after a through pass in a February game against Preston, Dooley collided with the goalkeeper. Gangrene set in and the leg was lost, one of the most exciting scorers gone from the field in the glad, confident morning of his youth.

When the prizes were not high the price of football success often was. Another scoring prodigy cut down in his prime was Alick Jeffery, the youngest man ever to play in the Cup proper when he was in Doncaster Rovers' side against Aston Villa on his sixteenth birthday, 29 January 1955. For a time it was all goals and adulation for this strong young striker. Then his leg and his career were both broken and he was declared unfit ever to play again. The insurance money was paid, with £4,000 of the £15,000 going to Jeffery soon to be dissipated, in drink and parties, as he searched in vain for the lost glamour. That remarkable Englishman, George Raynor, who became the most successful national coach Sweden have had, agreed to help the young man whom the doctors had written off. Raynor's quiet insistence, allied to a routine of exercises developed over many years, worked the miracle. He was declared fit for league football again. There was to be no happy ending, however. Jeffery could never recapture his form and was injured again. And for Raynor there was criticism, not congratulation, from authorities faced with awkward explanations to the insurance company.

Jackie Milburn was a centre-forward of a new type. The thrust and the courage were there, but he was more greyhound than bulldog. Here was a man who relied more on fleetness of foot than power of heading, more on strength of shot than robust physical challenge. Two goals which won a Cup Final for Newcastle exactly expressed the abilities which were so idolised on Tyneside. Against Blackpool in 1951 he raced through from the half-way line, beating the off-side trap, leaving Hayward trailing far behind, and hitting the shot firmly past Farm. Four minutes later little Ernie Taylor's skilful back heel rolled the ball into Milburn's path on the edge of the area. Without pause he sent his shot searing into the net. It needed only one characteristic racing run, one typically explosive shot to win the Cup.

Milburn's long leg always swung in a great arc as he hit these drives which travelled as swift and straight as light. The leg followed through fully stretched until it was at right angles to the body. Like so many of his contemporaries Milburn had practised endlessly from childhood with sponge balls, tennis balls, anything he could kick along streets or against walls. The smaller, softer, higher bouncing balls developed a more instinctive control in the young than the present practice of starting early with 'proper' footballs. The scoring instinct came early, but the practice was unrelenting. The mature Milburn still had his long and lonely sessions, kicking into an empty goal peopled in his imagination with three defenders on the line.

Stan Mortensen was the man on whom Milburn modelled himself, fascinated by his dynamic finishing when he watched 'Morty' play for Ashington early in the war. It was for Ashington, the rich Northumberland mine of footballers, that Milburn first played, when still an apprentice fitter in the local colliery of his home town. Soon he was asking Newcastle for a trial. They gave him two, offered him thirty shillings a match and put him straight into the first team. He began as inside-left or right wing. There was sense in that for Milburn's burning speed was over a distance, not that instant acceleration of the goalscorer over the first five yards. He himself disliked the idea of playing centre after a failure in the position when a schoolboy. But in the second season after the war Manager George Martin asked him to go centre-forward and Milburn was never one to put self before side. He had a sleepless night before his first game, but for Newcastle, his only club, it was the start of a golden decade, which saw them win the Cup three times.

In 354 League games Milburn scored 179 goals and in 13 matches for England he had 10. For his first International in 1948 against

Northern Ireland he was in the centre with his own idol, Stan Mortensen, as his inside right. That formidable pair collected 4 between them, but it was Mortensen who had the hat-trick. They were two of a kind, similarly talented and respecting each other's skill. When Milburn struck that crushing goal against Blackpool, Mortensen ran to shake his hand and say, 'That was a goal which deserves to win the Cup.' Like Ted Drake, these two were highly competitive players, who never let the urge to win undermine their sportsmanship or their sense of fun.

Milburn's one weakness was a reluctance to head the ball. He could do it well, when he wanted, as with a fine glancing header which set Newcastle on the way to another Cup Final victory over Manchester City. Usually he held back because his obsession as a boy for keeping on his light, damp football kit on freezing days had left him with fibrositis in the neck. So he was content to average 8 goals a season with his head and rely on those formidable feet.

Courage, energy and enjoyment were the distinguishing charac-teristics which made Mortensen rather special. His build was slight for a centre-forward, but his heart was outsize. Mortensen ran like a trotting horse. His shoulders were hunched forward, not like the other Stan's to baffle the tackler, but to absorb the jarring shock of collision. Give him a 'hospital' pass likely to involve a dangerous collision and Mortensen would chase it however hard and threatening the other man going for the ball. He would run at the heart of harsh defences with a gathering acceleration. Billy Wright watched him with awe in his England games. 'He had such thin, white, spindly legs and looked so frail you held your breath as he went in jet-propelled.'

Mortensen had the same remarkable energy which made Alan Ball such a useful member of England's World Cup winning team. But it was controlled by a more equable temperament, which shrugged off slights and laughed at misfortune. His play expressed a great joy in living, the carefree exuberance of a colt in springtime. For him every minute, every game was a bonus joyfully accepted. He regarded himself as living on borrowed time for in the war he had been dragged from a crashed Wellington bomber with severe head and back injuries not expected to survive.

Mortensen was the happy, resilient humorist who could still smile when his achievements were diminished by Matthews' long shadow, so that he was slightingly referred to as the 'other Stanley'. Even his most memorable performance went almost unrecognised. That emotional 1953 Cup Final is known simply as Matthews' match, the day the maestro won his medal. Although Matthews made that last killing goal on the stroke of time, it was Mortensen who won the Cup with three characteristic thrusts. He and Lofthouse were rivals for the England position and both had scored in every round of the Cup. Lofthouse scored again in the first minute of the Final, but Mortensen's swift shot brought an early equaliser. With twenty minutes to go Bolton were leading 3–1. Then Hanson in Bolton's goal momentarily lost his hold on one of Matthews' flighted centres. Before he could drop on the ball Mortensen had thrust in to stab it home, crashing into the post in his eagerness to score. Bolton now had their quota of cripples and if Blackpool could only force extra time the game was certainly theirs. As the minutes slipped away so did their chance. Then came a free kick just outside the area. The wall formed up, but Mortensen arrowed his shot through them into the roof of the net. That was the moment the Cup was won, although Matthews and Perry spared Bolton the agony of extra time.

In 25 Internationals Mortensen scored 23 goals, but there was one by which he will always be remembered. In the 1948 match in Turin, England faced a fine Italian side and a crowd desperate for success. In this feverish atmosphere Mortensen struck the immediate telling blow with an outrageous goal. As he careered through almost to the bye-line Bacigalupo moved to cover the cross. Instead Mortensen, still at top speed, hit a shot which swerved inside the startled goalkeeper into the near roof of the net.

As his speed waned, Mortensen became just another player dropping down from Blackpool to Hull, to Southport, to non-league Bath City to Lancaster City. There was nothing sad about the decline for 'Morty' was still playing and enjoying his football beyond the age of forty. In his fourteen seasons of League football he had hit 225 goals in 395 matches, scoring 197 of them for Blackpool.

The Munich air crash in 1958 left a tragic trail, one of its victims that most promising centre-forward, Tommy Taylor. He was shaping as another Lawton in that position, relying on all-round skills rather than any special qualities of speed, strength, or shooting ability with head or foot. Taylor was one of those all-purpose footballers who would have fitted neatly into Ramsey's scheme of play, and his early games for England were at inside left, as second striker. In nineteen appearances for England he scored 16 times.

His first match only lasted 23 minutes, the game against Argentina being abandoned because the Buenos Aires pitch had become a quagmire. England's record in South America is not too impressive but these were conditions in which English players revel. There was no score, but Taylor had already hit the bar and the Argentinians were clearly sliding to defeat when referee Arthur Ellis called the game off. The English team were not amused by the decision, and the unfortunate Ellis was greeted on the bus with a rousing chorus of 'Yellow Bird'.

Taylor scored in both his first two full games against Chile and Uruguay, but he was at his best at centre-forward at Wembley in May 1956, when England had their only win over Brazil. Taylor had two of the four goals, confusing the defenders by clever positional play and beating them both in the air and on the ground. With his short curly hair and round eager face Taylor looked the enthusiastic youngster, but he was mature and accomplished in temperament and technique. His knee had been suspect when he went from Doncaster to Manchester United, but, like his play, it was getting stronger all the time.

As England began their preparations for the World Cup Finals in Sweden Taylor again took a leading part in a crushing 4–0 defeat of France in November 1957. France finished third in Sweden, with Brazil the winners. Had Tommy Taylor, Duncan Edwards and Roger Byrne not died in the crash that winter England might not have had to wait until 1966 to win the Jules Rimet trophy.

Replacing him was no easy task and one of the contenders was the man who was getting so many goals for Middlesbrough, Brian Clough. Clough was a man of quick reaction in the penalty area where he loitered with intent. He pursued goals with the same driving determination with which he was later to pursue success as manager or feuds with those who crossed him. Clough was a poacher of goals like Gallacher, or Greaves, lithe, well balanced, with quick anticipation. The sharp face, framed by the short bristly hair, ferreted out the goal chances which he rarely missed.

In a mere seven seasons from 1956 to 1963 Clough scored 246 goals for Middlesbrough and Sunderland, yet only won two England caps. Selectorial madness is Clough's explanation, but it is surprising to read reports of the time blaming it on Clough's self-doubts and lack of confidence. That was not how it appeared to Walter Winterbottom. 'An essential part of a goalscorer's make-up is self-confidence and Clough was brimming with it.' He may even have had too much for his own good. While the World Cup side was re-forming, a disastrous 5–0 defeat in Yugoslavia caused speculation that Clough would take over from Kevan. In discussion Winterbottom found Wright and the senior players keen to keep the forceful Kevan, rather than risk a more individualist sharp-shooter. So Kevan was retained and Winterbottom had a quiet talk with Clough to forestall his disappointment when the team was later announced. Before the deadline for its publication Winterbottom was assailed by some of his players and some of the press, since news of the selection had already leaked. There seemed only one way that could have happened and the suspicion hardly improved Clough's standing.

It was not long, however, before he was picked, a fair debut in a drawn game with Wales being followed by a miserable performance in the match at Wembley lost 2–3 to Sweden. When he most needed to, Clough failed to take his chances. He was unfortunate, though, in being teamed with Greaves and Charlton as his insides. Those were three characters in selfish search of goals with no one to create them. When he broke a leg Clough was only 27, his goal tally 252 with even Rowley's record in his sights at the rate he was slapping them in. And as Manager goals have remained his first priority.

The name, centre-forward, was to go as the pattern of the game changed. There were only 'strikers' or 'target men' to challenge the back four and few of them were specialist goalscorers. Geoff Hurst was the best of the new breed, running and working with unselfish dedication, but retaining a keen sense for the opening.

'Nice guys never win anything' is sport's most overworked and most misleading adage. There has to be some competitive edge to the great players, but in football, Parker, Hapgood, Drake, Bobby Charlton, Greaves, Finney, Matthews, Meredith, Morton and a score of others disprove the words, which have played so malign a part in encouraging the shaken fist and driven boot. Certainly Geoff Hurst was the blueprint of a 'nice guy'. And he won the most important match of them all. Hurst's hat-trick in 1966 was the only one to be scored in a World Cup Final and it proved decisive in England's 4–2 win. Hurst, that pleasant, smiling man, never retaliated although he reached his peak in the decade of the late tackler, of defenders who took pride in 'biting the back of your leg'. There was little protection for the likes of Hurst until the stricter code of refereeing and discipline brought the hard men under control.

In his early days with West Ham Hurst was labelled an 'honest trier'. The characteristic puffing of the cheeks, that laboured stride, both gave the impression of toil and strain which had the crowd deriding him as a 'cart-horse'. Hurst's efforts looked the clumsier when compared with that clever, darting, birdlike forward, 'Budgie' Byrne, whose antics delighted the spectators. It was Johnny Byrne who looked the class player, and yet Hurst was to be of far greater value to West Ham and England.

Hurst could happily shrug off the spectators' lack of understanding because opposing defenders were just as slow to appreciate his special skills. He was a strong runner with great stamina, he could shoot hard with either foot, particularly his left, and he controlled the ball well off chest or thigh. His heading too was competent enough, but competency seemed all he had to offer. There were many others faster, or braver, or more subtle in their dribbling, or with the lithe, loose limbs which can hook in the awkward ball. Amid those born talented, Hurst was the man who had greatness thrust upon him. He is the catch in the throat for those who would deride coaching. For Hurst's special abilities were manufactured in the endless coaching sessions, stemming from his own determination to improve and his total belief in Ron Greenwood's new theories. From a perspiring wing-half with little future he was converted to a forward aspiring to an England cap. His special tricks were trained in as carefully as if he was a circus horse, rather than a puller of carts. There were two in which he was endlessly drilled. The first was in timing his runs to come in late and fast like Greaves. That was no natural instinct for Hurst, and Greenwood spent hours running beside him, or shouting 'Now' from the sidelines or even 'wired' to him to transmit instructions. The final pay-off of those hours of training came at Wembley as he stole unnoticed past the German defence, coming from deep with perfect timing to meet Moore's free-kick. As Hurst headed home beyond Tilkowski the usual arguments started among the defenders, 'Where did he come from? . . . Why didn't *you* pick him up?'

The other move drummed into Hurst was the 'near-post' goal. Traditionally the strikers had wanted the ball in the middle of the goal or the far side of it, giving them more time to home in and more goal at which to aim. By running late and diagonally to meet the shorter cross, Hurst could get to the ball before defenders. Then the glancing header or flicked shot, instinctively struck, had a fair chance of beating the equally surprised goalkeeper. For two or three seasons that move left defenders bemused, convinced it was someone else's fault or a lucky goal.

It was one such 'near-post' goal which killed off the Germans, the second in that famous hat-trick. Ball broke free down the right with his small, swift stride and pulled the ball back to Hurst, moving at the right moment to meet the pass. Swivelling to leave the sweeper stranded, Hurst lashed his shot against the underside of the bar, to bounce down over the line.

As the ball spun back out of goal and Weber came running from behind Hunt to head over the bar, Wembley was hushed in apprehension. Only the Russian linesman's decisive gesture unloosed the tumult of sound, the beautiful noise of victory. Many Germans felt they were cheated by the decision, since no camera shot finally proved the ball *was* over the line. One action confirmed beyond doubt that Hurst's goal was good. Roger Hunt was waiting there as the ball spun back, but instead of turning it in Hunt wheeled instantly away arms aloft to salute the goal he knew had been scored. But for an admirable linesman, that might have cost England dear. Hunt should have removed all argument and suspense by knocking it into the back of the net. He broke two of football's commandments: 'Play to the whistle', and 'Always make sure.'

Hurst's third goal gave proof of that extra stamina trained into him. In the final minute of extra time, when Wembley had drained so many others, he was still fit enough to take Moore's pass, run more than half the length of the pitch and hit so fierce a shot with his powerful left foot that Tilkowski barely sighted the ball.

Hurst came into the England World Cup side only because Greaves' shin was gashed in the game against France and he was out for two matches. In all probability Hurst was the one preferred to Greaves even when Greaves was fit for the Final. If results can justify a selection then Hurst's was splendidly confirmed as appropriate.

The only hat-trick in a World Cup Final could not have gone to a nicer person. It went to one whose ordinary qualities had been made extraordinary by conscientious training. These three goals were a justification of coaching. They also gave Hurst new confidence and personality. No need now for him to use Bobby Moore's name to get a table booking at an expensive restaurant. No need for him to hide away in England training sessions, as he had done at first when wondering what he was doing among the established stars.

From that moment Hurst's game grew in authority. When he finally passed out of League football and continued to enjoy the game as player-manager of Telford, he had scored 200 league goals for West Ham and Stoke, another 16 in his matches for England. The team man had been rewarded by individual success and individual acclaim, but he always remained the team man. When Hurst first felt he was in a rut at West Ham, and must move on, he put in his transfer request. Unknown to Hurst, Martin Peters had done the same half an hour earlier. When he heard that, Hurst was at once aware of the blow it would be to a club from which he had received so much. At once he withdrew his application – the gesture that was to be expected from this 'nice guy'.

Hurst left a gap that England had not filled ten years after that World

Cup triumph. They had no striker of his all-round ability, no mid-field creators capable of making his successors larger than life.

Scotland's greater success in the Seventies has entitled them to make critical remarks about English football. John Rafferty, then the leading Scottish football writer, made this comment in the *Observer* when Scotland, not England, qualified for the World Cup Finals in Germany in 1974. 'The English never buy hatchet men from us. Over a very long period, however, they have purchased our creative players. Maybe they have no shortage of hard men! But for years they have had no one who can pass like Haynes used to, sending those long balls which came sliding up alongside the running forward.'

Willie Ormond was a Manager who emphasised traditional Scottish skills in his selections and in his tactics. In looking at his style Rafferty pointed the contrast with English teams which have not been true to their traditions and basic strengths.

Ormond is a wingers' man and not just because he was one himself. He is one because he is simple and uncomplicated in his thinking. He says 'Why bunch in there when you can spread out?'

The reason for his simplicity is that he does not mix in circles of high velocity coaches and managers whose jargon would have your head full of magic.

Apparently it is too simple to give the answer to a packed defence 'Don't let them pack.' This is an age of overthink. When the truth is reached no one seems to want to leave it at that, but to carry on past the truth and arrive at some academic monstrosity. Everybody used to learn to read – very well too – by learning sounds. That was too easy and more complicated ways were devised until illiteracy prevailed.

So it is with football, particularly in England. The basics at which they used to be good have been forgotten. There has evolved an obsession with team work; players as individuals have been stamped on. It is not new patterns that are wanted but an increased emphasis on skills. That was learned as far back as 1953 from the Hungarians. What they need to relearn is the heading of Dean, the shooting of Lawton, the direct, lancing dribbles of Finney and the long precision passes of Haynes.

These strictures are apt enough now, but no Scot would have dared to make them in the year England won the World Cup. Apart from Hurst and Charlton, England did then have three insides whose contrasting skills covered the range of technical ability: Ball, Peters and Roger Hunt.

Martin Peters, with 21 goals for England in 67 matches, justified Ramsey's conviction that he was a player of unusual talent 'ten years ahead of his time in his approach to football'. Ramsey was talking in 1968 about the richness of talent in the England side of the day, but Peters had a sleepless night wondering if this was a polite way of saying he did not fit in any longer. Certainly it gave the opportunity to critics of Peters to be witty at his expense. In a typically caustic comment Malcolm Allison said on television during the World Cup in Mexico, 'Peters is the man who is ten years ahead of his time. So it looks as if we will have to wait that long for him to come good.'

Some, like Allison, felt Peters did not come good, because there was so little sign of striving and he so often disappeared from the game. Ramsey's view was the more perceptive. 'He is a great player. He has a wonderful sense of timing that would enable him to be outstanding at any ball game. His chief attribute, however, is to see situations and positions which lesser players don't notice.'

In another way Peters is a ghost, a 'Third Man', as much in the background as Harry Lime himself. At West Ham he was overshadowed by Moore and Hurst and even though he scored in the World Cup Final it was Hurst and Ball among the forwards who edged him out of the headlines.

As Greaves' career went into decline – he had lost pace after a jaundice attack in November 1965 – Peters was swapped for him in March 1970. But Spurs had to pay another £146,000 so much more highly was Peters then rated. Four years earlier he did not reckon himself more valuable. Like Greaves, he had been discovered playing schools football in Dagenham and Greaves had been his boyhood idol. 'I felt desperately sorry for Jimmy when he was not picked for the World Cup Final and the thought went through my mind, 'What am I doing here if Greaves is just a spectator?'

Peters might not be a goalscorer to equal Greaves at his best, but he has always been an elegant, graceful footballer with an eye for an opening.

Alan Ball is a different type of player, all aggression rather than evasion, never disappearing from the game, in which he is combatively involved for the full ninety minutes. Extra time in the World Cup Final called out the best in him. As others tired Ball ran and ran, even further and faster, until that star player, Schnellinger, nearly abandoned the chase. Those were his finest thirty minutes in all his 72 games for

England, where his effort and perceptive passing made goals for others but only 8 for himself. That is a poor return for a man who has passed 150 goals in League football and indicates the weight of responsibility born by Alan Ball in midfield for England. For his country winning the ball was his first task, with Stiles and himself the two mighty atoms who battled for it in midfield. His voice is so squeaky it might not have broken – but there is nothing else of the choirboy about him as he snaps into his tackles or drives on his team with high-pitched advice.

The explosive temperament that goes with his red hair spilled over once too often in Katowice in 1973. He intervened belligerently in a scuffle between Peters and a Polish player in that bad-tempered World Cup match and was rightly sent off.

In the hard men's world of English football Alan has always been an inspirational force, his own total involvement involving others. Everton, Arsenal and England all gave him the captaincy, Revie calling him back to the national team for his competitiveness and both the clubs recognising that his leadership qualities were not undermined by those flashes of temperament. Ball's life-style off the field reflected his temperament on it. Fast cars and race-horses have a fascination for him and he's always ready to gamble.

There was no gamble about his becoming an England footballer. He might have been put together for the game like some bionic man. His father, who was never in the first flight as a player or a manager, was determined his son should make it to the top. When his mother worried about his weak chest his father had him take up cross-country running, which built his remarkable stamina. And 'Big Alan', managing Ashton United in the Lancashire Combination, put young Alan in the first team when he was only 14. That was forcing him all right, for he was small for his age. And it failed in its immediate purpose, for Bolton, the club his family so wanted young Ball to join, rejected him at 15. Blackpool took him on, however, and on 18 August 1962, aged 17, Ball played his first First Division game against Liverpool.

Roger Hunt was the man who had just helped Liverpool back from the Second Division, where his 41 goals had made him leading scorer the previous season. Brave, strong and straightforward, Hunt was typical of the players who appealed to Bill Shankly as he took the club back to the heights. Liverpool successfully combined the creative skill of the Scots with the speed and determination of the English, virtues which Hunt so admirably demonstrated. And Shankly's emphasis on traditional values and the simple approach found a ready answer in

Hunt's play. He was fast, he was hard, he had a powerful shot and above all he had the spirit for the relentless pressure play demanded at Anfield. Shankly always demanded maximum effort – but confined his players to limited zones so that they had proper recovery time. He required compliance with the tactical plans but kept them so simple that unsubtle footballers like Hunt never had too much demanded of them. Hunt scored 245 goals for Liverpool and another 24 for Bolton Wanderers. Fair-haired and fair-minded, Hunt was an uncomplicated thruster at goal who gave defences no rest as he bored in at them himself, or came driving up to meet those crosses from the wing which have always remained an essential part of Liverpool's play whatever the current tactical fad elsewhere. Hunt had none of the elasticity, or the quick turn, of a Greaves, but he attacked the goal persistently and effectively, an archetypal Liverpool and England striker.

Hunt was the last of a breed that has been dying, to the detriment of the English game. Just as centre-forwards were rechristened 'strikers', England seemed to run out of those with the pace, power and passion the new name suggested. Instead of the 'hammerheads' of old there was Chivers, that big, strong man so full of talent, so lacking in fire. Rarely did Chivers operate at full throttle and yet his shooting and heading could be devastating when he exerted himself. When he left England to play in Swiss football Martin Chivers had scored 215 League goals. He had been a prodigy with Southampton, a mixed blessing for Spurs and England, who had so many hours of exasperation to offset against the memorable moments, the great goals. For England he scored 13 times in 24 matches and yet left that same sad aura of boundless potential not fully realised.

Joe Royle has been a similar disappointment. At 16 he came into the Everton side at Blackpool in place of the idol of Merseyside, the smooth, swift Alex Young with his graceful movement and neat dribbling. Harry Catterick was assaulted after the game by some Everton supporters, who could not understand how the Manager could have left out that whippet of a player for a clumsy-looking youngster. Royle, standing over six feet and broad in proportion, has in fact all the skills to be another Lawton, so light and fast is he on his feet. John Charles, that formidable centre-forward, saw in Royle a player with all his own qualities when young. But another comment by Charles in the twilight of his career may point to one reason Royle could not emulate him. 'Centre-forwards do not seem to challenge so hard for the header. My own forehead has been stitched forty times after deep cuts. You don't see any stitches on foreheads today.' And Royle's power has too often been concealed, as he goes apologetically for the header instead of demanding the ball as his right.

In 1972 he came into an England side, decimated by withdrawals, for the match against Yugoslavia. His heading still lacked power, but he was commanding on the ground, so fast and destructive that Katalinski, his marker, had to be substituted. He looked the decisive forward England needed, but it was an illusory flash of brilliance. Royle was soon to be dogged by odd accidents, in training, or from over-enthusiastic embraces after scoring, or from a stone leaping out of a lawnmower into his eye. As he moved on from Everton to Manchester City his international career became as accident prone, the chances of establishing himself never fully grasped. Mike Channon rates him the most helpful striker he has played beside, since he pressures defenders into mistakes and makes chances for others. But the selectors have been less convinced of his ability.

One forward who has not lacked pace, passion and self-assurance is Super-Mac. On Tyneside Malcolm Macdonald was hailed as another Milburn. He has indeed the same sprinter's pace, the same lethal power in his left foot, the same driving strength. But his range of skills has been too limited, his angle of attack, always looking for the ball on his left foot, too predictable. He had his moment of triumph with England scoring all five goals against Cyprus, but the failures in important matches were more frequent. And if Macdonald does not score goals, there is little else to his game. Even the kindly Joe Mercer, who was England's caretaker Manager after Ramsey, commented, 'There is no way anyone else can play off Macdonald because his whole game is geared to scoring himself. He is greedy for goals.' He was greedy all right the first time he met his old club, scoring a hat-trick to remind Newcastle of their loss in transferring him. His value was rated by Arsenal at £330,000 and though, predictably, the individualist needed time to fit into a side dedicated to method, it was not long before he was justifying the assessment. He has the spirit of the best of the 'English' centre-forwards, but not their range of skills. If only Macdonald, Chivers and Royle could have been made into a composite forward, there indeed would have been a complete goalscorer instead of three nearly greats. Macdonald's transfer fee rated him the hottest shot in the game after Bob Latchford when he joined the 'Gunners' with 149 goals already scored in League football. Yet there are other consistent goal-getters, who could hit the ball as hard without commanding so high a price.

Peter Lorimer and Alan Woodward are two wingers with the power to score remarkable goals, blasting the ball in from far out. The hardest driven shot I have seen was by Lorimer when Leeds were a goal down to Chelsea in an F.A. Cup Semi-final at Villa Park in 1967. With time running out a free-kick was rolled across. From 25 yards out Lorimer sent his shot skimming in before Bonetti could move. That should have been the saving goal, but it was harshly disallowed since some courageous Chelsea players had been standing too close to Lorimer, who could not repeat the thunderbolt. 'Lucky' Arsenal used to be the cry, but as so often in crucial matches this was 'unlucky' Leeds.

From Woodward came the other too hardest hit goals in my viewing – and both in the same match. As Sheffield United slid quietly out of the First Division in 1975–6 Woodward still surprised Derby's high-flying side. At the Baseball Ground he won the game with an angled 40-yard shot in each half. Boulton had clear sight of each, yet both times the goalkeeper was decisively beaten by the speed of the ball.

Derby themselves had two of the fiercest strikers of a ball. There was Alan Hinton, who brought with him from Wolves a well-trained left foot which raked in the shots and the crosses. Midfield, Hinton could be a timid player, his white boots seeming symbols of surrender against the crunching tackles. Near goal he was a changed and forceful personality, his searing shots and precise centres bringing goals in equal measure. Charlie George could shoot as hard, and at Derby his tempestuous temperament was better controlled. The promise of his play ran to waste at Arsenal because he was so easily upset. 'If they knee me, I butt them' was his eye for a tooth philosophy, which so often had him in trouble. It was a sign of talent squandered that he only reached his 50 League goals in 1977, despite being Derby's top scorer with 16 in the 1975–6 season. Yet some of those he has scored have been memorable indeed, none more than that which won Arsenal the 'Double'. In extra time of the 1971 Cup Final Arsenal and Liverpool were nearing stalemate with a goal apiece. Then Arsenal's coach, Don Howe, signalled to George to move further upfield as Graham tired. At once George took a pass, strode forward and hit the killing 25-yard shot too fast even for Clemence to touch.

There are still hotshots in plenty in the English game, but in the hectic flurry of its workrate the cool creators who give them their chances have been lost without trace. English football had once had its quota of them, like Clem Stephenson, who was the mainspring of Cup success for Aston Villa in 1913 and 1920. He was also the architect of Huddersfield's remarkable rise under Chapman, winning the league in three successive seasons from 1923. There was another Cup winner's medal with Huddersfield when Billy (W. H.) Smith's penalty won the 1922 Final and a loser's medal in 1928.

Ivan Sharpe, whose perception as player and critic was shrewder than most selectors', had him in his best-ever XI, but England capped him only once. As Sharpe commented, 'A greater club player and teamworker I have never known. A greater failure by England's selectors I have never known. For here, at this time we had a heaven-sent left-wing in Stephenson and long-legged, loping Smith, W. H., from Tantoby, and failed even once to choose them.'

Stephenson was a scoring inside at Villa, although not in the class of Bolton's Joe Smith, who had 315 goals in his career. Swarthy, strong and relentless in his pursuit of goals, Smith was one of the great dribblers and scorers of his day. He had 38 goals in 41 matches in one season and that was a record for any but a centre-forward until Arthur Rowley narrowly beat it.

Joe Smith, a thick-set, powerful blaster of the ball, was rated by David Jack as the finest shot of his time. He also had the competitive spirit which gives opponents and referees problems. In his book on soccer Jack gives this description of playing with Smith for Bolton Wanderers against a leading Viennese Club.

'In the first few minutes Joe Smith collided with an opponent as they both rose to head a high ball, and the latter fell, rather heavily, but unhurt, to the ground. It was obviously an accident, but without hesitation the referee ordered Smith off the field. He was too staggered for words for a moment, but when he realised the full import he said plenty – and bluntly refused to go off. Smith was the central figure in a circle of arguing, gesticulating players. The Wanderers officials had to appeal to their player to leave. The spectators cheered wildly when he eventually departed.' So it has all happened before!

In another game on that tour when the Devon fisherman in Bolton's goal, Dick Pym, was beaten from well outside the area by the Hungarian centre-forward, 'the Hungarian was applauded by the greatest marksman of that time, Joe Smith, and Joe was not given to throwing bouquets'.

On another tour in Switzerland Smith, Jack, and Vizard, the fine outside left who had such a formidable partnership with Smith, agreed to play for a Swiss side in a friendly against an Austrian team. Like many 'friendlies' this became distinctly hostile. Smith was heavily fouled and when he retaliated in kind the Austrians threatened a walk-off. Finally a penalty was given and Smith placed the ball with undisguised delight. 'His whole demeanour told of his intention to "break the back of the net". Few players of the time could hit a dead ball as hard as the Bolton captain – but when he framed for the shot he found the goalkeeper had deserted his post. He was eventually persuaded to face the marksman, who left him helpless with a more than usually fierce drive.'

On the Continent Jack encountered another inside left as expert as Joe Smith. The German Richard Hofmann scored three goals against England in Berlin in 1930. The Germans were leading 3–2 with a few minutes to go when Jack headed the equaliser. Of Hofmann he said, 'I have seen much cleverer footballers on the Continent, but none who knew better how to round off the excellent midfield play as his average of a goal a match in the International series indicates. Hofmann is regarded with justice as the best footballer Germany has produced in the course of fifty years of German football.' He has a lot of competition in the next fifty years!

Another player equally talented and nearly as neglected as Smith was Charlie Buchan. Buchan was a 'rippler', moving straight, but with the hint of a swerve which cleared opponents from his path. He looked like some latter-day Moses dividing the sea of defenders before him by his commanding presence. Buchan was not alone in this. Bolton's Westwood was similar in style, but with a more hectic pace than Buchan's measured stride. Then there was Billy Walker of Villa, another of these tall, penetrating forwards with a sure finish. Walker had 213 goals for Villa, while both Buchan, and his successor, David Jack, passed the 250 League goals. The dapper, elegant Jack was like Buchan too in bringing a more cultured image to professional football, rejecting the cap and muffler concept that still showed in the wage structure and in the treatment of the players.

Charlie Buchan, the schoolmaster who taught Arsenal how to adjust to the new off-side law and scored 272 League goals, won only 6 caps for England, all in his Sunderland days. The selectors classed him as 'too clever to play for England'. That was also their view of another Sunderland hero, Len Shackleton. In Shack's case there was more justification, for he was more the individualist, less the motivator of a team. At Sunderland those two fine players, Shackleton and Trevor Ford, had scant regard for each other and rarely combined. In one friendly match Shackleton went past four defenders and round the goalkeeper before laying the ball back for Ford to touch in. 'Don't say I *never* gave you a pass,' he called out in explanation of this isolated moment of co-operation.

England, who gave Shackleton just five caps, were not the only ones able to ignore his talent. Arsenal had him as an apprentice, where he did little but cut the grass and have to pose with the star, Bryn Jones, for a picture unkindly captioned 'This man cost £14,000. This man cost nothing.' And nothing was exactly what Shackleton had when Whittaker gave him avuncular advice that he was too small and too incompetent to continue in the game. As a final well-intentioned gesture he took the lad to see Highbury's latest marvel – a television set. That casual irrelevance maddened Shackleton, making him determined not to creep back north beaten and penniless. At the now defunct London Paper Mills in Dartford Shackleton found an employer who would let him play in the mill team and pay him above his rate for age. When Shackleton wrote his book *Clown Prince of Soccer* many came in for blistering criticism. Almost the only person for whom he had a good word was that mill Manager, the late Frank Langan. Shackleton made the perceptive comment that there had been many ready to help when he was famous, only Langan when he was unknown and in need.

Before a Wembley International Shackleton acknowledged the debt, revisiting his benefactor and his friends in the mill. On the field he repaid his other debt to Arsenal in full and in kind, humiliating them with the spectacular insolence of his play whenever he went to Highbury.

Jimmy Hagan was another clever midfield player and he was only once selected for England. But then he had to compete against the all-round skills of Raich Carter and Wilf Mannion. Later there was little Ernie Taylor, setting up the goals for Milburn and Mortensen, and George Eastham, with his deceptively long stride, winning freedom of movement for his fellow forwards on the field and all players off it. The *Observer*, getting Queen's Counsel's opinion that players' contracts were unfairly restrictive, helped Eastham win his determined fight to be allowed to transfer from Newcastle to Arsenal and so limit the restraints on players. And in his stylish play, even late in his career with Stoke, Eastham showed there were Englishmen with the creative skills to match the Scots, like John White, the 'ghost'. Before he was tragically killed, struck by lightning on a golf course, White had introduced to Tottenham that sense of anticipation, that stealthy approach which Peters was so successfully to emulate. Such creators are out of fashion now.

Colin Bell at least combined formidable work-rate with a trace of Haynes's passing and Peters's ability to glide into scoring positions. His injury left the England teams back at the feet of the tireless runners. Francis Lee had been the most inspiring of these with his arrogant self-confidence, his readiness to beat any number of defenders any number of times. Stocky, low-geared, and hard to shake off the ball, there was an assertive aggression in all Lee attempted. He brought colour and excitement to forward lines at Manchester City, and Derby as well as to England. It was never dull when Lee was around, and with his pugnacious outlook there was the odd unscheduled boxing match to be seen for no extra charge.

Lee scored 229 League goals and another 10 for England. In 1971–2 he was the leading First Division scorer with 33. Of these 13 were penalties, which he was as adept at winning as at scoring. A fast, tricky dribbler, Lee was often tripped as he bored in for goal. But his spectacular dives were sometimes of his own contriving and referees were soon giving defenders the benefit of every doubt. Lee was a battling, buoyant entertainer sometimes carried away by his own free expression.

England's captain of 1976 Kevin Keegan has many of the same qualities, but better disciplined. And whereas the 'runners' so often let themselves be channelled in the straight lines, which make life easy for the defenders, Keegan tries to use the full width of the pitch. He passed his 80 League goals before the end of 1976, a sharp and supple mover in the penalty area with remarkable spring in his legs to reach the balls that looked too high for so small a man. And he has looked happier searching out goals with Toshack for Liverpool, than trying to create them for England.

Kevin Keegan reminded Alf Ramsey of Geoff Hurst. 'He uses the whole width of the pitch. He and Geoff are among the few players in recent years to recognise this method of play.'

For his first Manager at Liverpool, Bill Shankly, Keegan is 'a whippet of a player, like a weasel after rats, always biting and snapping at your legs! He reminds me of Denis Law when he was 16. He's got everything, fantastic ability, two good feet. He's energetic and courageous and he has the will to win. Keegan's a perfect size, a fully-fledged middle-weight – the greatest fighters of them all.'

The Kop christened him 'Handy Andy', the man who was always there to help a colleague, take a pass, or score a goal. Keegan was spirited away from Scunthorpe by Shankly after a dozen other clubs had dismissed him as too small or too frail or too inexperienced for top-class football. Shankly recognised the skill, the restless energy and the combative determination which soon made him the darling of the Kop.

His manner is quiet, but Keegan has the steel that the goalscorer needs. After the successful 1971–2 season he said of himself in the *Observer*, 'Ambition, that's what drives me. I'll run until I succeed. I'm relieved when it's Saturday, you know. It's pressure all week, but I react opposite to most. When I get out there on the field it's a relief. All the talking is O.K. but I think *this* is what I am here for, to *play.*'

Keegan was aware of the aggression within him that had to be controlled and channelled. He said then, 'I must improve my temperament. If someone kicks me I must curb my desire to kick him back.' That was not achieved without an unfortunate incident or two, such as the sending off in the Showpiece Charity Shield game against Leeds at Wembley, when he and Bremner compounded the offence by hurling aside their shirts.

He has always worked to mature his attitude and his performance and the story so far has been of the rise and rise of Keegan. The outstanding success has been with Liverpool, rather than England where there has been no Toshack to steer the chances to him. And Keegan was always lifted by the atmosphere of the Kop, as Milburn used to be by the Newcastle crowd. The hero-worship brought its worries as well as its job. 'The only thing I feared in life was missing an open goal in front of them. I'd die rather than that happened. It's funny. Empty the Kop and it doesn't look anything. Yet when it's full you feel there's a million people there. When they start singing "You'll Never Walk Alone" it made my eyes water. Sometimes I've actually been crying while I've been playing.'

Keegan has achieved one of his 1972 ambitions. He said then 'I hope one day to get the pressure George Best got. Or Bobby Moore. I don't envy anyone who's got it, but those who have and start grumbling about it are fools, I think.' That is the balanced attitude which allowed Keegan to continue to enjoy his football and to take in his short purposeful stride the homage of a great city's football fanatics. And yet be free to move on when he judged it best for his career to go abroad to Hamburg. He had the pressures as ambition drove him and he throve on them. His domination of Bertie Vogts, the best close-marker in the game, helped Liverpool to win the European Cup Final. And it made him a truly international figure, the first English player to command a half a million pound transfer fee.

The dark-haired Keegan has many of the qualities which made a blond inside of an earlier generation, Wilf Mannion, the hero of youthful Don Revie. Mannion had 357 games for Middlesbrough and 26 caps for England, averaging about a goal every three games. Like Keegan he was an unselfish player making openings for others by his brave and tireless play. One quality particularly impressed Revie. 'What excited

me about Mannion was his balance. He had a beautiful body swerve
and went past opponents as if they weren't there.'

When England were beaten by America in the 1950 World Cup the
former Manager of the Italian team, the shrewd Vittorio Pozzo, had this
to say about their play. 'This did not surprise me greatly for England
seldom play up to their possibilities away from home and because they
have developed the safety-first principle to the detriment of the
individual. The concentration on "stopping them" – on not allowing the
opponent to play – has brought as a consequence a great scarcity of real
footballers. Rarely do you come across somebody playing real football
like Wilfred Mannion.'

How does today's game look to such a 'real' footballer? The *Daily
Mail* invited Mannion to watch Birmingham beat his old club
Middlesbrough 3–1 in the autumn of 1976. It was a game well up to
normal entertainment standards and he saw some resemblance to his
own swerving, decisive dribbles in the runs of Trevor Francis. For the
rest he was not impressed. 'There's so little natural skill and so many
manufactured robots out there nowadays. This was like watching a
Third Division match in the Thirties.' The new rarely satisfies the old,
and it was the searching queries and comments which followed that
were of interest. Mannion's football instinct had him pointing
accusingly to the chief weaknesses in the modern English game. 'Why
do they keep passing back? They don't seem able to use both feet any
more. . . . Why do they have to stop it every time instead of keeping it
rolling?

'All this funnelling back is nothing new. Sweden did it against us in
1947. But the speed of the game is dictated by the speed with which the
ball is moved. Before they could run back we'd always beaten them for
speed.' Old players are apt to recall the past with advantages, but the
records show Mannion helping Lawton to a hat-trick in that match
confirming his comment.

On the harsh realities of a professional footballer's life before the
ending of the maximum wage Mannion had once commented, 'The only
place for a retired footballer is the knackers' yard.' He himself had not
fared well in retirement and was frail of health. The game did not
encourage him back to watch another. 'I'd love to be playing again
today – but only for the money. I would not enjoy playing the football
we've been watching.'

Soccer 'slaves', the old idols might have been called in their day. Yet
in general there did seem to be more fun and less fear when they were
playing, fewer agents and more self-expression.

Six

Pick of the Scorers

There is a paradox about our top goalscorers. The goal is the star attraction of the game yet the highest scorer of them all was never a star, never played in a full England team.

The leading goal-getter in the history of the English League personifies the qualities which once made English forwards the terror of the Continent. Big, burly, bustling Arthur Rowley was the typical English scorer, courageous and hard-hitting, powerful in the air, lethal on the ground. His 434 goals remain a record – yet he never played in a full International for England. George Arthur Rowley's record is the more extraordinary as he was mainly an inside forward in the days when the inside's priority was foraging rather than scoring.

His first League match was for Fulham against Grimsby Town a week before Christmas in 1948. The word 'striker' was not then in the football vocabulary and the W formation, with insides feeding the wingers and centre-forward, was the main tactical concept in attack. Rowley suffered for being before his time, before full acceptance of two forwards lying upfield to threaten the heart of the defence. Despite the endless flow of goals, including 19 in his first 22 games for Fulham, he was classified as a goal-poacher who skimped the hard work expected of an inside. Even then there was a puritanical preference for work-rate rather than results. Rowley himself resented the implication that he did not do his share, just as he resented having only one intermediate International for England, particularly as he scored one of the goals in the 4–1 defeat of Switzerland 'B'.

On his own style he commented, 'It is unfair for anyone to say I am not constructive. I have always tried to keep in touch with my wing-half and I prefer inside to centre-forward because it gives me more space in which to operate. I move up only when I sense a scoring chance. My goals come from anticipation, not lazing.'

Arthur Rowley had, in fact, the same priceless assets as Jimmy Greaves – the feel for an opening, the ability to move in fast at the last instant, and cool confidence in hitting home the shot. Superficially the two were opposites, Jimmy Greaves so slight, so neat, so swift in acceleration – Rowley so ungainly, so ill-balanced, so slow to reach top speed. Yet both had the divine gifts for a goalscorer of intuition, timing and certainty in the finish. Both had to endure the senseless comment 'Unless he scores he's useless'.

When Rowley scored a hat-trick against Lincoln City in April 1953 he took his season's total to 39 goals, the record for any player other than a centre-forward.

How quickly the game changed! In 1962 Rowley had been averaging 30 goals a season over a period of twelve years. In 1976 only two players in all four divisions, Binney and Buckley, reached 20 goals for the second successive season. Was that all due to the back four and defensive tactics – or was it in part the destruction of initiative in a welter of drill and discipline?

Arthur Rowley and his elder brother Jack were both 'naturals', who were never overcoached, never forced into new moulds. With Manchester United, where Matt Busby encouraged the free expression which is a goalscorer's birthright, Jack also piled on the goals, passing 200 and scoring six times in his six games for England.

The more experienced Jack never tried to tutor Arthur. 'Jack did not need to tell me how to hit my shots. One can either crack a ball hard or one cannot. It comes naturally.'

The urge and instinct for scoring also came naturally to Arthur and flourished unfettered. Yet somehow Managers were always suspicious that the spring was about to run dry. Rowley was passed on from club to club, always to the detriment of the seller.

He started in his home town with Wolverhampton Wanderers, but made no impact. 'I decided early on that too much is expected of a local lad. I had to get away, even if only a short distance, so I went to West Bromwich.'

He was no sensation there either and was soon transferred, the reserve who was thrown in as a make-weight to complete the deal for Fulham's left-winger, Ernie Shepherd. For Fulham this proved an unexpected bonus. For Rowley there was the satisfaction that one of those 19 early goals was a last-minute winner, shot home in a snowstorm at the Hawthorns to end a run of eleven home wins by West

Bromwich Albion. That goal also brought Fulham the Second Division Championship at Albion's expense, Fulham finishing with 57 points, Albion with 56. What a bargain Rowley had already proved!

The following season Rowley broke a bone in his foot when playing at Newcastle. Fearing that they had had the best of him Fulham sold him in June 1950 to Leicester City for £12,000. Two seasons later Fulham were relegated and it was Rowley who started their slide, scoring 4 goals against them in their first away game. Six years after he joined Leicester Rowley had scored over 200 goals for the club.

Then he moved to Shrewsbury Town as player-Manager of this Fourth Division team. In his first season with them he scored 38 goals in 43 League games, winning Shrewsbury promotion and himself the chance to score goals in every division. In the next he achieved one more record, becoming the only player to score 20 or more goals in ten successive seasons, beating Dixie Dean's run of nine from 1924–5 to 1932–3.

Rowley's natural talent for goalscoring never brought him the fame or financial rewards that come the way of lesser lights in this goal-starved age. And it brought no recognition from England's selectors. 'Either my face or my style did not fit' is his sad reflection on a surprising omission. In 619 games Rowley scored his 434 goals and for him they had to be their own reward.

One who came close to Rowley's total was indeed a star. There is no doubt who was the finest forward as well as the outstanding goalscorer of the generations before the First World War. Stephen Bloomer was known as the 'greatest of them all' and his results proved it with 352 League goals plus 28 more in Internationals. For an inside right that was a phenomenal scoring record, the League tally unbeaten from 1914 until Dixie Dean passed his total in 1936–7, and the goals for England second only to Woodward's 29 until Lofthouse overtook them in the Fifties.

Bloomer had all the qualities of the goalscorer, a shot as lethal as Lorimer's, the deft touch of a Jimmy Greaves, the heading ability of a Denis Law, the body swerve of the instinctive dribbler and that sense of anticipation without which all other talents run to waste.

Steve was serving his apprenticeship in his father's blacksmith's shop in Derby when he made his impact in junior football. In September 1892 at the age of 18 he was drafted into the Derby County side for his first senior game against Stoke. Instant success was rewarded with being taken on the playing staff at 7s 6d a week. Three years later he won the first of his 23 International caps and was soon such a regular of the England side that he was only left out when the selectors wanted to experiment.

Criticism of selectors is not unknown, but the press really enjoyed itself when Humphreys of Notts County was brought in for Bloomer to play against the Scots at Sheffield. Bloomer had been their scourge for years and when this game was lost 1–2 the critics had no difficulty in identifying those responsible for the defeat.

Bloomer's career spanned 22 years until he played his last game against Bradford in January 1914. Despite his name he is only known to have made one footballing mistake. As soon as he retired he accepted a coaching appointment in Germany – just in time to be interned.

Bloomer's worth was measured in goals and like many of the great scorers he needed to lie low at times to induce a false sense of security in those detailed to mark him.

In the words of his own day, 'Never was Bloomer more dangerous than when he seemed to have lost interest in the game. All of sudden the electricity would run through him and in a twinkling the foe awoke to find three goals in the back of their net!'

Even the greatest players have their off-days and though these were rare for Bloomer there was disappointment when he did not score. The crowds, with their great expectations, were often restive when he failed to live up to their extravagant hopes. The 'destroying angel' was so idolised he was never permitted to be merely human. And yet he was anything but a 'Superman' in build.

Bloomer gave no impression of strength or athleticism, looking so wan and anaemic in the dressing room that he was known as 'Paleface'. At the end of his career he was still scoring as freely as ever. After playing for Middlesbrough he came home to Derby to the sort of rapturous reception that Brian Clough was later to stage for his new signing Storey-Moore – only to find, after parading him round the Baseball Ground, that the transfer was not valid. There was nothing illusory about Bloomer's return for the 1911–12 season. At once he took Derby to the championship of the Second Division.

On the left wing of that forward line was Ivan Sharpe, who wrote with his usual keen perception of the special characteristics which made Bloomer unique in his day. 'He was not a subtle or really scientific player. But he had the golden gift of splitting the defence with one arrow-like, pin-pointed pass. Just as he could make the pass while the ball was moving so he could shoot with a sudden touch. He scored most of his goals by *sudden* shooting. His great haul came principally from first-time shots. His was instantaneous marksmanship aimed at beating the goalkeeper's *eye*.'

That was the special knack of so many of the memorable scorers. Gallacher had it, so did Brian Clough, so have Gerd Muller and Ted MacDougall.

When Finland kept us to a 2–1 win at Wembley in the recent World Cup match Revie and his team apologised for their disappointing performance. In our own dejection at failing to pile up the goals we failed to give credit to the Finnish forwards. Whenever they were given a chance – and the defenders gave them more than they were entitled to – Clemence was stretched by a shot between the posts, while so many of ours soared wide. And when Nieminen scored it was with Bloomer's *sudden* touch, shooting from the edge of the area with no warning flurry. The ball was flicked quickly and quietly and the slow-paced shot still deceived Clemence into diving too late. The booming drive from far out may set the crowd roaring, but it is still the *sudden* shot that sneaks most goals, and makes scoring look simple.

Stephen was not the most co-operative of players, the natural individualism of the goalscorer heightened by the adulation. Sharpe suffered from the biting comments: 'Stephen was a tyrant. He said what he thought, and if things were going wrong his partner had no pleasant Saturday afternoon. "What d'ye call that? A pass? I haven't got an aeroplane!" This was a fair sample of a Bloomer explosion.'

Bloomer's 352 goals remained the record until passed by an even more formidable scoring machine. William Ralph Dean, goalscorer extraordinary, was for most people in the Thirties the epitome of the English centre-forward. So it irritated him the more that his crinkly jet-black hair, with its meticulously straight parting, should get him called 'Dixie', as if he was some strolling nigger minstrel of the football field. In Everton's high-spirited changing room he often had to endure finding a name card above his peg reading 'The Big Negro'. Had he only known it there was to be a certain appropriateness in that, since the intimates of the greatest goalscorer of them all, Pelé, also called him *Negrao* or 'The Big Negro'. So they shared nicknames as well as an insatiable appetite for goals.

Dean was at his most prolific when defenders were still adjusting to the off-side change, but as late as the 1931–2 season he scored 45 goals. By then most teams were copying Arsenal's 'stopper' centre-half, but none could stop Dean.

Inevitably, great teams decline and after four seasons of success Everton found themselves struggling in 1936, their attacking power no longer enough to carry an unorganised defence. Joe Mercer had just come into the side and he recalls the situation degenerating to the point where they had their first-ever collective team tactics talk. 'Usually tactics developed out of a talk in the corner with the coach or a casual discussion with other players. This was something new. Arsenal had just beaten us 4–0 and we realised it was due to method, not luck. When we were all assembled William put his heavy feet on the table, tilted his hat over his eyes and said, "Talk tactics as much as you like. That's not why we are losing. We are losing because you lot can't play."'

Dean had no time for tactical talks, but he was an instinctive tactician. As he was ever more closely marked he developed the ability to glance the ball down for a colleague, while the defence clustered round him. It was this skill which made goals for the insides.

After forty years' involvement with First Division football Joe Mercer still rates Dean as the best English forward he has seen. 'In today's terms he would be the ideal "target" man. He was always there for you to hit the ball to and he always did something threatening with it. He was as clever as Toshack at setting up chances for others with his flicked headers. No one has ever been a better scorer with his head than Dean with his soaring leap, his determination to get the ball, his power and his accuracy. He was very good on the ground too. What most people did not realise was how fast he was – as quick as Malcolm Macdonald today. We used to go in for 80-yard dashes in the summer and it was always Dean who won the prizes. He had the selfishness of the goalscorer, but he made it easy for others to play off him too.'

Fame never affected him and he made sure no others in the side had inflated egos. Tommy Lawton recalls walking into the changing room full of swagger and excitement from the thrill of hearing he had been chosen for his first cap. 'Sit down, Lawton,' said Dean. 'Stand up all the Internationals' – and in that side almost everyone stood up. It was a sobering moment which left a deep impression on Lawton.

'Dean did not look as polished as Greaves since many of his goals were contemptuously toe-ended in. But he had that same divine gift of timing. He scented his goals and protected his space by coming in late and fast like Gerd Muller has done so effectively. And he had such speed and power he could be unstoppable.' That is a fine tribute from Mercer, the man whose father was captaining Tranmere when Dean first played there, but who did not himself see him at his early peak.

Dean left Everton in 1937 for a short spell with Notts County. Then the man who had so cheerfully absorbed the hard pounding that was a centre's lot drifted on to Sligo. The Irish still found a 'terrible beauty' in his play and that was how so many defenders might have described him. Fame there had been in plenty, but no fortune for a man who was better known than Prime Ministers and more respected. So he followed the routine of the old footballers and took a pub, 'The Dublin Packet', in Chester. There he lost a packet rather than made it and the worry undermined his health. After a spell in hospital John Moores found him a job as a porter at Littlewoods, which he filled with his usual cheery efficiency. What a different world it then was for football's heroes and cult figures.

Shortly before his leg was amputated in 1976 Dean presented the Footballer of the Year award to Kevin Keegan at the Football Writers annual dinner. 'This,' he remarked, 'must be the first time any Evertonian has given a Liverpool player anything – except a good hiding on the field.'

Only Rowley has scored more goals in the English League than Dean's 379, all but 30 for Everton.

Dean made his debut for Tranmere in 1923 aged 15. Two years later Everton had acquired him for £3,000 and before he was 20 he had had sensational success. In 1927 he scored both goals in England's 2–1 defeat of Scotland at Hampden Park, their first victory there for more than twenty years. 'There was such a silence after my first goal,' he said, 'that I thought I must have been off-side. You could not believe 120,000 people could be so silent.'

Twelve goals in his first five Internationals, 98 in his first hundred League games for Everton were extraordinary scoring figures even in those happy seasons before defenders adjusted properly to the new off-side law. They were a slap in the eye too for the centre-half he faced in his first game for Tranmere. Twice the ball had been put through to him and 'twice I had put it in the net', to used his phrase which was as uncomplicated as his play. The centre-half then growled at Dean, 'You'll get no more goals, lad.' It was the sort of verbal intimidation much practised by the older professionals, but nothing was going to intimidate Dean.

The record which takes Dean beyond the reach of any modern forward is his 60 goals in the 1927–8 League season. It was a striking finish by Dean which brought Everton the Championship and himself the League scoring record. Until the last five matches Huddersfield's fine side had looked the more likely winners and Camsell's 59 goals scored in the Second Division for Middlesbrough the previous season seemed well beyond his reach. Then Sheffield United were beaten away,

3–1. After Gillespie had given the Blades the lead Dean's two second-half goals won the match for Everton. The first was a simple header from Kelly's free-kick, the next, his fiftieth, came from Troup's pass. 'Though the odds were against him,' Dean pressed on and swept past goalkeeper Anderson to score.

Then it was a home win against Newcastle with Dean outshining Hughie Gallacher and scoring once in Everton's 3–0 victory. Two great centre-forwards clashed again in the next match at Goodison. Aston Villa's Waring had been at Tranmere with Dean and the two publicly shook hands before the kick-off. Again it was Dean and Everton who came off best, winning 3–2 with Dean scoring 2 to Waring's 1.

Then came the crucial game away to Burnley who, earlier in the week, had beaten Huddersfield. Within thirty seconds Dean had scored, slipping between M'Cluggage and Waterfield to beat Down. But soon Page had equalised and Beel put Burnley ahead with the hundredth goal of his career. Dean's answer was to complete a hat-trick before half-time. 'Five goals in 28 minutes gave the crowd their fill of the one thing they yearn for,' commented the *Liverpool Football Echo*.

Beel levelled the scores yet again but at the end Everton raced away to win 5–3 as Dean laid on a goal for Martin, then chased a pass from Critchley 'like a whippet' to hit home his fourth. That assured Everton of the Championship and left Dean needing three goals in the final match at Goodison against Chapman's Arsenal – not a team to come bearing gifts on the field.

The *Football Echo* recorded the mood of the match. 'Referee W. P. Hartley gave Dean a hearty hand-grip' and 'it was as though 50,000 spectators were chanting "We want you to get goals."' But it was Shaw of Arsenal who scored a soft goal after two minutes having 'handled the ball and got away with it'. There was instant relief, however. 'It was left to the man of the moment to create another sensation. Before three more minutes were gone Dean had scored twice. The crowd's roar knew no bounds.' First Martin headed on a corner for Dean to nod the ball into the left-hand corner. Then as Dean tore through the middle the long-legged Butler crossed him and the accidental trip earned a penalty which Dean swept confidently home. One to go now for the record, but after that dramatic five minutes, the crowd was kept biting its nails for another hour and a quarter. They were not best pleased when O'Donnell put the ball in his own net to level the scores. And with some ten minutes left Dean and his colleagues seemed to have run themselves dry on this sultry May day. Then Troup took a corner and Dean soared high above the crowd of players. 'Out of the ruck of probably fourteen men Dean with unerring accuracy nodded the ball to the extreme right-hand side of the net.' That did it!

'There has never been such a joyful shout at Everton. The crowd went on cheering for eight solid minutes until the game's end. Dean was hugged by all his comrades and there was a threat of the crowd breaking onto the field. Two men did break past the police barrier and the referee had to bundle one man off.' The cheering did not cease even when Shaw equalised for Arsenal; and as Everton forced a corner in the final minute Butler and Paterson, the Arsenal goalkeeper, were too busy shaking hands with Dean to watch the ball. Or perhaps that was their way of ensuring he did not score yet again! Dean bolted from the field to beat the final whistle and it was left to O'Donnell to grab the ball for him.

Even the amplifiers were powerless to make the speeches heard above the tumult of noise as John McKenna, President of the Football League, presented the Cup to Warner Cresswell, Everton's captain. Herbert Chapman also presented a portfolio and gold pen and pencil to Charles Buchan to mark his last League game for Arsenal (his debut for Sunderland had also been at Goodison) and his transfer to journalism. What a pity he was not already writing for the *Daily News and Westminster Gazette* to record this historic match.

What headlines such a game would now make, but in 1928 the leading 'Nationals' could not be bothered to send a reporter there or include a match report! They did at least make congratulatory reference to 'the crack centre'. In its round-up of the day's play *The Times* commented 'That very brilliant centre Dean is largely responsible for Everton winning the championship. A very hard, eager player who can shoot with either foot, Dean has had to put up with a lot of "marking", but his strength and good humour have carried him through.' No mention even of that heading power which had brought so many of the 60 goals, while the best any other Everton forward could manage was Troup's 10.

Dean had not passed Smith's 66 goals for Ayr United in the Scottish Second Division, but he had beaten all other records. The man Dean so narrowly beat for the overall League record, George Camsell, had this to say in the *Football Echo* about his feelings and about the scorer's art.

I take it as a compliment to have my record broken by only one goal by England's centre-forward. During the last few seasons more and more teams have hit on the tactic of making the centre-forward the rapier to thrust home attacks. Not long ago most of the thrust came down the wings. Then we had the short-passing plan which resulted in three or four players keeping the ball going between them and advancing down the middle like a steam-roller. The best teams then adopted a combination of these, so that if one did not work they could try the other.

The introduction of the new off-side law saw a new tactic added as the centre-forward lay always ahead of his insides. As soon as he got the ball he was away with it straight for goal. That is how the demand came for centres like Dean, who could run like track athletes and shoot like cannons.

There are not many of these available and the teams which have them hold on to them. But the day of the tactician is not over. 'Dixie' Dean gives as good a pass as anybody, while Hughie Gallacher is still the wiliest of tacticians. If the opposing defenders say 'This is the man to watch' these players are able neatly to give the ball to someone else when they cannot do anything with it themselves.

On the knack of scoring Camsell made this perceptive remark. 'A centre-forward who is in front of goal when the ball is crossed is usually good at getting his head or foot to it somehow. You can stay with him like a shadow in midfield, but he will still give you the slip when the ball is in front of the net. That sums up the art of centre-forward play, if you are also always alert, and ready to receive a pass, and have learnt to give one too.'

That season of 1927–8 Dean had 82 goals in all, including the Cup, Internationals, and International trials. When he was still only 19 Dean had caused consternation on Merseyside. In a motorcycle crash in Wales he fractured his skull and jaw, to put his playing career in jeopardy.

After the accident it might be said that most of Dean's goals were served him on a plate – the silver one which pinned together that head which kept nodding home the centres.

Such was the Everton dedication to attack that at one stage they had five outstanding centre-forwards on the books, including Dean, Lawton, 'Bunny' Bell, and the forceful Harry Catterick. It was difficult enough to get a place in the third team! Folk hero though he was, Dean had even fiercer competition for England's side and was far from an automatic choice. There was the same remarkable embarrassment of riches for that position and in his ten years of success to 1937 he was chosen only 16 times.

His main rivals included George Camsell, scorer of those 59 goals in a season and 348 in his career. Camsell was the cutting edge of a forward line carefully collected by Middlesbrough which was the ideal to take advantage of the new freedom. Billy Pease and Owen Williams were international wingers, skilful enough to keep the backs stretched wide, while George Camsell hovered a yard or two onside, waiting for the through ball from his insides. Once the attacking centre-half wandered upfield Jack Carr would leave him stranded with the long through ball and Camsell was clear before the backs could close. So sure was his finishing that Carr would squat down and wait for the goal. 'All I did was to hit the pass, then sit on my "hunkers" and wait for George to score' was his terse description of the standard Middlesbrough move.

With those wingers, and goalkeepers who stayed on their line, Camsell scored many goals from close in – 'baby-liners,' as they were called. Anyone might have touched them home but the skill was in being in the right place, a skill Camsell combined with the cold accuracy of his finishing.

They were alike in so many qualities, and only in the power and accuracy of his heading was Dean clearly superior. After one Merseyside clash in which Dean had scored freely with his head he passed the great Liverpool goalkeeper, Elisha Scott, in the street and nodded a greeting – which had Scott instinctively diving into the gutter.

In all his career Joe Mercer found only four players who were quite unflappable, quite unmoved by the tensions, untouched by the excitements, of the big match. They were Jimmy Greaves, Denis Compton, Bill Dean, and George Camsell. Dean's comment to the lesser lights as they came out of the changing room used to be, 'All the best. Play your own games. Remember my wife and kids, but if in doubt hit it up the middle and I will put it in.' Camsell had the same happy outlook on his football and it won him nine caps, when allied to his ruthless efficiency as a finisher.

Dean scored two of his record 37 hat-tricks in his early Internationals. He had two goals in his first against Wales in February 1927. Then the two which beat Scotland at Hampden. Then hat-tricks against Belgium and Luxembourg, who were beaten 9–1 and 5–2.

He scored twice again in the 6–0 defeat of France. That was a racing start but not even Dean matched George Camsell's scoring consistency in Internationals. Dixie ended with 18 goals from 16 internationals, but Camsell scored as many in just 9, averaging 2 goals a game and scoring in every one in which he played. He scored 2 in his first on 9 May 1929 in a 4–1 win over France and one in the last, exactly seven years later when England lost 2–3 to Belgium in Brussels on 9 May 1936. With

Camsell scoring 348 league goals to Dean's 379 it is clear how unlucky he was to walk in Dean's shadow. As with Jimmy McGrory and Hughie Gallacher in Scotland, one bright star was to be eclipsed by another even more resplendent.

But there were a couple good enough to eclipse Dean and Camsell on occasions. Jimmy Hampson, Blackpool's polished forward who scored 290 League goals and who died so tragically in 1938, drowned in a fishing accident, was one to keep them out on occasions. Jimmy scored 2 of the goals against Austria's 'Wunderteam' and was unfortunate to win only three caps. Even more formidable an opponent was Tom (Pongo) Waring, who set a Villa record with his 49 goals in the 1930–1 season.

Like Dean, Waring started with Tranmere Rovers and like Dean he suffered from the sharp edge of Lancastrian wit, being labelled for life with an unflattering nickname. Pongo was a big dopey dog in vogue in cartoons at the time. Despite the fancied resemblance there was nothing floppy about his play. Waring was an individualist, often roaming wide, then coming in hard and fast to finish with power and purpose. He was as incisive and fearless in his comment as in his play.

When being paid thirty shillings a match 'Pongo' was taken to task by his manager for loitering upfield and not coming back to help. 'So I am to be a defender as well as a forward, am I?' said the aggrieved Waring. 'If you want me to do two jobs you can pay me sixty shillings a game then.' Perhaps today's overworked forwards might try the same tactics.

Mercer recalls listening to Waring's flow of derisive comment if his team struggled. None of the Villa idols escaped his scathing criticism. 'Look at Houghton and Broome, Joe. They are being paid the same as me and they aren't worth half of it.' Late in his career he played inside to an enthusiastic amateur in one game where his best passes were squandered. Then the referee held up play to shepherd a dog off the pitch. 'Hey, Ref.,' called Pongo in a voice that boomed over the field, 'can't you leave us the dog and take our outside-right off instead?'

In that great goalscoring season of 1930–1 when Arsenal won the League with a record 66 points, Pongo's goals gave Villa the satisfaction of scoring one more than their 127. And Pongo was at his most forceful against Arsenal. At Highbury, Villa were beaten 5–2 and L. V. Manning wrote in the *Daily Sketch*, 'I never hope to see a better match.' Waring scored both the Villa goals and the burly Pongo was even more devastating in the return match, taking the lead in the 5–1 defeat of Arsenal. John Arlott was training for the police in Birmingham in the Thirties and he recalls the pleasure with which he watched Waring, who was for him the best centre-forward of his day – fast, powerful, strong in both feet and irresistible near goal. Arsenal certainly could not resist him that game. The high-spirited Pongo made sure he was one up on them before he even took the field. Most players were in awe of the great Chapman, but Waring mocked him on arrival. 'You'd like to buy me, Herbert, wouldn't you? I am better than any of your lot.'

In the same impish spirit he undermined the confidence of Arsenal's spectacular, but highly strung goalkeeper, Charlie Preedy, who was already scared of this big, bustling scorer. 'I will get you this time, Charlie,' he growled at him whenever they stood close. Preedy was too nervous to be sure it was in jest. In fact Waring was always as fair as he was hard. He had the same sense of fun as a great Villa centre-forward of an earlier era, 'Happy' Harry Hampton, or 'Hurricane' Harry, the first clown prince of soccer, whose two goals won Villa the Cup in 1905 and whose 213 League goals for them is still a club record shared with Billy Walker.

Apart from Waring, Camsell and Hampson, Dean had to compete with half a dozen other prolific scorers such as Vic Watson, Joe Bradford of Birmingham, Fred Tilson, George Brown, Jack Bowers and Ted Harper, whose 43 First Division goals in a season was the First Division record until Dean bettered it. To be outstanding in such company has made his name synonymous with goals. There is no need now for him to be offended by his nickname. He has given 'Dixie' a new meaning. So 'Dixie' McNeil (at Hereford one of the few to score more than 30 goals in a recent season), 'Dixie' Deans of Scotland, and 'Dixie' Deehan of Aston Villa regard that tag with pride as echoing the master's flair.

Among the Scots at the time there was an answering richness of talent at centre-forward. Hugh Kilpatrick Gallacher had everything – except height. He was only 5 ft. 5 ins. yet such was the spring in his feet, the muscular power of his legs, that he could outjump most tall, ponderous centre-halves. He was as cocky as he was clever with the ball. On his transfer to Chelsea in 1930 he was wished good fortune. 'I don't need it,' said Hughie, 'I've done well with Airdrie. I've done well with Newcastle. And I'll do well anywhere.' So long as 'anywhere' was a football field that was fair comment.

Gallacher was born in Bellshill, Lanarkshire on 2 February 1903, the second son of an Ulsterman, who was farming there. He was to become as revered as Dean and held in even higher regard north of the Border. Hughie revelled in the applause and the adulation. Without it and without football the world held nothing but unhappiness for him. On the night of 11 June 1957 he took his own life, stepping in front of the Edinburgh to York express as it thundered over Dead Man's Crossing. The last word he ever spoke as he bumped blindly into a passer-by was 'Sorry'.

In his broken family life, in the impending charge of cruelty to his daughter, in his financial embarrassment, there was much for which to be sorry. In football there were times he had to apologise for his behaviour, but never for his play. Only Arthur Rowley and Jimmy McGrory have scored more than his 387 goals in English and Scottish Leagues. In twenty Internationals from 1923 to 1935 he scored 22 goals and won preference over his great rival, McGrory, who only managed seven caps.

The young Gallacher worked in a munitions factory in the First World War, and then went down the pit. The miner's work toughened him for the hard knocks which his pugnacity inevitably attracted on the football field. And the boxing he enjoyed sometimes came in useful there as well as in the gym. For Hughie played with the aggression of a Denis Law and could flare into violence.

As a junior he played with Tannochside Athletic and Hattonrigg Thistle before having a game for Bellshill, when he had gone to watch and they were a man short. Bellshill offered him a £10 signing-on fee, but he was never paid, which was to be the story of his financial misfortunes. After an early marriage came a protracted divorce which cost him £4,000 and left him broke. Gallacher enjoyed good living and was a stylish dresser, sometimes even wearing white spats. His expensive tastes were helped by some shrewd bargaining whenever he was transferred, but even so money was a perennial problem for him.

There were no problems on the field. He scored the winning goal with a 10-yard header two minutes from time in a match for junior Scotland against junior Ireland in December 1920. That led Queen of the South to sign him as a 17-year-old. Then, as he was convalescing after being on the danger list with double pneumonia, Airdrie offered him £9 a week and he was soon making his mark in Scottish First Division. In two successive seasons he scored more than 30 goals and in the first of them, 1923–4, Airdrie won the Scottish Cup.

There were demonstrations when in December 1925 Gallacher went to Newcastle for a fee of £6,500. In his first game he scored twice and made another goal for Stan Seymour. At once he was king of Tyneside. Such was the impact he made that next season he was Captain and Newcastle were League Champions. In all he scored 133 times for

Newcastle before moving on to delight Chelsea fans with another 72 goals. The moves came more quickly now as his game declined and he slid from Derby to Notts County, to Grimsby, to Gateshead, to disillusion and ultimate suicide.

What were the qualities which made him so deadly a scorer? Gallacher was like a combination of Greaves and Muller, with a cold certainty in his finishing and also the elastic, explosive action which let him touch the ball in from the most awkward postures.

In *One Hundred Years of Scottish Football*, by John Rafferty, Gallacher is described as 'A fast, elusive, jinky player very difficult to dispossess as he shielded the ball and worked towards goal. Close to goal he was sharp in taking a chance with foot or head, and slick in the short, cool pass to make the chance for others.'

He scored some remarkable goals, which have improved with the telling over the years. His own choice was one against Wales at Tynecastle Park in Edinburgh when he beat three defenders in a swift, mazy dribble before lobbing the ball over the goalkeeper. That was a typical individualist goal scored with a flourish. Yet the game for which he is best remembered was a perfect example of team play. It was the day in 1928 'the wee blue devils' beat England 5–1 at Wembley. That forward line of Jackson, Dunn, Gallacher, James and Morton included three as small as himself and England were left chasing shadows as the Wembley Wizards established their legend.

His pugnacity led him into trouble on the field and he was often ordered off and suspended. He was also accused of being drunk and disorderly on a tour of Hungary, but charmed the Scottish F.A. into exonerating him after his explanation that as the day was hot he had washed out his mouth with whisky and water. He was suspended for two months, however, after an angry exchange with a referee whom he felt was not giving him adequate protection against heavy tackles on a frosted ground. Asked his name Gallacher countered, 'If you don't know my name you have no right to be refereeing. What's yours?' 'Fogg', the official involuntarily answered. 'I know', said Gallacher. 'You've been in one all afternoon.' A fortnight after the suspension ended Fogg refereed the Scotland v. Ireland International and took no offence at any of the 4 goals Gallacher scored. And by coincidence it was Fogg who refereed again when Hughie had 5 for Derby against Blackburn.

The man Gallacher so often kept out of Scotland's team, James Edward McGrory, had an even larger haul of League goals, scoring 410 in 408 games, all but 13 of them for Celtic. The Scottish F.A. History has this comment on him, 'McGrory, broad shouldered and deep chested, had that mental attitude to goalscoring which is missing in many system-coached modern forwards. His mind was always on scoring. He also had the equipment to score. McGrory had great courage which sent him chasing and lunging at the half chance. He could head a ball more powerfully and accurately than anyone before or since. He could shoot with strength and accuracy and especially he could hook the ball, so that he was shooting early and before goalkeepers could get set.'

McGrory's own view was 'I got my goals through being in the right place at the right time. Much of goalscoring is in the mind. I was always looking for goals, thinking goals. There was no secret about my success. I played my heart out for my club and was always scared of being dropped right to the end.'

McGrory was brought up in the tough Garngad district of Glasgow, but he remained a pleasant, sporting personality with none of Gallacher's hardness or swagger. In his seven International games McGrory scored six times and in all he amassed 550 goals between his first match for Celtic on 20 January 1923 and his last in October 1937. In his second season after joining Celtic from St Roch juniors he was loaned to Clydebank as he could not yet command a place. He scored 13 goals for them before returning to Celtic to play outside-left, until he soon established himself at centre-forward. Like Dean he is chiefly remembered for his heading, but when he set the Scottish record with 8 goals in a game, against bottom of the table Dunfermline, not one was with his head. In February 1927 he beat the record previously held by Duncan Walker of St Mirren in a season which brought him 49 goals in only 33 games. Nine seasons later he scored 50 in 32 matches, passing on the way the total of 363 goals scored by Motherwell's Hugh Ferguson. To rub it in he scored four in five minutes against Motherwell.

Ferguson had been a scorer in the same mould, averaging around a goal a game. At the end of the First World War he sustained top form for six seasons, scoring, for Motherwell, 169 goals in 171 matches.

Such scoring meant in due course a transfer to the English League. Oddly, the most decisive shot of Ferguson's career was the one which took the Cup out of England for the only time. Seventeen minutes were left in the 1927 Final and neither Cardiff nor Sheffield United had scored. From a Cardiff throw-in the ball was moved to their centre-forward, Ferguson. With no room to manœuvre he hit a low diagonal drive straight at the goalkeeper. Lewis seemed to gather it safely enough and, under challenge from Davies, shaped to throw clear. But the ball

John Toshack celebrates a goal for Liverpool in a 'derby' match with Everton

Arthur Rowley challenges Charlton's Sam Bartram at Craven Cottage as spectators perch on the hoardings of Fulham's ground

OPPOSITE ABOVE Dean in typical goalmouth action in the 1927–28 season as he set the League record of 60 goals

OPPOSITE BELOW 'Dixie' is foiled for once by Spanish goalkeeper Zamora as England win 7–1 in 1931

Tommy Lawton, playing for Notts County, has the Millwall defence at full stretch as he gathers a centre

George Camsell of Middlesbrough, scorer of 59 goals in the 1926–27 season and of 18 in only 9 matches for England

OPPOSITE ABOVE Trevor Ford of Wales moves in as England's goalkeeper misses a high cross at Wembley in 1954

OPPOSITE BELOW Jackie Milburn scores the first Newcastle goal in a 4–2 defeat of Portsmouth in a 1953 sixth round Cup-tie at Fratton Park

Tom Waring evades a Tottenham tackle to score for Aston Villa at White Hart Lane in 1933

Hughie Gallacher, both arms outstretched, is outraged to have a 'goal'
disallowed for Chelsea at Stamford Bridge

Pegasus wingers converge on goal in the 1951 Amateur Cup Final as the
author watches Jimmy Potts's header

A precision centre from Stanley Matthews has Arsenal's McCullough and Groves stretching in vain at Highbury

John Tanner scores the second Pegasus goal in their 2–1 win over Bishop Auckland in the 1951 Amateur Cup Final

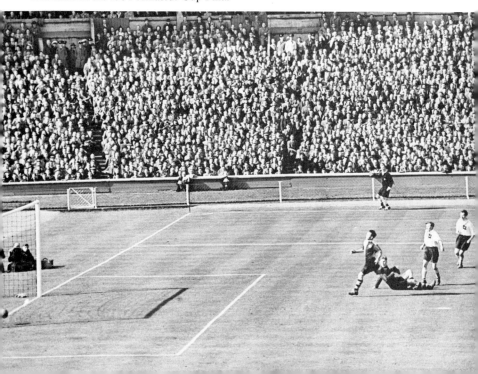

Derek Kevan heads a goal past Russia's Yashin in the World Cup Finals of 1958 as England draw 2–2

Ronnie Rooke leaps high to challenge goalkeeper Williams. Watching and waiting are teammate Logie (*right*) and Wolves' Billy Wright and Stan Cullis

slipped from his hands to trickle over the line. Poor Lewis blamed the greasy wool on his new jersey and ever after it has been an Arsenal tradition to wash the jersey before it is used. A shot by a Scot and an error by a Welsh goalkeeper, playing against a Welsh team, combined at last to take the F.A. Cup out of England.

The other Scottish forward to top three hundred goals, Bob McPhail, was a partner of Gallacher's in the best Airdrie team of all time with a forward line of Reid, Russell, Gallacher, McPhail and Somerville. McPhail then moved to Rangers in 1927 to become the partner for Morton at the club and in the national team. He was the big, strong, hard-shooting, hard-working type of forward – a sophisticated version of Arthur Rowley. McPhail had famous partnerships for Scotland with Jimmy McGrory when England were beaten in 1931 and 1933. Oddly, he only played once in the Scottish side with his old Airdrie clubmate, Gallacher. That was in 1935, when both were past their best, but the pairing worked well enough for England to be beaten again 2–0.

The pairing which brought McPhail many of his 307 goals was for Rangers with Alan Morton. Morton had 495 games for Rangers, scoring 115 goals for them and making countless others. Bob McPhail said of him, 'He was always going in a straight line – for goal. He could take the ball into the opponents' penalty-area quicker than anybody I ever saw. He never pulled his tricks until a game was won and then he gave the crowd the entertainment they wanted. In accuracy of the cross and the pass and in the art of dribbling he was Matthews' equal. In directness and goalscoring Morton was better. I would always rather play with him than Matthews, because he did not stop the game as Stanley did.'

McPhail was bound to be a bit biased. He had so many goals from the passes Morton cut back inviting him to hit them home. Theirs was one of the great goalscoring combinations and it put McPhail among the select fifteen players who have scored more than three hundred goals in League football in England or Scotland.

One of the ten to do it in English football alone was Atyeo. John Atyeo, scorer of 315 League goals and 5 in his 6 full Internationals, would have made an even greater impact on the game had he been a First Division player, rather than staying with Bristol City in the lower reaches. A West-Country boy from Dilton Marsh in Wiltshire, he could have established himself at the top when only 18, had it not been for his innate honesty, his amateur outlook.

Such was his natural games ability that he had played with young

England teams at both soccer and rugby to attract Portsmouth attention.

Portsmouth in 1950 had just celebrated their Golden Jubilee by winning the First Division Championship twice in succession. Peter Harris (scorer of 170 First Division goals, a record for a winger), Jimmy Dickinson (the model wing-half in his 764 appearances for his club), Jack Froggatt (who played for England at left-wing and centre-half), and Reg Flewin (who coached our Pegasus team as competently as he took charge of a penalty area), were at their peak. Yet so promising was young Atyeo that he was signed as an amateur and in early November was given a game in the first team.

The strong athletic Atyeo was a striking contrast to Portsmouth's most memorable scoring inside forward of an earlier era, tubby little 'Billy' Haines. It was Haines' thirty or more goals a season which had taken Portsmouth from Third to First Division in the Thirties. 'Billy' was a rustic West-Countryman who was always greeted on to the field with a chorus of 'To be a farmer's boy'. And now the failure to hold the West-Countryman, John Atyeo, was to be the start of the slide back to the Third Division, from which Billy Haines had once rescued them.

The following Saturday Atyeo was invited to play against Sunderland, but diffidently declined because he was already committed to play for his local club, Westbury United, in an Amateur Cup game against Bristol St George. Westbury's total population was only 4,000, not a tenth of those who would have come to watch him in those golden days at Fratton Park. But for 'Big John' his word and his loyalty to a club took precedence over his own career. He had promised Westbury that he would play in all their Cup-ties and would take them to the Championship of the Wiltshire League that season. Both promises were kept, but it cost him the interest of the leading club of the day. With the pick of the country's young players available why should Portsmouth chase after an 18-year-old who put his amateur team first?

Portsmouth's lack of sympathy and understanding cost them an outstanding player whom they could have had for a £10 signing-on fee. Nine years later, as the Club plummeted to the Third Division, they were to make a desperate and ineffectual attempt to buy him back for £15,000.

Portsmouth's lack of persistence left Atyeo to settle for a West-Country club. He still looked on football as a pleasure to be mixed with work and became a part-time professional with Bristol City. Ashton Gate was close enough to Westbury for him to continue working with a building firm.

Atyeo was physically the ideal of an inside forward who could be both striker and worker. Six feet tall, but always lean, a muscled 12 stone in weight, he was fast, hard and beautifully balanced. In the penalty area he was forceful enough to win the disputed ball, agile enough to take the fleeting chance. In midfield Atyeo was so strong and quick that he could forage with the industrious yet still be up to score the goals. Within two years he was leading Bristol to the Third Division South championship and Liverpool were offering £20,000 and two players for his transfer. He was now indispensable to Bristol – but not to his firm who, with a little intelligence, could have used some of that reflected glory.

After he had played in a midweek game for an F.A. XI against the Army, they told him to leave. 'They said the game was taking up too much of my time, that they could not rely on my services in consequence and it was placing a strain on other members of staff.' Atyeo resigned and within hours a Bristol City fan, who was a builder, offered him a post in his office.

Now that he had played so large a part in taking City back into the Second Division after twenty-three years his value was set too high for any bidder. Chelsea were put off by an asking price of £35,000. There was nothing, however, to deter England from asking for him and Atyeo was just the forward to make good use of Tom Finney's splendid service. In his first International against Spain in 1955 he scored himself and saw Finney add 2 more in a 4–1 win at Wembley. Then came the most vital goal of his career, as he headed home Tom's centre in the last ten seconds of a game in Dublin. That equaliser was sufficient to qualify England for the World Cup Finals.

The maximum wage of £20 per week ensured that his goalscoring feats would never make him wealthy. But the prudent Atyeo provided for his future by purchasing a grocer's business in Westbury Leigh only a few miles from his home. Football for him was always a part of his life, not life itself. He was the typical one-club man who would never look for a transfer, or the shady deals which accompanied them, to many players' profit. To the end he remained a Bristol City player, even though that almost certainly limited his England career.

A £35,000 asking price would not now deter the bidding for a man who could score 315 goals. As the pick of the scorers he would have his pick of the clubs.

Seven

The 'Nearly' Men

Besides the great goalscorers there are the 'nearly' men, all of whom left some distinctive mark. Goalscorers have never had it so good as in the Twenties and Thirties and it was then that many of them flourished. Ted Harper was one of those to cash in on the opportunity, a forceful centre-forward who set club scoring records for the season at Blackburn, Preston and Tottenham. At Blackburn his 43 goals in 1925–6 was the First Division record until Dean surpassed it two seasons later. Harper had 260 goals in the League yet it won him only one International cap. In March 1929 Tottenham bought him from Sheffield Wednesday in a bid to get back to the First Division.

Harper was past his best and did not make immediate impact. But how nearly he won them promotion in 1930–1. He scored 36 of the club's 88 goals that season, which stayed a club record until Bobby Smith equalled it, and Jimmy Greaves passed it. Tottenham's history by Julian Holland records, 'Had the season been completely injury-free for Harper, Spurs might well have gained promotion. For most of the season they held second place to Everton. But on 21 March at Swansea Harper badly injured his leg and from that moment Spurs fell away.' Such then was the value of a man who had no skill excepting the scoring of goals.

'In his time Harper had broken both legs and always played heavily bandaged. He looked lame even before he began to play. He was a very limited footballer, but before goal he was the deadliest centre-forward Spurs have ever had.' Some *but*!

As Harper fell away another fine young centre-forward, George Hunt, took over. He had 24 goals in his first full season, a century of them by the end of 1935, and International caps as well. The Spurs history enthuses over him. 'Hunt had all the penetrative power in front of goal that Eddie Harper had, but he also had more football skill than was usual among centre-forwards in the Thirties. He was a neat, good-looking player in a neat, good-looking forward line, which took Spurs back to the First Division.'

Dave Morris of Swindon was another in the English tradition of centre-forwards who bore and blast their way to goal. He was heavily built and of Jewish appearance, but with nothing of the Shylock about him. He gave his pound of blood and sweat as he led the Third Division South scorers in 1926–7 with 47 goals and had 38 more the next season. In all he netted 216 of his 291 goals for Swindon.

Morris was the ideal type to take advantage of those early years of free scoring under the new off-side law. He went hard, fast and direct through the middle. But these were golden years for the good goalscorers.

Another high scorer of the time was Tom Keetley with 278 goals in his 363 League games with Bradford, Doncaster, Notts County and Lincoln. But you don't recall a Keetley as an *individual*. They were remarkable as a *family*.

The Keetleys of Derby were to football what the Edrichs of Norfolk have been to cricket, a family capable of fielding their own team. There were eleven Keetley brothers and one girl, the eldest, William, being followed by Albert, John, Arthur, Lawrence, Sidney, Ethel, Joe, Tom, Frank, Harold and Charlie. At one time they fielded a complete Keetley forward line for the Victoria Ironworks team in Derby, with Frank, Harold, Tom, Joe, and John being supported by Arthur at left back and Sidney in goal. Nine of them played as soccer professionals, Lawrence and Sidney being the only exceptions, although they too were competent players.

During the 1920s Dick Ray signed five of them as forwards for clubs which he was managing – Tom, Harold, Joe and Frank playing together for Doncaster Rovers and Charlie for Leeds. Tom Keetley with 278 goals in 363 League games was by far the most prolific scorer but Charlie, the youngest, had 115 goals in 191 games, mainly for Leeds, while Frank once scored 5 goals in twenty minutes for Lincoln City and had 75 in all.

Between them these five brothers scored 509 League goals, with Harold getting 23 and Joe 18. But though they averaged over one hundred goals for each of the five, their total does not even give close challenge to the outstanding pair of scoring brothers – Arthur and Jack Rowley. With Jack scoring 207 and Arthur 434, the Rowleys had 641

League goals between the two of them – an unassailable record. Indeed they are the only two brothers both to score more than 200 each, and by a chance in a million each scored his 200th on the same afternoon, both in away matches in the Second Division. It was on Saturday, 22 October 1955 that Arthur scored for Leicester City at Fulham, reaching his 200th goal in the fifty-third minute of the game. Twelve minutes later Jack scored for Plymouth Argyle at Barnsley to reach the same total. In 1958–9 this pair pulled off another brotherly double, each winning promotion for the clubs they were managing. As player-manager Arthur Rowley took Shrewsbury Town out of the Fourth Division, while Jack's management led Plymouth Argyle to the championship of the Third Division. The Rowleys never did anything by halves!

Ernie Hine was another prolific scorer. He had 123 for Barnsley, for whom he played from 1921 to 1926 and again from 1934 to 1938, but it was with Leicester City in the years between that he reached International status. There he was mainly an inside right forming an instinctive partnership with England winger, Adcock. Hine had a greed for goals and lay well forward as an inside, even in the days of the 'W' formation. He was inside left to Cliff Bastin, when that fine winger made his unfortunate debut against Wales in the winter of 1931. Bastin was marked both by his club mate, the balding right-half Charlie Jones, and by right-back Williams. The 19-year-old did not get much help from his partner either. 'It was in part due to Ernie that I had such an undistinguished game. Unlike Alex James, who always stood well behind his centre-forward and winger, Ernie played very close to me. I found his style disconcerting. When I wanted to cut inside, he would usually be in the way,' wrote Bastin in his autobiography.

The close marking of Bastin gave space for Hine and he scored the final goal which brought England a 3–1 win after being a goal down. The fair-minded Bastin gave a more generous description of this. 'Hine's was an extremely well-taken goal. The ball came to him while he was standing with his back to the Welsh goalmouth, but he whipped round like lightning to flash it past Gray.' It was these fast reflexes, this instinctive knowledge of the unguarded spot in the goal which brought Hine 286 league goals.

Ernest Hine had many of them for Leicester, but the club's top scorer is Arthur Chandler, 262 of whose 282 league goals were for Leicester City. From 1923 to 1935 'Channy' was consistency itself and set up a record by scoring in 16 successive matches. He and Johnny ('Tokey') Duncan both scored 6 goals in a match for Leicester when defences were filled with Christmas generosity, Duncan against Port Vale in 1924 and Chandler in a 10–0 win over Portsmouth in 1928. Chandler's goals were scored in the morning in time to sweeten his Christmas dinner. Chandler was a hard, strong ferret of a player questing in eagerly after goals and never letting the chance squirm away.

Such was the competition then that a striker so functionally efficient as Chandler never won a cap, any more than that later Leicester goalscorer, Arthur Rowley. Between them they scored 716 league goals without catching the selectors' eye! Chandler went hard, but with more finesse than another expert goalgetter of the period.

James Cookson was a raw, rough hustler of a forward bludgeoning in his goals. But how effective he was. He made his debut in 1925 for Chesterfield and was the League top scorer in 1925–6, amassing 44 goals. Two seasons later he was scoring 6 in West Bromwich Albion's Second Division match against Blackpool, and he had 255 in his career. Cookson was the fastest man in League football to reach a century of goals in only his 87th game in December 1927, after moving to West Bromwich Albion.

Cookson was no longer in the Albion side of 1931. Instead there was another with a knack for scoring, W. G. Richardson. The 'G.' was wished on him in order to distinguish him from the other W. Richardson in the side, and was said to stand for 'Ginger'. 'Goals' would have been more appropriate, for his ability to knock them in brought West Bromwich promotion to the First Division that season. And in the Final it was Richardson who slipped 2 past Harry Hibbs to give them the Cup as well.

Those were the goals which beat Birmingham 2–1, in a battle of centre-forwards, with Joe Bradford scoring for Birmingham. Bradford was good enough to win 12 caps in competition with Dixie Dean and the other great centre-forwards of the day, apart from scoring 249 goals for Birmingham. Another Bradford, Geoff, was also a massive scorer for one club, with Bristol Rovers benefiting from his 245 League goals. Geoff was the first Bristol Rovers player to win a cap when he played against Denmark in October 1955 and scored a goal in the 5–1 win. Tall, dark and reserved, Geoff Bradford was a penalty-area pouncer who saved his energies for the scoring chance. These he pursued with the reckless courage of a Drake, never minding if he ended on his back or his face so long as the ball ended in the net.

Bradford's bravery was proof against every mischance. Blackburn Rovers rejected him as never likely to be a professional footballer and he made little impact at first with his home-town team. Only when Bert

Tann took over as Manager of Bristol Rovers did Bradford find the scoring touch. In 1953 the club won promotion to the Second Division on the strength of Geoff's 33 goals. Early next season, he was scoring with equal facility when a fierce tackle at Plymouth smashed his knee and sent him to hospital. It was thought his career was finished when he came out on crutches, but he fought his way back five months later. In January 1956 there was another serious injury, this time to his left leg. Again he was thought to be finished. Again he endured the weeks of plaster casts, the months of grinding rehabilitation exercises. And again he came back to score more goals. Whether he was played at centre-forward, or either inside, he was a striker who was irresistibly drawn to the penalty area. That was where this quiet man's anticipation, positional sense and killer instinct kept the goals flowing.

Scorers come in all shapes and sizes.

Wayman was one of those small, well-balanced centre-forwards, quick to anticipate an opening and very certain in his finishing. Put him through and the ball would end in the net without flourish, but with neat precision. In Newcastle's 13–0 defeat of Newport, Wayman scored 4 – after missing a penalty.

Charlie was an unathletic-looking figure, an unassuming player. That meant no caps for him, but it did not stop him scoring goals. In 1946–7 his 30 for Newcastle made him top scorer in the Second Division. Two seasons later 32 goals made him highest scorer in the League and set a Southampton record which Derek Reeves bettered with his 39 in 1960. And when the season ended in 1953 Wayman's 24 goals for Preston made him top scorer again in the First Division.

In the lower divisions Terry Bly was equally impressive. Tall, commanding in the air and insistent in his pressure, he scored 52 goals for Peterborough as late as the 1960–1 season. In 1959 he had been within a touch of making Norwich the first Third Division side to reach the F.A. Cup Final. His leadership of the forwards was vital in a run that ended only after a replay in the semi-final. Coached by Archie Macaulay, Norwich had every opportunity to beat Luton at the first attempt, but for once Bly was not on target. And in the replay Luton squeezed through to Wembley by the only goal.

Some players score goals with abandon yet still leave an indefinable aura of failure. Four such are Peter Harris, Jackie Sewell, Ronnie Allen and Allan Clarke. With Harris it was a failure to take his chances. With Sewell a failure of determination. With Allen a failure of selectors to give full appreciation to his special talents. With Clarke a failure to establish himself fully as an England player.

Peter Harris, the Portsmouth right-winger just after his club had held the Cup for the six years of war, was a man who could never open the door when opportunity knocked. As a club player Harris was in the class of Matthews or Finney. He had speed off the mark, and a jinking dribble that sent him down the wing like a startled snipe. His darting, sinuous runs made him look a natural for England, as he helped Portsmouth win the League in 1949 and 1950. Yet that ambition was to turn sour, as did his Cup hopes. When asked why he had become a professional footballer Harris said it was the only way he could think of to get into Wembley without a ticket. But even as a player he could not quite make it. In 1949 his startling miss, when he rapped the ball against the goalkeeper's leg from a few yards out, cost a semi-final replay and ultimate defeat by Second Division Leicester. And that May he was chosen for England against Sweden at Stockholm, only to be prevented from playing by a groin injury. That did not prevent one writer recording the view, 'Round about 1952 the name of Peter Harris will appear in England teams with the same joyful frequency as Stanley Matthews. That's a safe prediction.'

He had waited long in the shadow of that great winger, but on 21 September that same year he was picked to play against Eire at Goodison Park, Liverpool. Harris, Morris (Man. Utd.), Pye (Wolves), Mannion (Middlesbrough) and Finney were the forward line expected to score five. In fact it was Eire who won 2–0, the first team outside the U.K. to beat England at home. Such was the shock that only Finney survived for the next match and he was switched to the right in place of Harris.

Not until May 1954 was Harris to have another chance. Then he came into the team in Budapest and Hungary won 7–1! With that double of disastrous matches he was rated too accident-prone for another chance. Chance was the right word. Had Harris come in for two winning games in strong sides his name might now have something of the magic of Matthews. Instead memory fumbles to place him, his name a faint echo, like Portsmouth's First Division status. At least he had the excitement of those two seasons of glory at Fratton Park as the Pompey chimes swelled out to give wings to his feet. And there was that record 170 First Division goals from the wing with another 24 to add for Portsmouth on their slide down the Divisions.

When Harris was at his peak our Pegasus side played a floodlit friendly against Portsmouth, happily swapping goals to lose 6–3. It was a magical night for us, but the Portsmouth crowd, nurtured on Harris, was not so complimentary to the prematurely grey-haired man on the

Pegasus right wing. In the darkness beyond the lights I could hear the comments on my probable age and possible antecedents. As I walked back to take a corner a voice shouted out, 'Here. How old are you, Grand-pop?'

'Ninety-six', I called back sarcastically. 'Aye,' said the voice, 'and you're playing like it too.'

That night I was a double loser and could sympathise with Harris in his two failures.

There are 35 footballers who have scored 250 or more goals in the English League. One who should have been in that company is Jackie Sewell. Most players would be satisfied with 228 goals, but for Sewell that represented a failure to reach his full potential.

Goalscorers are said to be worth their weight in gold and that certainly was the view of Sheffield Wednesday when they bought Jackie Sewell from Notts County. Sewell had scored over 100 goals in his first four seasons of League Football and Wednesday paid £35,000 for him in 1951, a record figure at that time. With gold at £12 8s a Troy ounce they would have paid less for a golden replica of the 12-stone Sewell. The thought worried him.

'At school in Cumberland I was often in trouble for forgetting dates. But I will never forget that March fifteenth day in the Victoria Hotel, Nottingham. After signing up with Eric Taylor, the Sheffield Manager, that night was the longest of my life wondering if I had done right. When I opened the morning papers and found I had cost Wednesday all that money my worries started afresh.'

Players then did not get a share of the transfer fee, but they did have the anxiety of proving themselves to the new club and to supporters expecting miracles. Sewell was expected to save Sheffield from relegation to the Second Division in the six weeks that remained of the season. He did score in his first match, but Sheffield still lost and finally went down despite a resounding 6–0 defeat of Everton in the final game. The next season, however, they won the Second Division Championship and Sewell had soon gained five International caps for England.

When he left Notts County the old-timers there, like Tommy Lawton, told him, 'Forget the money. You'll repay every penny.' Yet he could not help worrying and this affected his play in the early matches. He was also troubled by a cracked bone over his left eyebrow which made the eye bloodshot and was a constant irritation. Such injuries are the price goalscorers pay for going hard for the half-chance, but each one tends to make them a little less eager. Sewell, however, was quick to settle and it was his instinctive partnership with the young Derek Dooley which brought Sheffield back to the First Division. But he was soon struggling to hold his place against the challenge of two other fine forwards, Albert Quixall and Redfern Froggatt. The bright promise of his Notts County days seemed stunted by the burden of that record transfer fee. And in his reaction to it he betrayed the lack of that self-confidence which so often distinguishes the great from the gifted. Once he became a marked man he lacked the hard determination to shake free.

Stanley Matthews was more skilful at conjuring goals for others than taking them himself, but he was the inspiration of that most dangerous striker, Ronnie Allen. At school Allen was an outstanding Rugby player, a scrum-half of infinite promise. But he lived in the Potteries and the magic name there was Matthews. It only needed a few visits to Stoke's Victoria Ground and Allen too was captivated by that stooped figure with the fluttering feet and the darting acceleration. Thereafter soccer was the only football he was prepared to play and his ability was instantly apparent.

At the war's end he was only sixteen, but already he was in Port Vale's first team, a fast, elusive right-winger modelling himself on his idol. He was still only a stripling, frail of figure, but quite fearless in his quest for goals. And while he had a hint of the master's trickery and ball control, he was also an effective goalscorer, powerful in either foot and accurate with his head.

With such a range of natural ability Port Vale had soon played him in every position in the forward line, while First Division clubs watched him with growing interest. After five years it was West Bromwich who won him away for £15,000. Albion had just returned to the First Division after twelve years and were having a hard struggle to stay there. Manager Jack Smith's main worry was the lack of a scoring centre-forward. Three were tried out in nine games without resolving the problem. As a last resort Allen was asked to play the part. It hardly seemed the right role for a man who was small when centre-forwards were expected to be robust and forceful. 'I will do my best, but you must give me a chance to settle into the position' was Allen's response.

He had always been a thoughtful player and now he evolved a new style that would suit his main assets – his speed and his elusive dribbling. There was to be no heavyweight confrontation with hard-bitten centre-halves. He would lie deep, roam across the field, pounce suddenly for the opening, or make one for others. He scored in his first game, coming in unnoticed and unmarked from a deep position. And he went on scoring so steadily and so regularly that he set a new record for the club and was to reach 250 goals in all League games.

Clubs did not then operate with a second centre-half and Allen's style of play was cleverly developed by Vic Buckingham to exploit two strikers against one defender. His midfield work allowed one inside to lie well ahead and with instinctive anticipation Allen would glide up unnoticed to make it two against one. He was a better exponent than Don Revie of the Hidegkuti style of deeply-lying centre-forward.

Allen was a centre-forward the defenders could never quite fathom or follow. He hovered in limbo as far as centre-halves were concerned and they were not sure whether to go with him or wait for him. All too often they lost him and his 274 League goals show how dangerous that was. But Ronnie Allen was as good at making them as taking them. Inside forwards fed happily off his telling passes and the confusion he caused made things easy for them. Three of his partners at Albion, Johnnie Nicholls, Derek Kevan, and Bobby Robson, all won caps before he did. And his clever prompting of the fast, unsubtle Nicholls sent him striding through for goals which almost gave Albion the double in 1954. They won the Cup and only injuries caused their long lead in the championship to evaporate at the season's end.

Allen's first cap for England was at outside-left in the 1952 tour. When, two years later, he was given his chance in the centre he bewildered Scotland just as he had bemused League defences. Scotland were beaten 4–2 at Hampden Park and then there were winning games against Wales and Germany, with Allen helping Roy Bentley to a hat-trick against Wales. But that was all. He had only five caps despite his clear ability. Yet he was always philosophical about the selectors. 'No two people see this game the same way and everyone is entitled to his own judgement.' The judgement of hindsight must be that England made inadequate use of his remarkable talent. His style baffled the selectors as well as the defenders.

Allan Clarke has had the greatest potential of any of the current goalscorers. In anticipating an opening, in cool certainty of finishing he has many of the characteristics of Jimmy Greaves. It is because he had the same potential as Greaves, the same neat balance and sharp reaction, that there is a tinge of disappointment about his career. By ordinary standards it is one of high achievement. Yet it has tailed off without the satisfying consistency of the great players. Clarke was at his best hunting in the burly shadow of Mick Jones and with Johnny Giles to create the openings for him at Leeds. Somehow he never found the same happy combination of support with England. 10 goals in 16

Internationals is no mean feat, but he had the potential for bettering that and for becoming a more certain choice.

'Sniffer' Clarke has nosed out more than 200 League goals and is among the top five of current scorers. That is a hard-won record at the highest level of today's expert defensive teams. It tells of his instinct for an opening backed by his special characteristic – the chilling confidence of his finishing. Typically it was Clarke who was asked to take the penalties at crucial moments in a World Cup game in Mexico and against Poland at Wembley in 1974. He stroked them home with evident relish, before wheeling to give that gladiatorial salute, arm stretched high above the long, slim body. And yet he always had to struggle for his England place.

Selectors, of course, have always been a little suspicious of the goalscorers, wondering if they will pull their weight in other ways. Only two men playing in 1976 had passed 250 goals. Ken Wagstaff had for long given width and scoring power to Hull as to Mansfield earlier, in the role of an old-fashioned winger with a lethal left foot. Yet First Division managers watched, wondered, and did not buy. And his career ended without a hint of an international cap. Kevin Hector got two, but both times he came on as substitute. Yet, the profusion of goals apart, he seemed to have all the right qualifications to play for England. His role was vital in Derby's success for his brave, surging runs disturbed defences and his sharp finishing turned chances to goals. He has been target man and scorer, working unselfishly for others, then grabbing goals himself. For Bradford, then Derby, he scored freely in all Divisions in which he played, and he should have fitted well into England sides dedicated to work-rate. No one ran further than Hector, who has always been prepared to go straight at the hardest defence to take the weight off others. In the World Cup match against Poland at Wembley Ramsey allowed him just two minutes as substitute to try and score the goal that would have qualified England for the Finals. And he was within an inch of doing it, as his header from a corner struck a startled Polish defender rooted on the line and bounced away.

Tony Brown is another of those whose one cap in 1971 seems an insult to his ability. With more than 180 goals for West Bromwich Albion by the start of 1977 he has more goals for one club than anyone else still playing. To me he has always seemed to have many of the qualities of Martin Peters. Brown is a strong and accurate finisher with a fine sense of anticipation. He is particularly dangerous with his runs from deep positions for he times them so well and has the acceleration to get into position before he can be picked up. Like Peters he has all-round skills, never shirking the defensive part of his role and being as perceptive in preventing goals as in scoring them. Perhaps he has been too consistent and too unobtrusive to win much international recognition despite his high skills. But then, as the records show, so many of the goalscorers remain 'nearly' men when it comes to national selection.

Eight

Men of the Moment

The way to goal has never been harder than today, the goal-getter never more closely watched, more protectively screened. But they are a resilient species, self-assured in their response to challenge. There is a touch of arrogance in most of them too, however well concealed. The mild-mannered Matthews used to enjoy destroying opponents, leaving them crushed in mind, beaten in spirit. He did it quietly, almost apologetically, where some of today's more spectacular forwards are ready to flaunt their skills, to revel in the humiliation of an opponent

Rodney Marsh still has this talent, his intricate dribbling and nonchalant shooting often a joyous revelation, a joke shared with a happy audience. But there is his sneering mood when he has the disdainful aggressive air of a showman casting sham pearls before real swine. It is then that he can divide his own team, or sting an opposition to bitter retaliation. He may mark their minds, but they will mark his shins in return. Like the comedian playing to a hostile audience, he often needs great courage to see him through his act.

The Jekyll and Hyde character in Marsh was never more apparent than in his transfer to Manchester City. When he was spirited away by Manager Malcolm Allison, Queen's Park Rangers were on the verge of promotion, City set for the League Championship. The loss of him kept Rangers down for they had the best defensive record in any League, but relied on Marsh to snatch the winning goals. His arrival cost Manchester City the Championship, for his extrovert play failed to fit in to a disciplined team. Yet Marsh is a compelling attraction whatever his mood. When he has the ball there is a new tension, a fresh air of expectancy, in the crowd. Sometimes the extravagant hopes are dashed, but sometimes he gives us those unforgettable goals as he leaves a trail of baffled tacklers, and winks at us while he sends the goalkeeper the wrong way.

Alec Stock, then his Manager at Fulham, summed him up. 'Almost thirteen stone of muscle, perfect balance, total assurance, complete mastery of the ball – he's got to be good, hasn't he?'

Not always – because it is not in Marsh's character to be good always, nor is it in Stan Bowles'. But when the mood takes him, Bowles is also the delight of spectators, the despair of defenders. There is that elfin quality in Bowles with which little Tommy Harmer – Harmer the Charmer – used to intrigue spectators at Tottenham. But Bowles can also be a precise and deadly finisher with the coolness of a Greaves. The challenge of top-class foreign opponents was the stimulus for one of his outstanding displays as Slovan Bratislava were held to a 3–3 draw with Bowles scoring twice in this away match for Queen's Park Rangers in the UEFA Cup in 1976. It was almost the Czechoslovakian team that Rangers were playing yet the ripples of apprehension widened round the little man. 'I knew I could upset the best of the continentals because they are frightened of a forward who runs at them. When they close-marked me and I beat them, they tried standing off. That was fatal. That gave me space.'

In the next round Bowles set a new scoring record, becoming the first British player to score 10 goals in one season of European competition. It was a typically impish goal which gave him that record. As he took the angled pass in the area Bowles wheeled suddenly back to strand two challengers, then curled his left-foot shot just inside the post. That brought Rangers a 3–0 win over a Cologne team, whose entertaining attack was not quite good enough to make up the leeway in the return leg. Givens, so sure in his finishing, made an ideal partner for Bowles, the pair more formidable than the two as individuals. But when Bowles broke a leg later that season the effect still hampered him a year afterwards.

When Matthews was left out of the England team puzzled foreign journalists used to ask 'He is ill then?' And when assured that he was dropped would say incredulously, 'You have someone *better* then?' The Czechs were right to express the same surprise about Bowles. But such players have rarely fitted happily into England sides. Unbelievably Len Shackleton, the Bowles of his day, the clown prince of Sunderland soccer, scored only one goal for England. Yet this was one of the best I have seen as West Germany were beaten 3–1 at Wembley a few months after winning the 1954 World Championship. Shackleton had just gone past three defenders, side-stepped the goalkeeper, Herkenrath, then lost control. Now he repeated the move at his own leisurely pace and this time chipped the ball into the empty net.

Bowles upset continental defenders by running at them, because in the intensive cover of the modern game 'shepherding' has become more important than tackling. There was a stark revelation of the change in our own skills when an England side launched itself into all-out attack against Finland in the 1976 World Cup match. Suddenly the defenders were left bare of cover as the Finnish forwards struck swiftly out of their own area. So they *had* to challenge themselves and win their own tackles. And a rare mess they made of it, mistiming and missing in a way that had old players like Billy Wright starting out of their seats to show them how.

Today covering and screening is so highly developed that it takes a Bowles or a Marsh at his best to go past three men in a cutting run to the heart of the penalty area. In a very different style Mike Channon has that ability and is more consistent in applying it. Before he moved to Manchester City his partnership with Ted MacDougall at Southampton proved an exciting pairing of two players of quite differing qualities and outlook. Between them they expressed the attitude and abilities which make for the successful striker unshackled by today's packed defences.

Mike Channon in full stride is as graceful as the horses he breeds and races, and as competitive. 'What fun is there in life if you are not competing? It would be very dull, wouldn't it? In a football match I have got to be in the game all the time, not just lurking in the penalty area waiting to score. There's so much enjoyment if you are taking people on all the time. Outside football, horses and horseracing are all that excite me because that's a continual challenge too.'

Soccer is as vital to Channon as spinach was to Pop-eye. It expands him, gives him a strength and assurance beyond the reach of everyday life. And he has had the sense to recognise that this is his life-force, to surf along in the enthusiasm that rides him to the top. There are none of the doubts or distractions which diminished George Best, none of the world-weariness that kept Martin Chivers from being an outstanding striker. Of him Channon comments, 'At Southampton Martin had more potential than any other player I have seen. Ron Davies was a great goalscorer, but he needed others to put the ball on his head. Martin could do it all on his own when he wanted to. But often he just did not seem interested.'

There is wonder in Channon's voice as he contemplates a man who had all those gifts and failed to use them to the full. For Channon is the natural ninety-minute player. As Southampton's Manager, Laurie McMenemy, put it, 'He will keep on trying something to the end no matter how badly he's been playing, how many moves have failed to come off for him. You never see his head go down. You never substitute him because he may still win you the game in the last minute.

'Against Carrick Rangers, in the Cup Winners Cup, we cannot do a thing right in the first half. It's a small, bumpy pitch and they are rightly rushing us off our game. We cannot put a pass together and Mike looks the worst of them all. In the interval I tell the team they cannot go on being that bad. Some still go out thinking it's not their day, that nothing's going to go right. But Channon sets his teeth and runs straight through them from the kick-off, determined to prove who has the superior skill. And in no time he's won the match.'

Channon is almost as free a talker as McMenemy, but his summary is briefer. 'They pay me a lot to turn a match and that's what I keep trying to do.'

With his engaging smile, his boyish enthusiasm, there is only the unmasked competitiveness to justify McMenemy's comment. 'Goalscorers? They are all hard, mean and selfish. And it has to be in their character. They have to be like it off the field as well as on.' Perhaps Channon is still a little too nice to be an outstanding scorer. 'If he took all the goals he makes for himself he'd be better than "Dixie" Dean,' said McMenemy without rancour. The killer touch has been lacking, although he has scored more than 150 goals. But Channon is working on it with Manchester. 'My instinct was just to blast the ball in the net and that's wasted me lots of goals. Now I try to be more thoughtful and precise about it.' He wastes goals for himself, but makes them for the team by a lot of unselfish running and passing. 'I wish I could be one of those players like Jimmy Greaves who got twenty goals a season tapping the ball in from two yards out.' That does not happen to Channon because he is usually the one who has rolled it across for someone else to tap in from two yards.

A few phrases of soccer wisdom echo down the years with unchanging truth. One that is too often ignored comes from that scorer extraordinary of Derby County's early years, Steve Bloomer. He commented, 'The half-backs should give more support to the forwards for the forward needs all his energy for scoring goals.' Channon is liberal in his expense of energy, restlessly ready to run rather than wait for the goals to come or the ball be passed to him. That makes him a less prolific scorer than he might be and governs his idea on the ideal supporting partners. 'Who do I like playing with? The man who gives me the early ball, of course, so that I have time and space to work it. Since everyone started talking "possession" football you don't get the early pass so often.' Johnny Haynes and Mike Channon would have made a wonderful combination in the England side, with Haynes the unrivalled hitter of the long instant pass too often squandered by the slow-witted, or the slow moving. For years at Fulham Haynes had to endure his best passes being allowed to run to waste by that endearing left-winger 'Tosh' Chamberlain, of the explosive shot but lumbering run. Every time Chamberlain's name was on the team sheet Haynes' manner clearly expressed 'Not him *again!*' What a pleasure it would have been for Haynes to have seen Channon listed instead in his forward line.

Channon is a present-day example of another of Steve Bloomer's guiding principles: 'Some players are frightened of shooting for fear of missing, but a forward should always be prepared to take chances.' That is the way Channon plays, always ready to chance a shot, or chance a difficult pass or chance a tricky dribble. 'Some good footballers can only do the straightforward things perfectly. You go to watch Channon because when he's in the play you never know what the finish of the act will be. There's usually a twist at the end' is McMenemy's view of him.

England had trouble enough beating Finland in the World Cup match at Wembley, but it was the unexpected from Channon which finally brought two points and a narrow 2–1 win. He beat defender after defender in the area before making an easy opening for Royle. 'I was looking to get a shot in and when they screened the goal I just kept turning and twisting until I could win space to pick out a man in a scoring position. "Pick out a man!" That was something Terry Paine kept drumming into me.'

Paine, that durable campaigner who lasted longer than anyone else, 806 matches in League football before his first 'retirement', was the formative influence on Channon. 'Paine had so much experience and there is no substitute for it. That's what changes a good footballer into a great one, or keeps an old player going when he's lost his speed. He was always trying to pick out a man in a scoring position – "Don't worry if it doesn't come off nine times as long as he scores the tenth" was his philosophy. And he never missed a small point whether it was pinching half a yard at a throw-in, or widening the angle for a shot. "Think of it before they do", was his theme, "the great player never gets caught a second time."'

For all the elegance of his lancing dribbles and gazelle-like running Channon has no time for the artistic flourishes. 'Skill is doing the right thing at the right time. And if that means kicking the ball over the stand, then kick it over the stand.'

But Channon has the higher skill to do more than that, to win a game on his own against all the odds by doing the *unlikely* thing. He is the man to snatch a 1–0 victory in an away match with a sudden lonely break out of defence. And it is in character that the goal that gave him most pleasure was one against Coventry when he took a pass on the edge of his own area and went the length of the field on his own, slipping every tackle and beating the goalkeeper. At the core of Channon's play is the loneliness and determination of the long-distance runner. And if that has occasionally cost him his England place, it has also put him in the top ten English scorers. How strange he should be discarded when we had such a dearth of goalscorers.

The pairing with Ted MacDougall brought together two strikers of contrasted ability. MacDougall, flat-footed, ungainly in movement, is a predator of the penalty area. Only there does the adrenalin flow and the reflexes sharpen, quickness of thought giving him the first touch. Says McMenemy, 'I brought him to Southampton because he has all the scoring qualities that Mike lacks. He gets the unlikely goals close in with nudges and flicks and deflections. The ball may bounce in off his bottom, or the back of his neck, but that's part of his game. The crowd may deride him and call him lucky, but he's got the confidence to know it's only results that matter.' And that confidence has taken him close to 250 League goals.

In training MacDougall stumbles round the track as if in need of an oxygen cylinder after a couple of laps. His speed is in the three-yard burst in the penalty area, in the quick reaction that gets his toes to a ball a defender is sure he has covered. He has in fact many of the qualities that Hugh McIlvanney observed in the young Scottish striker of high promise, Andy Gray, top scorer with 29 goals in his first full season in the First Division.

Goal-scoring in football, like knock-out punching in boxing, is a talent that makes itself violently obvious while remaining somewhat mysterious. Of course, as Jimmy Greaves thrillingly demonstrated throughout his career, technical excellence helps an executioner to do a nice clean job. But Greaves was not typical of the most successful British strikers. For every Mack the Knife of the penalty box there are several who attack like sharks, seeking to spread scarlet billows of alarm wherever they go. Denis Law may yet be canonised as the patron saint of such predators, the most dramatic personification of the quality that sets the great finisher apart from all other footballers; a scarcely definable instinct for homing in on the jugular of the opposition.

Some of the most exciting glimpses of that instinct the English game has had in many a day have been provided recently by a young Glaswegian whose conversation is inclined to degenerate engagingly into a listing of his inadequacies as a player. Andy Gray had established himself as one of the two most prolific scorers in Scotland before moving from Dundee United to Aston Villa for £110,000. Already he has indicated that he can be just as destructive of the tighter defences in the First Division.

The fact that Villa were able to sign him for so modest a fee indicates the extreme difficulty so many English clubs have in deciding if a Scottish player's assets will retain their validity south of the Solway. Some of them seem to believe that in Scotland goals are given out with the stocking tie-ups.

Jock Stein, the Celtic manager, has never doubted Gray's ability. 'This is a real one,' he said before Gray left Dundee. 'He's got tremendous effective aggression. You can hardly keep him from getting a telling touch on anything that comes across the goal. He's marvellous in the air, although he's only about five feet ten and on the ground he can get round and go at people and he can work well off other players.'

While at Kingsridge School in Drumchapel (a sprawling housing estate on the outskirts of Glasgow that may not justify Billy Connelly's description, 'a desert wi' windaes', but it is quite raw enough to be set alongside the traditional breeding grounds of Scottish footballers) Gray played for Scotland under-eighteens against England and Wales, scoring against the English at Firhill.

At seventeen he went straight from school to Dundee United, was in the first team after only three outings with the reserves and, despite missing nine weeks of his first season because of a cartilage operation on his right knee, he knocked in 20 goals. In the following season, 1974–5, he took 26 League and Cup goals and was joint top scorer in Scotland with Willie Pettigrew, the Motherwell attacker.

Many lads who have done much less in the game than he has would be ready to give lessons in swaggering to Jimmy Cagney. Gray, one of four brothers, who lacked nothing of the alertness Glasgow is in the habit of teaching its sons, could hardly be mistaken for a shrinking violet. The face under the high sweep of blond hair is strong and unafraid, the blue eyes free of agitation.

His modesty is simply modesty, not the tip of an iceberg of inferiority. Mention of his ball control brings from him a hissing, explosive laugh. 'Yeah, it's something special all right,' he says.

'Playing the ball to me is like hittin' it off a brick wall. When it reaches me that's another attack broken down.' The exaggeration is outrageous, of course, for he does plenty of damage on the ground, but the corollary of this self-deprecation is that he works long hours on his control and improvement is inevitable. 'When I can't do something at training I tell the lads I'm at my best with the real thing, under pressure. That's my story and I'm sticking to it.'

He is particularly hard in his assessment of his right foot. 'Have you seen it? It's a beauty, isn't it?' When reminded that he has managed some important goals with that right, he says, 'Yeah, that was just to kid the defenders on.'

Pressed to try seriously to identify his strength, he is equally refreshing. 'Well, I do think I'm a bit aggressive. I throw myself about in the box, cause a flurry here and there. And I don't think my timing in the air is too bad. I can get up to the ball and make the right kind of contact even against much taller lads.

'One thing I like about my manager, Ron Saunders, is the way he keeps on my back even when I'm doing quite well. That's how it should be. I like to be driven on and I like to drive myself on. Maybe if I've got one outstanding quality, that's it. I don't give up. No matter how badly I'm playing. I'll offer myself for the ball, try to get involved, try to put it where it counts. I won't let my head go down.' That at least is a timeless quality of the great goalscorers.

Nine

The Forty Club

There are just five British players who have scored thirty or more goals in International matches. And a nicely balanced forward line they would make, no matter what the tactical formation. Finney, Greaves, Lofthouse, Law and Charlton – what a fine blend of aggression and subtlety.

Three of them scored exactly thirty goals, but the other two went on to pass the 40 mark. Greaves had 44 in only 57 matches for England, Charlton 49 in 106 matches.

April 1973 was the time of goodbyes as Manchester United and the football world saw the end of the highest scorers in the history of English and Scottish football. Bobby Charlton and Denis Law retired together, the valedictory notices full of affection and gratitude. Perfect gentleman and volatile fighter, model of good manners and explosive scourge of defenders, in their contrasting characters both these two had graced the game and delighted the crowds.

The passing of such players must momentarily leave its mark. And their loss was weighed not by the funeral orations from Press and public, but by the relegation of Manchester United the following season. It would hardly have seemed right if the stars had not so obviously fallen from their courses as the mighty departed.

Bobby Charlton, with his record 49 goals for England, and his 106 caps exceeded only by Bobby Moore, always had a special place in the public's affection. He was the Cliff Richards of the game, the wholesome young star who never lost his power to charm. Charlton spanned the generation gap, pleasing all ages in the family, all classes in society, all regions of the country. He was the footballer everyone loved to love, the man born to be King of the game.

There was the footballing background through the relationship to the Milburns and the right birthplace at Ashington in Northumberland – 'Go to the pits and whistle for a footballer' was the advice to the early Managers – and to come from a mining family completed the perfect pedigree.

The precocious talent was soon evident and in 1953 Bobby went to the best place for its development – Old Trafford. Matt Busby had improved on the Wolves' expert organisation for spotting and grooming the young. With Cullis continuing the Buckley tradition at Wolverhampton, these two clubs dominated the fifties until Manchester United gradually established their supremacy on the field and in the nurturing of their own talent. The Busby 'Babes' became a succession of young stars, their debuts thoughtfully stage-managed in the strongest of teams and, preferably, least vital of matches. Bobby's came after only three years of forcing in the United nursery and in his first match he scored two goals from centre-forward against Charlton Athletic.

In another eighteen months he was helping to destroy Scotland 4–0 at Hampden Park, that explosive left foot thundering out its warning to goalkeepers with one flashing drive. But the carefree morning of his career was already shadowed by the trauma of the air crash. When he should still have been the youthful prodigy of a great side he was suddenly survivor and elder statesman, the man on whom United relied. His inspired play and the frenzied tide of emotion swept Manchester to Wembley with their hastily rebuilt team of promising youngsters and elderly rejects. In that Final of 1958 emotion was not enough against Bolton Wanderers and Nat Lofthouse's two goals. Nor was Charlton's inspiration – but how narrowly that failed to sway the match. At the time I recorded in the *Observer*:

> There remained Charlton to save the game for United and it is a measure of his remarkable advance that he came near to doing it. Bolton's superiority was unquestioned but twice he nearly snatched the game from them.
>
> In the first half he sent Hopkinson diving to save, brilliantly, a shot of ferocious power. In the second his shot which might have turned the match slapped against the inside of the post to rebound straight to the goalkeeper.
>
> A year ago Charlton would have manoeuvred the ball awkwardly and automatically to his left foot, but now these shots were hit with equal felicity and ferocity with either foot.

Already he had had to assume a responsibility beyond his years and he was one to take any responsibility seriously. Not surprising then that he should come to wear that slightly harassed, slightly baffled look which would have been more appropriate in those who had to mark him. The long bony face seemed prematurely lined and as the hair thinned the right hand still kept nervously sweeping back into place the straggling lock on his forehead.

The look of bewilderment was not entirely misleading. For Charlton, forced so quickly, still lacked confidence in his own great talent. He could not command a place in England's World Cup team, though he was in the party in Sweden that year, and the next he still had difficulty in establishing himself.

There was too much flair, too much individualism, when he was teamed with Clough and Greaves in a singularly ill-balanced and short-lived combination of inside forwards. It is strange to re-read a report of the time by Basil Easterbrook. 'As we saw against the young Hungarians at Goodison Charlton can go from bad to worse and come near to utter despair when luck or the bounce of the ball are against him.'

And again, despite his scoring the second goal when England lost 2–3 to Sweden at Wembley, 'Charlton must be dropped. He is having a bad season and it will not serve either him or England to keep him in until he snaps out of it. Not one of his famed power drives was even near the target.'

Even outstanding players have their periods when nothing runs for them and then they are the more harshly judged because more is expected of them. As experience matured Charlton's skills and revived his confidence few indeed were the bad games to offset the triumphant ones. Of the many matches he signed with his personality, one stands out, that memorable floodlit scene at Wembley as United became the first English club to win the European Cup. No staged *Son et Lumière* performance has achieved more dramatic effects as we supplied the constant roar of sound, Charlton and Best the magical light.

The mood before and after that great match was summed up by Hugh McIlvanney. In prospect he wrote in the *Observer*

Perhaps the trick is to retreat to a cottage in Wester Ross with a case of whisky or half a pound of aspirins. That way we could anaesthetise ourselves next Wednesday and wait for the result of the European Cup Final to filter through, hoping that its emotional effects would be softened by the delay.

However, there is no escape. We will have to sit there at Wembley and watch United wrestle with the most significant assignment in their history, just one thrust away from the realisation of their obsessive ambition, one slip away from failure and a bleak residue of gloom. . . .

Judging United purely on a technical assessment of their recent form the danger of defeat might appear considerable. Now that Law is a hospital case, United's list of outstanding footballers, of names that would be meaningful anywhere, would fall short of that offered by Benfica.

In answer to Best, Charlton, Crerand and Stiles one must say Eusebio, Coluna, Torres, Augusto, Simoes and possibly Graca. . . .

Heart may be United's greatest asset at Wembley and their courage should give them time to settle to their own splendid natural game.

And on the day they did just that. After forty-five meaningless minutes with the referee Signor Lo Bello permitting too much mayhem on Best, Eusebio and Charlton, there was still no score. Twelve minutes later Charlton scored one of the more unusual and most decisive goals of his career. As he begged for the ground pass Sadler floated over a cross and Charlton neatly headed home the slippery ball. 'It glanced off my bald patch,' he explained. In the last quarter of an hour United had to fight desperately after Graca had moved up to hit home the equaliser. For once Stiles lost Eusebio and there was the great forward through on his own. His shot was struck with all his usual force and accuracy, but Stepney only a few yards away dived instinctively to his right and held the ball – a miraculous piece of goalkeeping which made Busby certain at last that United would win. And in extra time they had Wembley roaring as if this was a Beatles Concert as Best and Kidd completed the 4–1 destruction of Benfica.

Charlton was so tired he missed the celebratory dinner, but less than twenty-four hours later he was still caught on soccer's wheel preparing for a match against West Germany.

He was sitting in the lounge of the Esso Motor Hotel wearing football boots and shorts. His socks were at his ankles, his eyelids were heavy and the narrow strangely affecting face beneath the isolated strands of yellow hair was more deeply lined than usual. For a moment it seemed he might have come straight from Wembley without changing or sleeping. It took the blue track suit top and the England insignia to remind us that he was beginning a new cycle, that for him great victories merely lead to more battles. He must pick up the laurel wreath on the run. . . .

It became clear afterwards that Charlton, Stiles and Stepney are not only being sustained by euphoria, but insulated by it. The reality of Wednesday night is taking time to seep into their minds.

'It's just dawning on me now,' admitted Charlton, his eyes looking beyond me to the memory of those two incredible hours at Wembley. Inevitably his thoughts dwell on the last 15 or 20 minutes of regular time when United almost as one man slowed to a stagger and Benfica began to reach confidently for a prize which should have been swept irrevocably away long before.

'We were really gone. None of us could run. It was a terrible helpless feeling. My legs were killing me, both of them. It wasn't like ordinary cramp. They just sort of seized up and there wasn't a real stoppage in that last quarter so you didn't have a chance to get down and give them a shake to loosen them. It was murder.' He slapped his calf muscles as he spoke studying them critically as if they might yield some reason for their perfidy.

'When they scored it looked on for them, considering the state we were in, but we held on somehow and when full time came they lost their advantage. It was starting all over again and we had a breather, a chance to get ourselves going again. We were flopped out there like dead men, but we were ready to go when we had to. Matt said, "Just keep going; you can still beat these." We were more like ourselves again when extra time began, we got a quick break and they could do nothing with us. . . .'

Extra time was the supreme test of spirit and United, sharing the advantage of massive home support which had assisted England through the same ordeal in the World Cup, responded magnificently, Benfica, understandably, caved in.

Charlton, Stiles, Best and Stepney were the great players on whom a great victory was built. But they acknowledged their debt to the others. 'What about Brian Kidd? He was like Roger Hunt, working for everybody. And John Aston with those runs? What a game he had. Paralysed that poor fellow Adolfo.' And Crerand whose intelligence and perception meant so much and the inimitable George Best, who made up for his earlier indiscretions with his brilliant goal, and Dunne, and Foulkes – indeed all of them and most vitally perhaps Matt Busby who expressed everything that had to be expressed when he said 'That's it. We've done it.'

Charlton had heard both Ramsey and Busby say that in the two most memorable matches of our time and it was his spirit and skill, as much as anything, which had allowed them to say it.

Bobby Charlton's last game was in a Stamford Bridge strangely contorted, the stadium three-sided with the new white-elephant stand in constructive desolation. It had been a muted season for Chelsea, their games without atmosphere until Charlton came for his 606th and final League match for United. Then they roared their welcome and willed him to get the two goals he needed to reach 200 in League games. He needed only to finish as he had begun, but there was to be no memorable ending; the game was undistinguished, the goal tally still 198.

That is an unsensational total for so accomplished a player, but it is not by League goals we remember him. Three that best illustrate the wide range of his scoring talent are forever impressed in my mind. They were scored for England and they took us to World Cup victory in Britain in 1966.

For ninety minutes of frustration England had failed to score against Uruguay, even Greaves lost in the maze of defenders. Next it was the Mexican Maginot Line blunting England's anxious forwards. For another 37 minutes the wall of Chaires, Pena, Nunez and Hernandez held firm with close support from del Muro behind and the other five in front coming back to help. Crowd and players grew ever more restive, spirits drained as Hunt's header hit the net only for the goal to be disallowed.

That was the crucial moment Charlton chose for one of the great goals of his career. Getting the ball near the half-way line he accelerated smoothly away, veering always to his right. As the Mexicans held off the tackle, screening the goal, Charlton spun without warning to smash his shot against the far stanchion high above Calderon's groping right hand. That was the Charlton of explosive power with the Lorimer-like shooting which made his name as a youngster. But Charlton now was thirty, the hair thinning, the face serious, the mind steeped in all the arts of goalscoring. And it was a quite different method which won the breathless semi-final against Portugal.

It was the night when Charlton made even Eusebio look second rate. Under Nobby Stiles' snapping, snarling challenge the Portuguese goalscorer supreme became as ineffectual as a man trying to thumb a lift from James Hunt on the last lap of the Japanese Grand Prix. A late penalty was all Eusebio could contribute, while Charlton's inspiration flowed free, lifting us to the Final. The cool fantasy of his play overawed his opponents as much as his two smoothly-struck goals.

As his confidence soared Charlton brought off the impossible with easy assurance. The back-heeled passes and angled flicks were all inch-perfect, the deceptive swerve and sudden acceleration left his challengers trailing. The splendours of his game had the Portuguese anxious but admiring. It was an enthralling performance, his escapes from the tightest situations as baffling as Houdini materialising through his brick wall.

The first goal after 31 minutes was fashioned from one of the few ragged moves in a game of fluent attack. Ray Wilson's pass was too far ahead of Roger Hunt pounding optimistically through the centre. But as so often the determined Hunt harassed a defender into error. Pereira darted from his goal and slid dramatically at a ball he could so safely have dived on. It cannoned away off his fluster of legs straight to Charlton, the one player who could have taken the fleeting chance with total composure. Nerveless and unhurried he stroked the ball back past the stranded Pereira, past the tangle of other players precisely into the centre of the net. It was not a shot so much as a coldly accurate 25-yard pass struck with the right instep.

His final killing thrust came in the eightieth minute, the perfect finish to a sweeping move. Brother Jack started it with a pass out to Ball on the touchline. From his short pass Moore switched the attack across to Cohen moving up on the right. It was played forward again to Hurst, who fought gamely past Hilario's tackle, then pivoted to pull the ball back from the line. The pass was rolled in front of Charlton who ran onto it without checking to hit another instant, lethal shot. Augusto sportingly congratulated him on this masterstroke that killed off his team and a Swedish newspaper suggested immediate knighthood, which all at Wembley would have welcomed.

Those goals were doubly effective, playing their part in beating Germany in the Final as well. They made the Germans fearful enough to chain back Beckenbauer to stay on Charlton's toes and while they watched him Geoff Hurst stole in for his winning hat-trick, which brought England the Cup for the first time.

The instant reactions and reflexes of the goalscorer are now called 'fast muscle'. It's a pity that expressive term was not in use in Jimmy Greaves' day. Benny Hill, no doubt, would have characterised him as the 'fastest muscle in the West', an appropriate title for the best sharp-shooter our game has known.

Greaves was the most heavily marked man of his time yet he was so quick on the draw that he could still get in his shot – and to such effect that he passed his 100 goals before he came of age at twenty-one, and scored 491 first-class goals in all.

The memory that sums up Greaves in my mind is a goal that never was. That fine Tottenham team of 1962 had reached the semi-final of the European Cup but had lost the first leg 3–1 to Benfica in Portugal. Twice more the ball had been in the Benfica net, but the goal was disallowed each time for questionable off-side decisions.

With the 'glory, glory, Hallelujah' chants resounding from the floodlit White Hart Lane three goals seemed well within Spurs compass for the second leg. But suddenly Aguas moved easily past defenders too early committed to attack, and drove home a low, precise shot beyond Brown. Now it needed a strike by Greaves to give Tottenham hope. His close marker had clearly been told to stay goalside of him *always* and wherever Greaves went he moved in front of him. I was sitting level with the Portuguese defensive line when a cross came over from the right. As the centre was struck Greaves was a yard behind. As he reached the ball and glanced it home he was four yards clear of anyone. Inevitably he was given off-side, his movement too fast for the eye of the linesman. Spurs won the match all right, with Cliff Jones thundering in one shot and Danny Blanchflower stroking home a penalty with a coolness no one in the crowd could match. But it was not enough, for Benfica still won on aggregate as that final, needed goal obstinately eluded the net. That off-side decision may well have cost Tottenham the European Cup, yet Greaves accepted it with the unruffled calm of one who had suffered this way so often before. It was not a calm I could share. Spectating strains the nerve more than playing, for the foot-baller can find relief in activity. My son had come with me to watch and as the tension mounted in those final minutes he could not bear to see it through. So we had to walk away early, hoping in vain to be pursued by that thunderous roar which would have greeted any goal.

Johnny Dixon, the inside forward who captained Aston Villa to victory in the 1957 Cup Final, used to know himself as the 'blur'. Coming off the field he would make the satisfied comment 'All they saw of me today was the blur'. It was not too apt a description of his own play, but it was the right one for Greaves. Like Matthews he would wait until the last second before going, but when he went he was just a blur for the first five yards.

As sharp-shooter Greaves had three killing qualities. Like Steve Bloomer he would shoot from the holster, catching the goalkeeper unawares with no warning given by searching eyes or leg drawn back or stride checked. Greaves's England captain, Johnny Haynes, was once asked, 'How does Jimmy keep bobbling them in?'

'He shoots a couple of seconds before I even think about it' was the definitive answer from a player who was himself a useful goalscorer.

And he had the uncanny knack of finding the net. As Billy Wright commented about him, 'How often do you see the forward with arms raised in agony as his fierce shot brushes just the wrong side of the post. You never saw Greaves like that. His shots were always inches the *right* side of the post.'

To that he added an instinctive sense of anticipation and the confidence to move late for the chance. So many forwards are too eager to seize the opening, moving so early that they have to check as the ball comes, or get picked up by the marker. Gerry Summers, who so often had to mark him, made that the lesson he tried to coach into his forwards when he was managing Oxford United. 'I was in the stand once watching Greaves when the winger got away and a great gap opened at the far post. The opening was so obvious that I thought he must see it too. But there was Greaves loitering far back apparently oblivious. "You've missed it. You've left it too late," I kept saying to myself. Then suddenly Jimmy moved smoothly and swiftly forward to meet the ball without challenge and slide it in without even having to check his stride. I knew his play well but I still could not believe he would reach that ball. That was why he was so difficult to mark. Just as you thought you had played him out of the game he would beat you to a ball you thought you had covered.'

Others might study and analyse the Greaves technique, but he himself was in blissful ignorance of his own art. Like Matthews it came out of him under pressure. From his schooldays he remained a child of instinct never consciously absorbing coaching lessons or changing his method. As he puts it, 'Goals obsess me. I like scoring them. But I don't know how I get them. I have never consciously schemed a goal. The only thought that ever records itself is when the ball crosses the line and my brain says: "It's in!" I don't know how or why I get my goals. I only know that I want them so badly that I ache for them sometimes.' That ache has Greaves still playing quietly and happily in the Southern League, still enjoying the game even in obscurity.

Greaves thrived on the ball played early and long with Danny Blanchflower and Johnny Haynes the only two with the wit and control to execute it to perfection.

'Blanchflower's play suited me because he was constantly looking for the gap for the thirty yard pass down the middle. That's the pass I liked

– the one that gives me the chance of a quick dash on goal. It's the move in which Johnny Haynes and I linked up so well.'

That explains why Greaves was at his best with Spurs and England and why the spread of the back four formation, with its two centre backs, deprived him of his favourite opening. As Blanchflower said sadly, 'It killed the creative wing-half too. How do you give a good pass to a man who has two marking him?'

Nothing could kill the Greaves instinct for goals, though the appetite was dulled in his periods with AC Milan and West Ham. At no time was it sharper than in that purple period of English football when Greaves had 11 of the 40 goals scored by England in six matches from 8 October 1960 to 10 May 1961. Northern Ireland 5–2, Luxembourg 9–0, Spain 4–2, Wales 5–1, Scotland 9–3, Mexico 8–0, the victories rolled on. And Greaves was teamed with his ideal centre-forward, the powerful Bobby Smith whose boisterous play made space for Greaves. From their Chelsea days there had been a special understanding between the two. The talents of both were at their peak in the game against Scotland when full revenge was taken for that famous drubbing by the 'blue devils' in 1928.

This was my account in the *Observer*:

The Scots were butchered to make an English holiday as Haynes's triumphant team swept decisively to the Home Championship and into the record books with this massacre of their bewildered opponents. Appropriately this was the anniversary of Culloden, perhaps the only other battle in which the Scots have been as savagely mauled. 9–3 is their biggest defeat since the first International was drawn 0–0 in 1872. It is also the highest score ever at Wembley Stadium.

The Scots, however, were not disposed to go quietly as they struggled to free themselves from England's grip at the start of the second half. But no sooner did they pull back two goals and threaten England's authority, than they were beaten into abject submission by six more scored in half-an-hour.

There was no questioning the wisdom of keeping together this England side which played so well last autumn – and looked as if they had been playing together ever since. Their understanding and anticipation was uncanny, and this was the foundation of their success, the secret of the casual ease of many of their most delightful moves.

Thirty-two goals in their last five matches indicates where

England's strength lies, but their forwards have never yet played so commandingly and so attractively. This wealth of goals was no easy offering, for Scotland pride themselves on a sound defence and, before the game, were more concerned about the ability of their forwards.

England's 4–2–4 formation, in its normal interpretation, is a defensive system yet it has been brilliantly adapted to form the springboard of attack. With Swan and Flowers blocking the centre it is Robson and Haynes who act as the transformers, changing the current of play in midfield and switching the ball instantly to the feet of the other forwards.

The killing power of the line is in their universal ability as goalscorers, and in their speed of thought and movement. All have that sense of position which carries them into the open space and they can rely on getting the ball placed perfectly into their stride at the precise moment the defence is split.

This was teamwork such as we have not seen from an England side before. The understanding was apparent as a long pass from deep in England's half reached Greaves moving unchallenged through the middle. For once he dallied too long and McNeill caught him with a saving tackle.

The respite was brief. Greaves flicked on a pass to send Smith free on the wing, and moved up to take the return. With the centre blocked Greaves pulled the ball back to Robson, striding up to the edge of the area to drive the ball low under Haffey's dive. Then Haynes, as if equipped with some private computer, calculated the pass to the exact inch to meet Greaves, stealing in between backs and goalkeeper to turn the ball into the empty net.

Scotland were passing just as neatly, but they lacked the changes of pace and direction which gave England's happy wanderers the knack of roaming to the right place at the right time. The best example of their close co-operation came as Douglas raced back to tackle Scotland's left-winger then pushed the ball forward for his own back to run the length of the field.

Armfield's low centre slipped past Haffey, but Smith, his head still singing from a clash with McNeill, failed to give the touch that would have turned it in. But Smith never lacks persistence and at once he drove in a shot which poor Haffey could not hold. Greaves, inevitably, was there to tap it home.

At the start of the second half the Scots marking was closer with Mackay and McCann not so often caught out of position in midfield.

For a time they seemed to gain the measure of England as Law, Mackay and McNeill, accepting that Scotland could not match England's skill, tried strength, their tackling ferocious, often illegal. Soon Mackay drove a free kick at the wall of defenders to see it deflected past Springett into the net. With England unsettled Wilson quickly squeezed the ball past Springett glancing in one of McLeod's centres.

Now as McLeod's dainty dribbling took him all too frequently past Middlesbrough's McNeil England were at their testing time. The response was swift and final. As Wilson tried to delay a free kick on the edge of the area Greaves suddenly flicked the ball to Douglas, darting in behind the wall to shoot gently past Haffey. The goals then came almost too swiftly to record. A pass by Greaves, a side-step and powerful shot from Smith and it was 5–2. Then Wilson sent the ball trickling through a maze of legs to roll past the unsighted Springett. Before the echo of the Scottish cheers had died Haynes had moved up to drive home two powerful shots from the edge of the area.

Immediately Greaves with insolent ease, Smith with hearty gusto, took advantage of two defensive errors to make it 9–3.

Other goals should have followed had Greaves not given the ball an affectionate pat with his hand before hooking it into the net or Charlton's certainty of shot deserted him after two swerving dribbles had taken him clear of challenge. Nothing further would have been added to the picture of England playing the football their Manager, Walter Winterbottom, must have dreamed of and has worked so patiently to perfect. No wonder Johnny Haynes, the England captain, was chaired from the field after receiving the International Trophy from the Queen.

And no wonder my Scottish colleague, the late John Rafferty, picked Greaves and Haynes as the decisive influence.

These men, Greaves and Haynes, won the game and had they been in Scottish jerseys the result could well have gone the other way.

They were a perfect blend. Greaves was ever running clear inviting the ball to be sent ahead of him. Haynes, lying deep, had the spirit to fight for the ball, the speed to work clear, the precision to lay on the chances for Greaves. The Chelsea man has the sublime forward virtue that he seldom misses. It all seems so simple and, indeed, it is if you know how – but the simplicity conceals the intelligence and accuracy with which the pair works.

With Haynes, with Blanchflower, with anyone, Greaves was simply unique as a goal scorer. His record is his proof.

Greaves is slight to look at, but very strong from the waist down, a characteristic shared with Gerd Muller, Hughie Gallacher and many of the little men who steal the goals. The power there gave him the sudden quick movement which so disconcerted those who thought they had the ball screened from him.

The unusual quality in Greaves's scoring was that he was always well balanced. Some small men get their goals from the oddest of positions, the weirdest of contortions. With Greaves it was the opponents who twisted themselves at awkward angles while he stayed sure-footed. His presence in the area set up shock waves of apprehension, making the defenders stretch for balls that were beyond them. If they missed, Greaves was lurking perfectly positioned and perfectly poised. That was why his goals always looked so simple.

In the first-class game he scored 491 times, 357 of the goals coming in First Division games. Greaves once commented, 'I never knew if my supporters prefer to remember how I played for Chelsea or for Tottenham – or to forget how I played for West Ham.' He had 124 goals for Chelsea, 220 for Spurs and an unlucky 13 for West Ham.

As unlucky and more unhappy was his brief period with Milan. The over-dictatorial, over-defensive Italian League was not for him. They could buy his skills and his 9 goals in ten games, but not his mind. That independence of thought and action was better harnessed for England by Winterbottom than by the organisational expert, Alf Ramsey. Although Greaves stands only 5 ft. 8 ins., and weighed only 10½ stone at his fittest, his 44 goals in 57 matches make him the giant among England's goalscorers.

Ten

Scottish Selection

Hugh McIlvanney made this selection of the best of Scottish finishers.

In the folklore of Scottish football extraordinary goals totals tend to be associated with goalkeepers rather than forwards. The 7 yielded to England at Wembley by Fred Martin in 1955 and the 9 that went past Frank Haffey in the equivalent international half a dozen years later are the fabric of black legend. If you ask a middle-aged Scotland supporter to name the finisher who has made most impact on him he is more than likely to say Jimmy Greaves. There is indeed only one Scottish forward of the last thirty years capable of pushing from our minds the jostling images of all the damage inflicted on us by the beautiful deadliness of that great talent. The one-man antidote is, of course, Denis Law, and his achievement in emerging as one of the supreme goalscorers in the history of the game is all the more remarkable because to do so he had to violate his native tradition.

Law came to us a fully fledged hawk from a country more noted for its bantams and its peacocks. As bred north of the Solway, bantams and peacocks are, it should be emphasised, killer species. The first can tear the heart out of opponents, as such as Billy Bremner and Dave Mackay have so often done, and the second, as represented in their different ways by Jim Baxter and Jimmy Johnstone, can lure and dazzle their victims into vertiginous collapse. These men were the heirs to the traditional glories of Scottish football: cunning, imagination, spirit and superb skills in midfield; bravura, spontaneity, an affinity with the ball and an incorrigible impertinence in attack. It is a philosophy of the game that is rooted in the fact that the Scots, far from justifying the world's view of them as dour pragmatists, are an inveterately, self-destructively romantic nation. The language of their football can never be disciplined or punctuated by anything as practical as goals.

Alan Sharp, a novelist and screenwriter whose past in Greenock remains more basic to him than his present in Hollywood, has made a lifelong and agonised study of that language (agonised because he acknowledges that Scottish football has always been an intrusive metaphor for the psychological limitations of himself and many of our race) and it was he who best answered those who criticised Scotland in 1967 for resting on a one-goal lead over an England side handicapped by injuries. 'When the English are on top their natural expression of it is to hammer in goals,' said Sharp. 'We'd love to score plenty, too, of course, but our instinctive way of showing we are in complete control is to go along the wing bouncing the ball on the instep, making an ass of anybody who comes in to tackle.' That was hyperbole but it made the point, and Alan Sharp has elaborated convincingly in a recent essay. 'I suppose if a poll were to be conducted among those I consider my general contemporaries as to who was the greatest Scottish player they ever saw, the outcome would be Jim Baxter. Maybe the question would have to be framed to dissuade some of them from being rational or objective, to exclude comparable talents like Charlie Cooke, or superior commitments like Bremner, or more utter instinctiveness like Wee Johnstone. But if it were put right the answer would be Baxter. Now if one considers Baxter's game, and if folklore is your thing, then it will be clear that Scotsmen value things in this world far above success, or integrity or intelligence. They value most what Baxter had, they value the completely held conviction of their own superiority. Baxter's game was the consummation of that fallacy. There was in him, consciously, sub-consciously and unconsciously, the belief in his singular genius.'

It is here that Denis Law may be regarded, after all, as a representative rather than a violator of the tradition. He was a paradox, a player whose style of goal-scoring was a unique blend of economy and theatricality. If, to borrow an analogy from the *corrida*, Baxter was a supreme artist with the cape, Law was a corresponding master with the sword.

He killed with an individual, unmistakable flourish that never failed to send a tremor through the blood. He, too, had a compelling sense of his singularity, a conviction of his own irrepressibility that seemed to radiate from his lean, electric presence. In him Scottish football, for once, resolved its central dilemma, satisfying the national hunger for panache while at the same time meeting the practical demands of the game. The Scots would obviously welcome anyone who was a great scorer of goals but they could exult only over someone who was also a scorer of great goals, as Law consistently was. 'There are quite a few tremendous finishers in this game,' Jimmy Murphy, then the assistant manager of Manchester United, said to me several years ago. 'Who could ask for a deadlier man in the box than Jimmy Greaves or a more aggressive, effective striker than Geoff Hurst? But if I had to send out one fella to score a goal to save my life, there's only one man I'd consider. It would have to be that Denis. You would feel that if he didn't do it, it was impossible in the first place. When did you ever see a man who was so hard to keep out, whose talent was so hard to subdue and whose spirit was so hard to break? You would have a chance every second he was on the park. There might be half-a-dozen boots swinging at the ball and that blond head would appear in the middle of them and knock in a goal. Or he would do one of those climbs, as if he was being jerked above the defence on a wire, and the ball would be smashed down into the net before the goalkeeper knew what was happening. Or he would explode into an opening that nobody else had seen, making all the others look as if they were nailed down, there would be a little side-footer and he would be back in the middle waiting for the ball to be centred by the time they realised what he had done to them. The defence hasn't been invented that could cope with this fella. He's tortured them wherever he's played, from the moment he came down from Aberdeen to Huddersfield as a skinny boy with glasses. He did it with Huddersfield, with Manchester City, with Torino – where all the heavy treatment from the Italian defenders couldn't keep him down – he's done it in internationals and he's done it so unbelievably with United that he's a god to the Old Trafford crowd and will always be a god to them long after he's stopped kicking the ball for us.'

That last prophecy was readily vindicated when Law came out of retirement to play in a testimonial match for Pat Crerand at Old Trafford. Crerand is a close and valued friend but Law was reluctant to turn out because he had always promised himself that once the years began to erode his extraordinary athleticism, once he was no longer able to meet his own fierce standards of performance, he would put away his boots and never go near them again. He appreciates that many old players gain and give considerable pleasure by creaking around in charity matches or in the odd casual Sunday game but that is not his way. 'Anything that lad does,' says Sir Matt Busby, 'he wants to do right. Half-measures appal him.' In the end it was Busby's intervention (a gentle leverage based on the respect and – let's not sidestep the word – love that so many of those who played under him retain for the boss of bosses) that persuaded Law to come out of the tunnel that night with

Best and Charlton and Stiles and Herd and the other heroes of an earlier time. Before he agreed to do so, however, he trained for weeks, running the darkened streets of a Manchester suburb in the taxing company of one of his four sons. There is something quietly moving about the thought of Law, who is secure in anybody's pantheon of the game, undergoing such pain in such a cause. 'It was six or eight weeks of purgatory but it had to be done,' he says, and the narrow, intelligent and usually mischievous face turns serious at the memory. 'People say you shouldn't bother about testimonials, they're just for a lark. Well, the game has never been that way for me. I've never been willing to risk making a complete fool of myself.'

There was no danger of that when he took the field to do his old friend and admired ally some service. He entered the arena as he always did, swivelling his head to take in the whole stadium, hunching his shoulders and pulling his sleeves down over his hands as he trotted towards the action. Despite the presence of those other magnificent footballers, it was to that slim figure that our eyes moved in expectation of something unforgettable. Best and Charlton always had more refined technique, a more dazzling virtuosity, and who dare say they ever lacked an aura of the dramatic. Yet it was Law's name the crowd chanted, to him their blood warmed. They knew what they were doing. He embodied the dream of the heroic in all of them. The words of Lady Jean Busby came to mind. 'Many, many marvellous players have worn the Manchester United shirt but there can only ever be one Denis.'

That night he scored a goal and just failed to take one that would have belonged with his finest. As usual, the cheers for his achievements were acknowledged with the gestures of an emperor, one who had, for an hour-and-a-half at least, re-inherited his empire. His behaviour in such moments has surprised and embarrassed him when he has seen it subsequently on a television screen. 'It's like looking at a stranger and I can hardly bear to watch. It seems such an extravagant way to go on. And yet when I'm out there it's the most natural thing in the world. The adrenalin is flowing and I suppose I'm kind of high on it. I've always been two different people on the park and off it.'

Anyone acquainted with Law's ways will accept the substance of that last sentence. Off the field, Law remains a forceful personality but his intensity is generally expressed without flamboyance. He can, if the company suits him, be exuberantly light-hearted, a mickey-taker of endless ingenuity and persistence. Equally, he can be damagingly forthright in argument. He is no shrinking flower. But in the main his private persona is very private indeed. There are times when he seems to crave remoteness, even from the family to whom he is devoted. Certainly, he has never sought any truck with the usual garish haunts of successful footballers, preferring a quiet beer with the one or two players he found most congenial or, as likely as not, with friends from outside the game. At his golf club he would be discovered drinking tea in the boiler-room with the assistants (drinking tea is an addiction with him and when Pat Crerand was a neighbour in Manchester he felt inclined to alert the Guinness Book of Records when Denis came to call, which meant on most days of the week). Though now a regular attender at both Old Trafford and Maine Road, he was never a keen watcher of football in his playing days, nor an eager debater of its theories. A conversation with him on a plane on the way to an important match might well be devoid of football – apart from a few scathingly simple judgements – and had every chance of developing into a general knowledge quiz. His appetite for esoteric bits of information almost equals his thirst for tea.

There was never anything esoteric or even complicated about his approach as a performer. He applied his vast natural gifts (the elasticity that enabled him to leap like Nijinsky and explode like an Olympic sprinter, the unbreakable nerve and the spontaneous comprehension of opportunities) to exploit the basic geometry of the game. On the way to goal he favoured the swift one-two exchange of passes that leaves defenders stranded within the triangles created by sharp attackers. 'Puskas was a master of the method,' he says, 'and it didn't let him down too often.'

Law was never one of the purer strikers of the ball and he scored few goals from long range, but once close to the target he was direct as gunshot, though infinitely more graceful. His uncanny swiftness was probably to be seen at its deadliest when a goalkeeper made a fumble, a situation that occurred with profitable frequency when David Herd was blasting away alongside him for Manchester United. 'Herdie hit the ball so hard that the goalkeepers often failed to take it cleanly,' he recalls happily. 'When that happens, if your reactions are quick enough, you should get to it before he recovers. He will be upset by the shock of the shot and his own mistake and the forward should be favourite.' Law's voice assumes an almost schoolmasterish tone as he adds: 'A goalkeeper who drops the ball has really got to be punished. If he is not, somebody is botching the job.' Anyone who suspects that this pronouncement is unjustified should think back some years to a marathon series of Cup ties between United and Sunderland, to one moment in the second replay when Herd drove the ball in from the right and Montgomery, in the Sunderland goal, fumbled briefly at the near post. Law was on the edge of the box but before Montgomery could rectify his small error the executioner was in and the ball was buried. It is because of memories such as that, and what they imply, that this chapter has been largely a tribute to the player this writer at least believes was the greatest finisher Scottish football has produced. The status is all the more natural because Law took so much pride in scoring for Scotland and the goal he finds perhaps his most memorable was a header at Hampden Park, against England of course. 'You seem to rise a foot higher when you are wearing that jersey,' he says. It scarcely needs to be said that there has always been deep in his nature something even more fundamental than patriotism that made him jump higher and strike quicker than the next man. Law recognises that it showed in the days of his adolescence when he wore glasses to correct a squint. 'Cock-eyed was the word they used where I was brought up. When I took the glasses off the eye went right into the corner and you can imagine what I had to take on account of that. Kids can be very cruel. From a very early age I went out to show that I wasn't going to be trampled on.'

Sometimes he may have appeared to trample rather harshly on other players but a man whose whole mode of operation leaves him so vulnerable to serious physical injury and whose effectiveness depended so much on being 101% fit was bound to have an aggressively protective attitude about his limbs. Law admits that his concern about taking the field absolutely sound was so extreme that it might have given the impression occasionally of incipient hypochondria. 'Naturally, I played often enough when there was something wrong, maybe a bad ankle, but I never felt good, was never able to shake off the sense that I was a lot less than I should have been.' It followed that when he was sound he did not take kindly to people who were intent on changing that. He is not at all a vicious character but on the park he had that quality beloved of the boxing cognoscenti in the East End of London, he could be 'nice and spiteful'.

Denis Law could, to put it straight, be everything that a scoring forward should be. It would be a ludicrous injustice to fail to acknowledge the brilliant others that Scotland has produced. The list would have to begin far back beyond the inspired and inspirational contributions of those great centre-forwards, Hughie Gallacher and Jimmy McGrory, and of Alex Jackson, who took 3 of the 5 goals claimed by the Wembley Wizards in 1928. In more recent eras it would have to include Jimmy Delaney for verve and fearlessness and destructively intelligent positioning, Tommy Walker for his cool elegance, Jack Dodds for his purposeful rumbustiousness, and Bobby Johnstone and Lawrie Reilly as representatives of a Hibernian forward-line that surely had no superior in the entire lifespan of British football. Smith, Johnstone, Reilly, Turnbull and Ormond (yes, the same round and friendly little man who became Manager of Scotland) made a devastating combination and even in that company the terrible precision of Johnstone and the harrying, tireless combativeness of Reilly made them outstanding.

Later still we had Graham Leggatt, another classic opportunist with an instinct for space, Alex Young with his delicacy of touch and exceptional calm when clean through, Alan Gilzean, also a touch player, and Joe McBride, who will be an obscure name to many but did some prodigious scoring for Jock Stein's Celtic until injury cut him down. Today there is Kenny Dalglish, a player without exceptional pace or power, but with an inborn instinct for making and taking goals which Liverpool valued at almost half a million pounds; and there is Andy Gray, a genuine phenomenon for Aston Villa and Scotland, but it is probable that neither he nor any of those who have gone before him will resent having Denis Law to carry their banner.

Jimmy Murphy was right. If you wanted a man to score a goal to save your life you would send for Denis. Even if he did not save your life, he would sure as hell brighten your last moments!

Eleven

The Best of the Irish

'He's almost as good as Billy Gillespie' used to be the highest tribute to an Irish forward. The Sheffield United inside-forward was as constructive a schemer as Alex James, yet so sharp a shooter that he became Ireland's leading scorer as well. Not even Joe Bambrick, who scored 6 goals in one International against Wales in 1930, could better Gillespie's 13 goals in his twenty-five appearances.

Gillespie was the Kojak of his day, a balding, dynamic boss of a player whose team called him the 'General'. He was the master-mind of Sheffield United's fourth F.A. Cup victory when Tunstall's solitary goal was enough to beat Cardiff in 1925. And it was Gillespie's subtle prompting which helped centre-forward Harry Johnson to many of his 309 League goals.

Gillespie was renowned for his long diagonal passes to the wings which sent them flying away for Johnson to turn home their centres. His was an early version of the tactics which brought Wolves such success in the Fifties and Gillespie used it to equal effect for Ireland.

Billy Gillespie played his first International in Belfast on 15 February 1913 and a memorable debut it was. He scored both goals in the first-ever Irish win over England. That 2–1 victory was the start of an international career which ended less happily seventeen years later. In his last game in 1930 it was England who won 5–1 though his Sheffield partner, the fair-haired young Goliath, Jimmy Dunne, scored the consolation goal.

Dunne had 4 goals in his seven Internationals for Northern Ireland, 14 in fifteen matches for the Republic of Ireland. No other Irishman has matched this forceful centre-forward's consistency, except Bambrick with his 11 goals in eleven matches.

But it was another inside-forward, Peter Doherty, who was to become the darling of the public despite a career shortened by the war. As vivacious as his red hair promised Doherty was an inspirational force on the field. He swept Manchester City to a League championship, then in the first post-war Cup Final brought Derby County their first win.

His combination with the other inside, the silver-haired, silver-tongued Raich Carter, whose style was as silky smooth as his voice, was a memorable pairing making the goals for a typically forceful centre-forward, Jackie Stamps.

In all Peter Doherty scored 197 League goals. One perfectly expressed the courage and dynamism of the man who never admitted defeat. The match was an International.

At Goodison Park, Liverpool, on Guy Fawkes Day 1947 there were fireworks indeed at the end of England's match with Northern Ireland. The English forward line, which had just taken 10 goals off the Portuguese, had been so well held that the score was 1–1 with only a minute remaining. Then Matthews darted away past Farrell, past Johnny Carey, and slid the centre into Lawton's path. The shot seared past Ted Hinton, the goalkeeper Fulham had recently acquired for nothing. That should have settled it.

Hardly had Ireland kicked off than Eglington slipped past right-back Laurie Scott and drove across a despairing centre. It looked far from Doherty's reach but he raced in, hurling himself at it, twisting and diving to get his head to the ball. That last touch of the game gave Ireland the equaliser, while Doherty crashed on his back to lie dazed and barely conscious. Frank Swift and the Irish trainer had to help him from the field.

Doherty had to chase every chance even when Manchester City were already assured of the championship in 1937. His compulsive bravery had him running headlong for just such an equalising goal against Birmingham City, his collision with Harry Hibbs sending the goalkeeper to hospital. It was typical of his competitive nature that he should admit afterwards that he had fisted the ball in and was surprised the goal was allowed.

Impetuous in challenging for the ball in play he was slow and deliberate in taking penalty kicks. He favoured placing the ball rather than blasting it, but his main preoccupation was to ensure that the goalkeeper was too nervous and unsettled to guess the direction of the kick. So he would fiddle with his stocking tie-ups, keep replacing the ball on the spot and continue distracting the goalkeeper until he began to move apprehensively on his line. As soon as he moved enough to expose one side of the goal Doherty slotted the ball there with instant accuracy. No wonder he missed so few, and scored so many!

Doherty, particularly anxious to do well in his first game for Manchester City, was unfortunate enough to find himself up against Bill Shankly, an old hand at putting down bright young opponents. The marking was tight, but it was the talking that also put Doherty off his game. Wherever he went the gravelly voice muttered in his ear, 'The North End's a grand wee team, a grand wee team. Ye've no chance.' Psychological warfare came easily to Shankly, who has always found people take seriously his tongue in cheek comments. Doherty certainly was serious and totally committed.

Blanchflower, one of the most astute and inventive players of our age, was fascinated by Doherty, one brave spirit responding to another. 'Doherty had a tremendous competitive spirit, so bold it dismissed outrageous odds against it. When he trained us for the World Cup in 1958 I marvelled at his example. I could run for ever, but even though he was nearly forty Doherty would pass me three times on the way. But mainly we reacted to his sheer enjoyment of the game.

'Doherty showed us how quickly the outlook could alter once a team became united in its desire to improve things. Anybody can become better once they set their minds and energies to that end.'

These two did, indeed, work miracles, giving Irish football some of its finest hours. So thin were the reserves of talent that there was no possibility of naming the full first list of 40 possible World Cup players and only 17, not the permitted 22, were considered good enough to go to Sweden. Yet with magician as Manager and conjuror as Captain, Ireland kept pulling the victories out of the hat. Theirs was no fist-shaking defiance, they simply laughed away the odds.

In November 1957 Doherty's side won 3–2 at Wembley – the first time the Irish had beaten England in thirty years. With Blanchflower prompting his forwards there was a goal for each of the insiders, Simpson, McIlroy and Sammy McCrory, that prolific scorer of goals in the Third Division who was playing in his first International at thirty-three. There was something of the luck of the Irish in the result as post, bar and leprechauns frustrated the English forwards despite their wealth of chances. But this was a team to ride its luck and there was nothing fortunate about the remarkable saves by Harry Gregg.

Then it was the formidable Italians who were defeated in the decisive World Cup qualifying match, the first time Italy had ever failed to reach the Finals. The game should have been played on 4 December, but the referee, the Hungarian, Istvan Zsolt, was stranded by fog at London Airport. With the ground packed with excited spectators it was agreed to play a 'friendly' when the Italians rightly refused to accept the only available referee – an Irishman. What recriminations there would have been had Ireland won through with their own countryman in charge! Tommy Mitchell of Lurgan had a difficult enough time as it was trying to control this most unfriendly of friendlies.

Twice Northern Ireland came from behind with Wilbur Cush, the little 5 ft. 5 in. utility player, snatching the two equalising goals as makeshift inside in place of McCrory.

The Italian team of all the talents was also one of all the temperaments with the South American stars like Schiaffino and Ghiggia making an uneasy blend. Mitchell was understandably hesitant to take firm action as tempers flared in the final minutes and the game became a brawl with bodies scattered across the pitch and the crowd, hostile from the start, baying for vengeance for the brutal assaults on their own players. Blanchflower could control his own team, but no one could calm the Italians, who were fortunate to leave the field without disaster.

Drained of passion on their return the Italians were also drained of fight, letting the game slip quietly away after Cush and Jimmy McIlroy's 2-goal lead had been whittled away through Uprichard's nervy error in goal.

The Irish had not taken their football or themselves too seriously, but for others it was a mistake not to do so. Czechoslovakia were beaten by Cush's goal in the opening match, then Germany, the Cup holders, found themselves held to a draw. And how nearly were they beaten as Gregg foiled Seeler's every effort after Peter McParland had given them a 2–1 lead. Just as the outstanding goalkeeper seemed to have tamed the world-class marksman Seeler beat him at last with a searing shot from 25 yards.

Peter McParland, scoring 5 goals of Ireland's 6 goals in the competition, established himself as a forward to rank with the best that have worn the emerald green shirt with pride. The Aston Villa left-winger was in the Billy Liddell mould, strong running and aggressive. Switching from left wing to centre-forward he confused all three defences, scoring a goal against Argentina, 2 against Germany and the 2 which won the play-off against Czechoslovakia. The season before he had deprived Manchester United of the double in a Cup Final they were expected to take in their easy stride. It was McParland who went striding in early to collide with goalkeeper Wood, cracking his cheekbone. And it was McParland who added insult to injury by slamming the 2 decisive goals past Jackie Blanchflower, who had to take over Wood's sweater.

For the Finals in Sweden I was teamed with Danny Blanchflower, the two of us covering the matches for the *Observer*. That was typical of the independent-minded Blanchflower, who was later to startle Eamonn Andrews by walking out on 'This is Your Life', instantly dismissing its tawdry emotionalism. The 'populars' no doubt would have paid him far more, but in those days of 'ghosted' articles Blanchflower wanted to write first for a paper which would establish beyond doubt that his words were his own. Not that there was ever much doubt of that from so articulate and imaginative a person.

When asked what ingenious tactics had brought the unfancied Northern Ireland team to the quarter-final Blanchflower's answer was unmistakably his own. 'It's a new system. We equalise before the other side has scored.'

In the *Observer* his description of the feelings of a World Cup player came as unmistakably from that original mind.

In the highly intense world of professional football the sun rises and sets with alarming suddenness. The world turns over every twenty-four hours, but not with the smooth astronomical rhythm that compels our planet. It just gives a quick impulsive spin, and the character who has been basking in the summit sunshine unexpectedly finds himself clinging desperately to the South Pole with cold, bare fingers.

The difference of performance between winning and losing a game is often a razor's edge, but the difference of feelings that accompany victory and defeat are always poles apart. Playing in the World Cup competition one is more aware of those feelings. At this level a football match is no mere sporting occasion. The player carries on the field responsibilities that would weaken the knees of a Cabinet Minister. He is there to represent his country and he knows that nothing short of victory will satisfy all those who share his nationality.

It is some consolation to realise that players of other countries fight the same fates and share the same feelings. I shall not forget the evidence of quiet despair as the Czechoslovakians retreated from the ground after we had defeated them last Saturday. And I will always remember the extreme exhilaration of the Argentinians as they defeated us last Wednesday. Yet in their moment of triumph I believe they felt kindly towards us.

In some quiet way I was pleasantly surprised to read that the Russian goalkeeper had chased the referee after he had awarded a penalty to England last Sunday. It was a little reassuring to think that even the much drilled and disciplined Russians could not entirely control their despair.

All the teams that had had to play-off for a place lost their quarterfinal matches, which followed on too quickly for them to recover. Northern Ireland were especially hard hit by injury, with Gregg having to keep goal when he could barely limp. France, with that deadly duo of strikers, Kopa and Fontaine, eliminated them with 4 crushing goals. But they had had their fun on the way and humbled some of the world's leading football nations.

That 1958 team was one of the great Irish sides and, apart from Peter McParland, there were two outstanding forwards in Bingham and McIlroy.

Jimmy McIlroy was the prompter of others' goals, a player of subtle perception, seeing an opening as easily as he beat a man. The inside then was still regarded as the workhorse, but McIlroy had a flair for attack and all his energies went into the creation of goals. He had also a little-used asset – the ability to change pace and move at searing speed without seeming to do so. That is the quality that marks out the best of the moderns, like Cruyff, yet McIlroy rarely exploited a skill that might have made him a prolific goalscorer. For he was the expert at winning space. He says, 'It's surprising how easy that is if only you check and look when you get the ball instead of instantly moving in towards defenders as so many forwards do. . . .'

McIlroy had every skill except the knack of easy scoring: 'I could do anything in midfield, but I tensed up in front of goal. How I envied Jimmy Greaves with his happy confidence. He didn't worry if he missed because he *knew* he would score next time. For me a goal was a sigh of relief, the many missed chances an agony of remorse.'

Billy Bingham, became as vital a part of the Irish team as Danny Blanchflower, each of them winning 56 caps. With Danny it was difficult to predict how he would play for he was always willing to experiment, to take chances, to be tripped up by the ordinary, while searching for the unusual. Bingham was the opposite, a consistent winger without peaks or troughs of performance, always good, never brilliant. He was fast and elusive, like most small wingers, but sharp of wit and shot.

The workman of the line was Wilbur Cush, whose title 'the Mighty Oak' referred to the size and strength of his heart, not his stature. A pygmy in build, a giant in endeavour, he was the tireless, willing player of all positions that every good side needs.

Johnny Crossan was to prove a more effective goalscorer than McIlroy and almost as constructive. Crossan had 10 goals in his 23 Internationals. This small, tricky inside-forward was always on the move on and off the field. He was with Sparta of Rotterdam when he played his first game for Ireland, scoring one of the goals which beat Poland 2–0 in 1962. When with Sunderland he made a major contribution to the 3–0 defeat of Uruguay and a 4–1 win over Albania, scoring twice in the first match and getting a hat-trick in the other.

He was a Manchester City player when he scored a crucial goal in the 2–1 defeat of the Netherlands in 1965. And it was as a Middlesbrough man that he played in his final match some two years later, helping to beat Scotland in Belfast. It was not surprising he was so much in demand by League clubs for he scored 232 goals.

Derek Dougan was unfortunate not to be part of that team at its best. He was in the World Cup party, but never played in Sweden. No doubt, like many a self-confident performer, he attributed his omission to a remarkable lack of judgement by the Manager and rated Doherty accordingly. Certainly he never responded to him and the Irish side looked on Dougan as 'Geronimo', the young brave who had to be independent and go his own way.

A striker needs to be lifted and given opportunity by a strong team around him. Dougan made muted impact at international level, since there was no such supporting ability and only as he matured did he fit in with the limited talent Ireland then possessed. Too often he and Best had to be a forward line in themselves. Yet Dougan had qualities enough to have made him an outstanding striker. His height gave him advantage in the air and he was also master of those flicks with the head which make openings for others. On the ground he worked the ball with clever control and had the stride which could leave challengers trailing.

Most of the long striders and slow turners are easy to shepherd since they have to commit themselves to moving one way and find it difficult to alter course suddenly. Dougan was an exception. His toes pointed in as if bent by years of flicking passes with the outside of the foot. And this seemed to give him the ability to make these startling swift changes of direction, which throw the defender.

When Joe Mercer was managing Aston Villa he had spent long hours developing Gerry Hitchens into a goalscoring forward to catch the eye, instead of one with 'a left leg you could use for firewood'. Knowing how Mercer prized Hitchens, his Chairman rang him apprehensively to ask his view of a surprise offer by Inter-Milan Directors of £85,000 for Hitchens. What should he do? 'Lock the door and keep them there till they sign,' said Joe. 'I can buy you an even better forward for £15,000.' And that indeed was what it cost him to get Derek Dougan.

Dougan went out of his way to be unconventional in dress and sometimes in performance. When with Blackburn Rovers he asked for a transfer on the eve of the Cup Final with Wolves – and might already have been given one for all the impact he made on that match in 1960.

But footballers generally have reason to thank Dougan's independence of mind when Chairman of the Professional Footballers' Association. Even as player/manager of Kettering he continued to take on authority and opposing teams with equal relish. Reprimanded by the F.A. for advertising Kettering tyres on his kit he counter-attacked by pointing to the advertising on England team track suits. There is too much character in Irish football and Irish footballers for there to be many dull moments when they are involved with the game.

In the World Cup qualifier of 1976 Blanchflower was to bring back to Ireland in his first match as Manager of the National Team the same spirit he himself had shown in Sweden eighteen years earlier. The task was the daunting one of taking on Holland, Cruyff and all, in Amsterdam. This time he was the catalyst in the final transformation of another unique Irishman, the most gifted and wayward of them all, George Best. Best had been written off as great player run to the bad, the prodigal son who had recklessly squandered his inheritance. Fulham's Alec Stock and Danny Blanchflower perceived that Best had at last come to terms with the fact that football was the 'one talent which is death to hide'. This was how Hugh McIlvanney saw Best touch greatness again as Ireland drew 2–2:

> The result may have been first-cousin to a miracle but the football played by Northern Ireland in Rotterdam last week had the wholesome smell of naturalness about it, a freshness to revive senses dulled for so long by the odours of the embalming chamber. While the English game, as represented by Don Revie's national team, seems to be in a mummified state, bandaged into its own preoccupations and decaying assumptions, the Irish under Danny Blanchflower go out to meet the world with a strong pulse and the glow of a sensible optimism on their cheeks.
>
> Blanchflower's obvious advantage is that as the £2,000-a-year

part-time manager of a country that is considered peripheral in international football he is not burdened with the dread of failure, the compulsion to take out insurance, that afflicts those who have more extravagant resources. 'If we can't be a bit adventurous, who can?' he asked across the breakfast table at a Rotterdam airport motel on Thursday. If the football world thought of them as nobodies, he suggested, then at least they could be interesting nobodies, brave and aggressive nobodies, nobodies with enough wit and enough heart to behave like somebodies.

That principle had been brought marvellously alive at the Feyenoord Stadium the previous evening. It is true, of course, that the Dutch were unlikely to categorise any side containing George Best and Pat Jennings as nonentities. Yet it is equally certain that Cruyff, Neeskens, Haan, Krol, Rensenbrink and all the other stars whose names read less like a team to be opposed than a firing squad to be faced, could never have expected the flood of quality that all but submerged them in the first half.

Best's contribution was magnificent and crucial. To anyone who had seen him a year ago his very appearance was a marvel. Then the thickening of legs and torso appeared to be chronic but now he is trimmed down to within a pound or two of 11 stone. In the supreme days of his youth 10 st. 10 lb. was his deadliest weight and even without the years of dissipation and neglect he would surely have added three or four pounds at his present age of 30.

The slimness has restored to him much of his old flexibility, that elasticity of body movement which, when allied to his freakish sense of balance and the incredible precision of touch in both feet, allows him to slide past defenders as readily as if he were a snake and they were rooted trees. He did plenty of that on Wednesday, particularly in the first 20 minutes or so, a period in which his confident declaration of his talents established the mood of the match.

Everything he did in that spell, the sinuous, cumulatively accelerating runs, the firmly struck passes and violent shooting, had a quality of deliberate statement. 'Did someone mention world-class players?' he was saying, in effect, to Cruyff and the others. 'Well, how's this for starters?'

Naturally, not all of the old brilliance was there. Those murderous explosions of pace that once ensured that a beaten defender was left without hope of recovery are still missing and probably always will be in the seasons that are left to him.

One of the warmest tributes to him came inevitably from another hero of the occasion, Pat Jennings, his regular room mate on Irish trips and a great goalkeeper whose deepest admiration is reserved for two goal-scorers, Jimmy Greaves and Best. Jennings himself made extraordinary saves and without his excellence Northern Ireland would not have stayed in a situation where young Derek Spence's late goal earned an unbelievable draw. McIlroy, a forward of class as well as vigour, also did splendidly.

But the platform from which the Irish launched themselves, however briefly, into orbit was the genius of Best.

The merit of that performance was underlined when Holland toyed so contemptuously with the England team at Wembley a few months later. For Ireland Best responded to Blanchflower's enthusiasm as his Manager had once responded to Peter Doherty.

Twelve

Welsh Winners

The spirit of Welsh football is legendary, the dragon spitting fire at its challengers, consuming them in the intense heat of enthusiasm. Yet the outstanding footballer and most formidable goalscorer to represent Wales was one of the calmest players. John Charles, the 'gentle giant' with the figure of a Goliath, the demeanour of a Galahad, earned his reputation as the chivalrous knight of the game.

As centre-forward he scored 15 times for Wales and as centre-half he saved perhaps twice that number of goals. Charles towered over Welsh football and over the English League. In his days with Juventus the Italians christened him 'King Charles' and gave him the freedom of their country. Even there he never used his strength in anger at the petty obstructions and passionate outbursts in the Italian game, of which it was said 'when they tackle, they tackle to kill'.

Like some renowned gun-fighter Charles was the natural target for lesser lights aiming to make their name. The supreme accolade of greatness was paid him in the World Cup of 1958 when he became the prime target of the professional tacticians. 'Stop Charles' was the order of the day, with the end justifying the means in opponents' eyes. So the Lilliputians hacked Gulliver down as later they were to swarm over Pelé or Eusebio. Greatness brings its own perils on the football field, but Charles was never provoked to retaliate on his tormentors.

My memory of him centres on just such a day of battery and of his triumph over petty men and petty tactics. It was in Sweden in 1958 as Wales played off against Hungary for a place in the quarter-final of the World Cup. Three draws had won Wales that right.

In the first game against Hungary, in the small Sandvicken Stadium close to the Arctic Circle, Charles had inspired the Welsh fight-back and scored the goal that matched Bozsik's. Since he had achieved that despite vicious tackling and elbowing, in the play-off the Hungarians marked him for destruction.

Whenever there was a corner one player pinioned his arms while another smashed into him from behind. He would not retaliate and he had no protection from the Russian referee, who mystified us afterwards by saying he had been playing the advantage rule. He was careful not to answer the question – whose advantage?

Wales were soon a goal down as Budai sped away and Tichy hit home the centre. Before half-time Charles was hit and kicked in the back once too often for him to survive and he hobbled painfully away. Soon he came limping back and still contrived to float over a threatening centre. Allchurch raced in on it, swung his left leg and smashed the volley past goalkeeper Grosics. With Bowen driving them on, an inspired captain drawing an inspiring response, there was now a fine dispassionate fury as the Welsh outplayed the Hungarians in skill and spirit.

The crippled Charles stayed on as talisman and the Welsh became a team of Charleses playing with impeccable sportsmanship and deadly determination. While John Charles focused the attention and drained the resources of the desperate Hungarians, the other red shirts surged through to victory. Sixteen minutes from the end Medwin slipped away on his own, sped past Saroso and flicked the shot home. This was Wales' hour of glory and if it was short-lived they won even more respect on their day of defeat.

Without the crippled Charles in the quarter-final they held the brilliant Brazilians to a single goal, scored by a little-known 17-year-old – Pelé. His winning shot was covered by Kelsey only to be diverted by Sherwood's heel. That was the best performance of Welsh football, the best by any British team in the World Cup until England won it. If only John Charles had been fit might the established master have gone one better than the young prodigy? Might Wales have beaten two of the great teams of Europe and South America in successive matches? Charles certainly was the one man who might have made the miracle happen.

Many sides had reason to fear his strength, but none the abuse of it. Unusually light on his feet for a big man, there was no stopping him as he soared to meet a centre with the challengers bounced aside by that barrel chest. Some of his most entertaining duels in the air were against England as Billy Wright tried to match his spring, the whippet straining against the bulldog.

Once only was Charles goaded to fury. In an International against Austria in 1955, which became a by-word for roughness, his brother Mel was carried off on a stretcher after an outrageous tackle. John had been as aloof as always from the vicious in-fighting, although already injured himself. Now he took his share of a battle that left the dressing rooms looking like casualty stations. Even in anger he was unselfish, stirred to violence only to avenge Mel.

Those two have a claim to be the best pair of footballing brothers, for Melvyn was a fainter carbon copy of John. And it is Mel who holds the individual goalscoring record for Wales with 4 in a match against Ireland in April 1962. Cardiff had recently bought Mel from Arsenal, where cartilage trouble had prevented him being the formidable centre-half Highbury had needed. Cardiff, however, wanted him to score goals to save them from relegation, but for once Mel could not get the ball in the net. In the middle of his lean spell came his 4 for Wales, all the goals of a 4–0 win.

Yet the two are not quite a match for the Charlton brothers. Jack was a far more effective centre-half than Mel, and although not so versatile, he had six goals for England as well. That was one more than Mel achieved for Wales despite the four in a day. John and Bobby were both unique and who can fairly compare their contrasting talents?

John was yet another of Major Frank Buckley's 'discoveries'. As a youngster of twelve he had been in the Swansea schoolboys side which reached the quarter-final of the English Schools Trophy. At fourteen he joined Swansea Town, not yet big of body or reputation, but described as a 'slip of a boy'. It was fortunate for him that Buckley was the man to spot his potential early and shape his career.

One of Buckley's coaching concepts was to make every player equally competent with either foot and ready to play in any position. So the apprehensive youngster who had been playing left-half found himself down to play right-back for his first practice game with Leeds. Versatility was trained early into the man Buckley called 'his greatest find'.

As he gained in strength Charles overcame all the disadvantages that handicap the outsize player. He trained himself to have the speed, balance and swiftness of reaction needed in the rush of League football. So his size became bonus. In the penalty area his height and weight made him a commanding figure in attack or defence. A high ball was his ball and no one could stop him getting it.

When later he moved to Juventus his play acquired new depth. For Charles the Italian system of 'bolt' defences and close marking brought a further revelation of his own talent. He could screen the ball under close challenge, centre it skilfully, use it perceptively. 'I discovered that football is not played with players moving away from each other. It is played with players moving into spaces, moving close to the man with the ball. And it is not played at breakneck speed all the time.'

After the run, run, run, the work-rate requirement, the long passes of the English game, Charles adapted to the Italian style with the easy adjustment of the born games player. This made him the complete footballer who took Juventus to three League Championships and two Cup wins and with a presence that brought calm and stability to the emotional atmosphere of the Italian game.

When he decided to return to Leeds, Juventus offered him £18,000 to stay for just one season more. Sadly, his talents had passed their peak and he was not the force that Leeds had known before. Charles moved on uneasily to Roma, to Cardiff City and then to Hereford United in the Southern League.

In first-class football he scored 270 goals as well as proving himself an outstanding centre-half. Even in the twilight of a great career in the semi-obscurity of the Southern League, his play gave expression of his own enjoyment of the game and left others free to enjoy theirs. There were none of the old pro tricks of cutting others down to his pace or using his strength to cover the lack of speed. 'He nothing common did, nor mean' would have been a better epitaph for him than for the other 'King' Charles.

On Easter Monday 1949 Charles had played his first League game aged seventeen. Twenty-five years later he was still playing for the sheer enjoyment of it, turning out for Merthyr Tydfil. He was asked why he did not go out like others while still at his peak.

'Perhaps they had no wish to play,' said Charles. 'But I do. I love every minute of it. So why pack it in if I can still be useful? As for playing on public parks with few people watching – so what? You are not suggesting it is beneath me, are you? It can never be beneath the dignity of a footballer to play football.'

John Charles was the most remarkable product of Welsh football, yet it was Italy which made him internationally famous, ranking with the best in the world. Some of his best games, however, were for Wales and in the 1955–6 season he came close to driving them to the Home Championship. England were beaten at Ninian Park for the first time in seventeen years. At the start, when Finney and Matthews seemed to have the freedom of Cardiff, their brilliance ran to waste, so tightly did Charles seal the centre. And it was Charles who in turn put England under siege, sending his forwards surging in so fiercely that Tapscott raced clear to beat Williams, and Cliff Jones added a second with a characteristic flying header. Charles also achieved an unstoppable headed goal – into his own net. So completely had he dominated the game that he could afford that one error.

In the final match they needed only to beat Ireland to win the Championship. That was some 'only' against a side with Blanchflower and Bingham to probe any weakness. Yet Charles set up victory for them with an irresistible run that left a trail of stranded tacklers. His final pass made the goal for Clarke, when Trevor Ford stepped over the ball to complete the defence's confusion.

But now Blanchflower kept sending Bingham darting in behind Hopkins' back and even Charles could not cut out all the lancing centres. The equaliser was stabbed home at last by Jimmy Jones. There could have been no centre-forward who looked a less demanding opponent for Charles. Balding, tubby, his thick thighs straining the seams of the shortest of shorts, Jones looked the caricature of a centre-forward. Yet he denied Charles total triumph when he escaped him that once. It made no difference to the critics' verdict. 'When we review this game now and in the future the final summary is inevitable – the John Charles match.' And when we review John Charles the final summary is just as inevitable – the best all-round footballer to play for Wales and, with Trevor Ford, their most dangerous goalscorer.

The most effective and entertaining forward in their history was an equally phlegmatic character. Billy Meredith was once the great attraction of Welsh football, as Stanley Matthews was to be of English. And 'once' covers a long time for he played top-class football for thirty years. Meredith joined Manchester City in 1894 aged nineteen, acquired by them from Chirk, his home town just across the Shropshire–Wales border whose citizens threw one of the Manchester officials into a horse trough for daring to remove the local idol.

He played his last competitive game for them in 1924, turning out only twice in the League side, but being picked for all the Cup-ties. Still his stamina was remarkable, although almost fifty. The tie against Cardiff at Ninian Park went into extra time, but it was the young back marking him, not 'Old Skinny' who tired. And as Meredith broke free the winner was scored from his impeccably precise cross. In April 1925 he made his final appearance playing at Maine Road in a combined team of his own choosing against a combined Rangers and Celtic eleven. It was a 2–2 draw and a game worthy of the old master.

There is a remarkable similarity in the careers of Meredith and

Matthews. These two memorable right-wingers both played until they were around fifty. Both made their reputation with one club, moved on in their prime, then returned to the team of their youth when past the normal footballer's age of retirement.

Their styles, however, were very different, with Meredith the more direct, the more keen to score. Tall and gaunt, Meredith was as ungainly as Matthews when walking relaxed. But as he broke down the wing he too was transformed into a swift, graceful runner who could cross the ball with neat precision. The sudden cut in, the dash for goal and the shot on the run, were, however, a formidable part of his game. So too was the Meredithian back-heel, a joyous double bluff which foxed countless defenders. He would lean in towards the tackler, then dart past on the outside just like Matthews. But as often as not he would have backheeled the ball, as the mesmerised defender turned to follow him, leaving inside or half-back with space to spare.

His career record is staggering. With World War I costing him four lost seasons, and a year's suspension for taking illegal payments depriving him of another, he still played 670 League matches, almost equally divided between Manchester City and Manchester United, and scored 181 goals. For Wales he played in 48 full and 3 Victory Internationals, but scored only 10 goals. Wales' opponents then were limited to the three home countries, but he might still be holding the record for caps had his clubs been more co-operative. He was selected for 71 consecutive Internationals between 1895 and 1920, but the demands of his clubs, particularly City, so limited his appearances that it is Ivor Allchurch whose 68 caps hold the record for Wales.

The year's suspension – along with seventeen other City players – was for accepting 'illegal' bonuses of 5s. or 10s. a match. It led to his transfer to United, immediately the suspension ended in 1906, and gives an interesting sidelight on the values of the time. Meredith was for years the greatest attraction in football yet his average wage was £4 15s. a week with £1 a match for Internationals. In today's high-priced game there are loud complaints of the 'pressures'. But these minimal wages brought their own 'pressures'. In his early years Meredith continued to work in a pit in North Wales to earn enough for himself and for the allowance he always sent to his impoverished parents.

This was his schedule for the week in 1895 when he won his first cap. Friday night he suffered sea-sickness in a rough crossing to Belfast. Saturday he played against Ireland and endured another uncomfortable voyage that night. Monday he was in London playing against England. Tuesday down the pit in North Wales. Wednesday playing a League game for City. Thursday and Friday there were more shifts down the pit and on Saturday he was at Wrexham to play for Wales against Scotland. 'Pressure' is nothing new for a professional footballer.

Meredith coached at Old Trafford for a few years from 1931 and always retained a warm attachment for United until his death in 1958.

Yet the game which gave him most pleasure was not concerned with the League Championship titles of 1905 and 1911 or the Cup victory in 1909 with United; nor with the day he had a Cup Winner's medal with City in 1904; it was a game for Wales. In 1920 they played England at Highbury when Meredith was forty-four. Before the match he and the Welsh team made a presentation to T. E. Thomas, the retiring Headmaster of Chirk School, whose passion for football had been rewarded by no less than forty-nine Welsh internationals, five of them playing that day, having been his pupils. Meredith played with all his old panache and for the first time in their history Wales beat England. Even the unemotional Meredith, so cool on the field, so reserved off it, was moved to tears. It was the proudest moment of his career and his last cap for Wales.

Meredith was a footballing freak and this greatest of all Welsh wingers, perhaps of all Welsh forwards, is remembered by two quirks of personality – his quill toothpick and his method of taking penalties.

For him the toothpick, which was always in his mouth, served, like today's gum, to keep his throat from going dry as he chewed away at it. And when goalkeepers were briefly allowed to stand on the 6-yard line for penalties Meredith made them look foolish by standing stationary with his toe under the ball, then lofting it gently over their heads into the net. With the heavy balls and heavy toe-caps of his period that was quite a feat. But Meredith was quite a player.

Ron Davies was another to score 10 goals for Wales, playing for them in twenty-nine Internationals. 'Big Ron', like John Toshack, was a man whose heading power could take or make goals against the best defences. The low hard centre driven across goal is a dangerous move which threatened to make obsolete the high lob into the centre. But as defenders packed even more closely on the ground the tall men were still able to beat them in the air, making the cross to the head fashionable again. Ron Davies was one of those who was adept at nodding them in, or backheading across goal, or glancing the ball down to the other striker's feet.

Ron was born at Holywell in Flintshire and in the local school team he was overshadowed by another tall player, Mike England, later to be such an effective centre-half. It was England who made the impression while Davies was still so self-effacing he was once sent home for not speaking to anyone for two weeks. Davies had just started as an apprentice moulder at a steelworks when John Harris, who had been impressed by the play in a school match, took him on at Chester at £3 a week as a 15-year-old. Being picked to play for Chester at seventeen in the 1959–60 season was hardly football's greatest honour. They usually finished bottom of the Fourth Division. But in that hard school Davies learnt the skill which was to bring him most of his 276 League goals. 'I was then a better player on the ground,' he has commented, 'but they made me jump hurdles wearing Army boots. It was murder, but it learnt me the trick. There may be little room on the ground, but there is always space in the air if you can get higher than the others.' And that was what Davies did with such efficiency first at Luton and then at Norwich. But it was his move to Southampton in 1966 which brought him to the fore. Newcastle United had been interested, but finally bought a similar type of player instead, Wyn Davies. 'They bought the wrong Davies,' said Ashman, the Norwich Manager, and he may have been right, good though Wyn was. Certainly Ron made an instant impact at Southampton with Martin Chivers beside him and Terry Paine lobbing those accurate crosses on to his head. In his first season he was the League's leading scorer with 38 First Division goals and another 5 in cup-ties made him the top scorer in Europe.

For Wales he became the focal point of the attack with Dave Bowen, the Manager of the National team, enthusing over his ability. 'I think he is one of the greatest in Europe.' And in May 1969 he confirmed that view with two spectacular headers against Scotland and one against England, only for Wales to lose 3–5, and 1–2.

Sometimes Ron was Wyn's rival for the No. 9 shirt, sometimes they were partners, two tall strikers together giving the centre-backs a testing time. But three of a kind seemed too many when Toshack was also teamed with them. The man who wins the ball in the air needs a sure finisher to feed off his headed flicks.

The best finisher Wales have had was the man who truly struck sparks as he flamed at the defences. Trevor Ford was as hard as ferro-concrete, as fast and fierce as a wind-swept bush fire. He was the goalkeepers' nightmare and referees had their whistles poised as soon as they saw him. In his Sunderland days Manager Bill Ridding lamented, 'He is the best forward I've seen, but referees don't give him a chance. As soon as he touches the ball they warn him and undermine his confidence.' It took a lot to undermine Ford's confidence. Off the field he was the typical salesman, smart in dress and wit, assured, talkative, companionable. On it, only the unwise needled him.

Derek Ufton, playing in one of his early games for Charlton at wing-half, occasionally picked up Ford as he wandered across and the experience made a deep impression on him. 'He chatted amicably with me, but kept saying, "Your centre-half is really niggling me today. I am not going to stand much more." Finally he said, "I have had enough. You watch when the next high ball comes down the middle." And as Ufton watched Ford went in like a tank, the granite head clashing with the centre-half's to have him carried from the field with a cut above his eyebrow. "But I enjoyed playing against him at centre-half later. With me he was always hard, but always fair."'

For Wales Ford scored a record 23 goals in 38 matches while his controversial and profitable transfer trail took him from Swansea to Aston Villa to Sunderland to Cardiff. Derek Tapscott of Arsenal was the tearaway inside in the Welsh team who best reflected Ford's personality.

But his ideal partnership was with the 'golden boy' of Welsh football, that calm, immaculate inside-forward, Ivor Allchurch. When Allchurch had his first game for Wales in November 1950 Ford scored twice against England. That game was lost, but they were teamed with happier result for another significant match.

The Welsh F.A.'s 75th anniversary match was played on 5 December 1951 at Cardiff and they defeated an Eleven from the Rest of the United Kingdom by 3–2. Exhibition match this may have been, but it was a showpiece for the talents of Trevor Ford and Ivor Allchurch. After only two minutes Allchurch headed in Ron Burgess' centre. Then it was Trevor Ford racing onto Allchurch's through pass to beat Cowan. Ivor Allchurch scored again after half-time, slipping the ball in after Morris had headed against the post to put Wales three up. Charlie Fleming, the frail East Fife forward with the cannonball shot got a couple in the final half-hour but Ford and Allchurch had already won the match between them.

International football was for Allchurch the spur to greatness. For Swansea or Newcastle he was always a consistent footballer, whose thoughtful, measured play was a delight to watch. But for Wales he was the magnet for passes, a creator of chances, an inspiration to forward lines of limited talent. And when opportunity offered his shooting was cool, precise and powerful. Yet there was nothing passionate about his football. Like John Charles he was a gentle, graceful player, unhurried and unemotional. And as with Charles he was too much in love with the game to leave it as his skills waned, continuing to play in non-league football until he was forty-seven.

Ivor Allchurch had many partners to benefit from the telling passes he hit with all the accuracy of a Johnny Haynes. He was a strong finisher too, scoring 22 goals in his record 68 Internationals.

There is one remarkable goal in Welsh history which featured three of their outstanding players. The scene was Ninian Park on Saturday, 17 October 1959. England were just sixty seconds away from victory, leading 1–0 from a characteristic Greaves goal. Kelsey had brilliantly parried Clough's 26th-minute shot, but as he groped after the ball there was Greaves to stab it through his fingers into the net. And with England still attacking at the end we were already composing our introductory paragraphs recording their victory. There was some hasty rewriting required in the pressbox as Nurse intercepted the ball and sent Phil Woosnam off on a long loping run past the half-way line. From Woosnam the pass went to Ivor Allchurch, the 'golden boy' of Welsh football, who had rusted unburnished for most of the match, so effectively had Flowers screened him. Now he slid a telling pass out to Cliff Jones by the left corner flag. With no room for manœuvre Jones hit a deep cross with that powerful left foot. As the ball raked across the crowded area there was 18-year-old Graham Moore rising high above the rest to head home. That goal in his first game established Moore as an exciting prospect. But the bright promise faded and it was the old heads who had fashioned the goal – Woosnam, Allchurch and Jones – whose names will linger in the memory down the years.

Cliff Jones had many of the characteristics which made Finney outstanding. He was fast, a clever dribbler, and he could shoot like lightning with that strong left foot. But the picture his name conjures up is of a winger moving in fast to leap above the defenders and head home a cross from the far side of the field. He was a thrilling player to watch and a vital part of Tottenham's finest team. Phil Woosnam was a thoughtful, intelligent inside, expert in the smooth short-passing game expected of a West Ham player. With his close-cropped hair and intent expression as he ran, a little crouched and leaning forward, he looked as much the academic as the athlete. These two sides of his personality have made him the ideal man to mastermind the steady growth of football in America, where it is now being played with even more flamboyance than in the valleys of Wales.

The two forwards who have made most impact on the recent revival of Welsh fortunes have been Leighton James and John Toshack, that old tactical combination of a clever winger on the flank playing to a good header of the ball in the centre. The two matches which best expressed the effectiveness of the pairing were the 1973 World Cup games against Poland in Cardiff and England at Wembley.

The Poles, who were to finish in third place behind West Germany and Holland, were well beaten, unable to cope with James's pace and dribbling skill. Toshack had been moving wide to help, but in the second half he stayed in the centre, seeing the wingers could do the job on their own. And soon he had flicked the ball on for James to score the first in the 2–0 defeat of an outstanding side. It was the same combination which ruined England's chances of qualifying for the Finals by holding them to a 1–1 draw. Leighton James, busy as ever, switched over to the right, glided past McFarland and turned the ball back for Toshack to sweep into the net.

The pair was prominent again as Wales beat Hungary in both Cardiff and Budapest, a double never achieved by England. With Luxembourg also beaten twice, 8–1 on aggregate, Wales became the only home side to qualify for the 1976 Finals of the European Nations Cup. From 27 October 1971 to 14 May 1974, when they lost 0–2 to Scotland, Wales scored only 4 goals in 14 matches. In the next 8, including the games against Hungary and Luxembourg, they scored 18. And in a World Cup qualifying match in 1977 Czechoslovakia were beaten 3–0 with Leighton James back to his best after being dropped. The fire had returned to the Welsh forwards.

Thirteen

The Complete Forward

For me the most memorable of all the goalscorers, the completest forward of them all, was Tom Finney. In part that is personal prejudice for I was captivated by his skills from the time we played together at the war's end in Sixth Armoured Divisional matches in Italy and Austria. But consider the many talents which made him unique as both goal-maker and goal-taker. Finney was equally at home on either wing, or at centre-forward – or even, in emergency, at inside. He is one of only four who have scored 30 or more goals for England – and the only winger to do so.

In his career he scored 187 goals in 431 games for Preston. Yet his most passionate admirer, Bill Shankly, points to goalmaking as his main talent.'Ye canna match Finney. No back ever stopped him reaching the goal line to make the killing pass back. And he had the art, lost to the moderns, of centring accurately when running at full speed.' In Shankly's terms he walked on egg-shells, ran like a gazelle, headed like Denis Law, shot like Bobby Charlton. Above all he was the natural winger, master of a position which brought so much colour, excitement and goals to the game.

One of the more entertaining confrontations on the football field was between the massive George Young, Scotland's formidable defender, and the thin, wiry, elusive Finney. I can picture him still in an International at Wembley trapped by the corner flag, hovering and hesitating over the ball, while the impassive Young screened his every move. The unintelligent in the Wembley crowd were already shouting 'get on with it' when Finney suddenly went gliding past like a mongoose striking too swift for the cobra to follow. The pass was cut back from the goal-line, the ball swept into the net. It was no surprise

The young Pelé is smothered by ecstatic Brazilian players after scoring the only goal of their quarter-final match against Wales in 1958

Pelé scores the fifth goal in Brazil's 5–2 defeat of Sweden in the World Cup Final in Stockholm

Duncan Edwards kicks clear after Scotland's Lawrie Reilly has forced the ball past Wright and Hodgkinson. Edwards also scored the winner in this 2–1 England victory in 1957

Three defenders are not enough to stop Jimmy Greaves

John Charles, falling back (*centre*), heads a goal against England watched by
Billy Wright and Mel Charles in 1956

Di Stefano (in white) scores his second goal in Real Madrid's 7–3 win over
Eintracht at Hampden Park in the 1960 European Cup Final

Finney slides in to score England's third goal against Wales at Wembley in 1956 as substitute goalkeeper Alf Sherwood dives too late

Bobby Charlton leaps for joy after scoring his second goal in England's 2–1 win over Portugal in the semi-final of the World Cup in 1966

That's Nat Lofthouse that was. Manchester United's Harry Gregg has been charged into the net for Bolton's second goal in the 1958 Cup Final

Geoff Hurst gets in where it hurts against Scotland in 1967. The result hurt too with England beaten 2–3

Roger Hunt heads home his second against France in the 1966 World Cup Finals

Johan Cruyff scores in the 4–0 win by Holland over Argentina in the 1974 World Cup Finals. Note the care with which the easy chance is taken

Mike Channon weaves through the Scottish tacklers as England win 5–1 at Wembley in 1975

Andy Gray hurtles in to head the winner in an F.A. Cup-tie at Leicester in 1977

The smile on the face of the tiger as Denis Law salutes another of his goals

then that Young was also an admirer of Finney's talent. 'Tom was even better than Matthews, being two-footed and a magnificent header of the ball. Finney – a rarity among artistic players – was also a powerful tackler who worked hard all the time. He was the complete footballer.'

Young found that Finney set quite unusual problems. 'When he operates on the left wing he works the ball with his right foot and when he switches to the right he dribbles with the inside of his left.'

This skill which so upset opposing backs was no natural talent. When ordinary training stopped at Preston Finney went on practising hour after hour on his own kicking the ball against the shed mainly with his weaker foot. In practice he used to wear a soft shoe on his strong left foot and a boot on the weaker right to ensure *that* was the foot he used until both were almost equally powerful.

The hours of practice at Preston had ingrained the habit in Tom. Even with all the distractions and delights of Italy and Austria at our disposal at the war's end he had us training endlessly for army games of little import. Heading tennis was a favourite of his and his mastery of the game used perfectly to demonstrate the power of his legs, the nice balance of body and mind. We were both 5 ft. 7 in., but he always seemed a foot higher than me as he sprang lightly up to head the ball hard down over the eye-level net.

It was impossible to play with a man of his ability and intelligence without learning something from him. He taught me one move that was to make him so much more effective than Matthews as a scorer as well as a creator. When wingers tended to stay wide he would cut in and shoot with the opposite foot, preferring to play on the right so that he could hit the ball with his stronger left. He had another special trick for shaking off a pursuer. As he turned inside he would move across him then suddenly slow. The chaser had to check and in that instant Finney accelerated away to lose him for good.

Finney's scoring talent was clear to see from his first full International against Ireland in Belfast in September 1946. England won 7–2 and Finney had his goal as well as making them for others. He scored again in Dublin, his solitary goal eight minutes from the end snatching a win against the run of play. Next it was his goal at Hampden that set Scotland on the way to defeat. In four of his first five Internationals he scored goals to assert a vital advantage over Matthews, whose injury had first let Finney into the side.

Had Finney not been switched to the left Matthews might never have regained his place. Finney himself won 76 caps and never lost his knack for scoring vital goals.

Two games stand out for me for their emotional settings in the countries where I had first seen him play. There was Milan in 1948 with the whole of Italy longing to assert itself – to find consolation in victory at soccer for defeat at war.

The tumultuous crowd was instantly stilled by Mortensen's remarkable goal. But it was Finney, poised and precise, who crushed the final Italian challenge with two killing goals.

Years later in Vienna there was the stirring match that both Austria and England saw as being for the championship of Europe. With the score 2–2 it was Finney's shrewd perception and instant pass that sent Nat Lofthouse charging through for a memorable and decisive goal.

When Finney was asked to choose his own greatest game he made a characteristic comment before describing the 5–3 win over Portugal in Lisbon in 1950. 'I reflected uneasily I might seem conceited if I spoke of a game in which I shone. But I made the decision I think most honest.'

So it always was with Tom. Frank and sporting, he was a team man at heart, but always confident enough when the responsibility came to make his own way to goal.

In that game against Portugal he put an early penalty past Ernesto after being brought down in full flight. Bentley gave him an opening for his second. His third he remembers was the best of his career, but felt it was a little 'selfish' to go round the fourth tackler before scoring himself instead of passing to Milburn. England then were 4–1, but a rousing Portuguese rally had the stadium in uproar as two goals sliced into the England net. Finney gives credit for final victory to right-back Ramsey. 'Here his genius showed itself. Here was one player, perhaps the only one, who refused to be rattled. He was so cool, so calm, so rational, his influence brought us back to planned football.' But in fact it was Finney's clever play that tested the Portuguese to destruction. He was upended yet again in full flight for goal and slid home the penalty. Four goals in an International was a record harvest for a winger.

He might as easily have chosen that game in 1947 when Portugal were beaten 10–0 in Lisbon, destroyed by the skills of Finney on the one wing, Matthews on the other.

'That was the first time in my life that I had played on the left-wing although I had experience at left-inside. Bobby Langton had been injured in our previous game against Switzerland and Walter Winterbottom asked me to make the switch.

'Everything went right for us from the start and the whole forward line had an instinctive understanding. The Portuguese had some expert individual players, but no organisation. The backs stood square without the one on the far side to the play covering in behind the centre-half. So we only had to beat our man and there were great gaps in the middle for Lawton and Mortensen.

'The goalkeeper was the local hero in Lisbon, regarded as world-class. It was not long before his fans were throwing cushions at him and he was so demoralised he had to be substituted.' Finney would not mention of course that his own right-back, Portugal's captain, was similarly demoralised and substituted.

We were discussing that game on the eve of England's World Cup match against Finland in 1976 at Wembley with a flood of goals confidently predicted. 'The Finnish players won't have the class of the Portuguese we massacred, but it will still be much harder for our forwards. Defences are so much better organised that they will be lucky to get four where we got ten!' He was one of the few not surprised when two was all we could manage.

With four at the back so quickly reinforced by three more in the modern game there are special skills needed to break through. It needs a man who can beat two or three tacklers in a quick close dribble as Channon did to set up England's winning goal in that match. Or it needs quick precise passing which lances through before the cover can be thickened up. The first skill was inborn in Finney, the second was drilled in later.

'At first I was too much the individualist, fascinated with dribbling. In one practice game when I was a youngster at Preston the coach, Bill Scott, suddenly stopped play and came over to me. "Would you like me to buy you a ball of your own? You don't seem to want anyone else on your side to use it."

'Then came one of the few coaching demonstrations that had a real impact on my play. He made two of the others stand ten yards apart, then faced me from the far side of them. "Now dribble the ball to me," he called, and I had a difficult time evading the two who closed in to tackle. Then he sent me back. "Now pass me the ball," he said and in a second it had slid to him without hope of the two intercepting. "By all means beat a man when you *have* to. But always remember how much quicker and simpler it is to pass a ball to someone than dribble it to him."

'So to the dribbling and shooting practice was added precision in passing and the awareness of when to hold the ball, when to part with it.'

Some fine players live by instinct alone, doing magical things without knowing how. Finney was always well aware of just what he could do, his intelligence as sharp as his instinct. I had early experience of that when our Divisional side played a touring team of top-class professionals sent out to Italy to give exhibition matches to the troops waiting impatiently to be demobilised. The game was in Padua and unusually the ground was frozen hard, though it was late spring. The professionals with their careers before them were not prepared to risk injury, walking as delicately as Agag while the less talented performers on our side flung themselves boisterously into the fray. Finney was already on the verge of International honours, but he never held back and scored the only goal before the interval. As nominal captain of our side all I could then say was 'well played' whereupon Tom politely but firmly took over, dissecting the opposition, suggesting a change of tactics, organising a 5–0 victory that had the exhibition team departing in an agony of injured pride and bitter complaints about the conditions.

That match always summed up for me three of the Finney characteristics – courage, shrewd tactical sense and a boyish enthusiasm for the game which never staled over the years. The courage had been expressed in another way. His craftsman's skill could have ensured him a permanent place in the rear echelons as the army slogged its way up the prickly spine of Italy. But Tom had to be at the centre of action and talked himself into driving a 'honey' tank, eager to take on the German 'bolt' defences of the Hitler or Gustav lines. The 'honey' was fast and manœuvrable like Tom. But in Italy there was nowhere for light tanks to manœuvre out of range of the 88 mm guns that lurked in the olive groves or in the foothills. To *ask* to drive one was cold courage indeed.

Finney had the ideal approach to coaching and training, with a wholehearted relish for any practice that would improve his skills. Some only enjoy showing off their strengths, but he was as persistent in analysing and eliminating weakness. So the boy who modelled himself on Alex James became the man who could score with the facility with which James created chances.

Finney never allowed himself to be the slave of training routine or tactical instruction. He always set as much store by natural instinct and natural ability, sharpened though these might be by advice and practice.

The attacking forward can be judged only on the goals he scores, the openings he makes for others. The rest is irrelevant however smooth the passes or intelligent the positioning. It is not enough to do the simple thing consistently well. There has to be something else of subtlety or strength to make him outstanding. So he must always be free to experiment, to make errors, to try the improbable provided always that he has the 'feel' for scoring. Finney had that knack and the confidence to follow an instinct that homed him in on goal as if driven by some private computer.

Whatever he undertook Finney attacked with the same concentration, the same logical thought. When between matches in Austria, we stopped the truck to have a couple of hours' fishing Finney had to learn the sport, rather than watch. Before we moved on he had caught three trout and was casting like an old hand.

The Preston plumber, as he was called, was as good at business as at football. In the days when his earnings from the game were limited to the maximum £20 a week, rather than the fortune he would make now, he needed to build up a lucrative plumbing business with his brother. He runs it still in Preston, a nice blend of manager and craftsman who deals as competently with a balance sheet as with a repair.

Finney's standards are of a generation when there was pride in performance and great store set on loyalty.

Inevitably he was a one-club man for twenty-three years. When Palermo offered him £10,000, a villa, a car and a large salary to play two seasons for them Finney rejected the riches of those days when the Preston Board asked him not to go. With him to prop them Preston only once slipped into the Second Division. That was in 1949 when Tom had his jaw broken in a cup-tie with Leicester and was out of action. In a couple of years they were back again, missing the League Championship in 1953 only on goal average when they finished level on points with Arsenal. They missed the Cup the next year when West Bromwich Albion beat them in the final.

This was the final that followed 'Matthews's match', that great emotional moment when the people's favourite won his medal at last. That same season my team, Pegasus, won the Amateur Cup at Wembley before a 100,000 crowd. I hoped 1954 would complete a trilogy of Cup success for my three favourite right-wingers. And, indeed, it was a right-winger who scored the winner three minutes before time. Sadly it was Albion's Griffin who made it 3–2.

Finney's cool critique made himself responsible for the loss. 'The team were used to playing to me and I was up against a back I could usually leave standing. But on the day our left-winger was having a fine game and I was being well contained. Yet they kept working the ball to me and, as captain, I should have made them change their game, switch the attack to the left.'

Finney was almost certainly cheated of his Cup ambition by his own kindness. He found it hard to say 'no' to the endless requests for tickets or interviews, and even to a dinner on the eve of the final. This ceaseless involvement left him drained and listless on the day that mattered most. Football never runs smoothly even for its masters. Those two disappointments were matched by another. Finney was a member of England's World Cup team unbelievably beaten by the U.S.A. 'I still cannot get over it. We were playing on a small bumpy pitch before a handful of spectators. Control was difficult and there was no atmosphere to raise one's game. We were so sure it was a walk-over as we kept hitting the bar and the post. Then they scored a break-away goal as Gaetjens unexpectedly glanced in a shot Williams had covered. We kept trying to play football. But nothing would run for us and we got more and more desperate until we ended as a rabble. There was a feeling of utter desolation as we left the field.'

Even for such a player as Finney there was total truth in Blanchflower's comment on professional footballers. One minute he might be enjoying the sunlit summit of the world, the next in despair, clinging with icy fingers to the South Pole. Yet however the ball bounced or the world spun Finney looked always utterly composed, completely self-reliant.

My last World Cup memory of him is a happier one from Sweden in 1958. Until the Munich air disaster we had a team that should have won that competition. Even without Manchester United's Roger Byrne, Duncan Edwards and Tommy Taylor it was still good. Yet here were Russia leading 2–1 with five minutes to go in our first match. The Gotenburg Stadium was hushed as Finney faced Yashin for the vital penalty. Yashin, that great bear of a goalkeeper, leapt forward arms wide to narrow the angle, but Finney's shot slid quietly into the corner.

His skills brought him such a hammering in that game that, to our sad loss, he could play no more in the competition. Yet bruised as he was he could still take that decisive penalty with cool certainty.

That too is a fair picture of Finney over the years. He was the target for all the tacklers and there were many who cared little how they stopped him. He too was a fighter for the ball, as Young remembered, one who never shirked a challenge. But there was no need to check the record to know he was never sent off, never booked, never reprimanded. With his ascetic face, his short crinkled hair, his good humour, he was of an era that had little of today's fake dramatics, instant anger and crafty gamesmanship.

Tom Finney was already 35 when Preston switched him to centre-forward to play the waiting game there with the same authority that Bobby Charlton was to show in his later years. Finney had the vision to control the play from midfield, still the speed to break unexpectedly from deep positions to score. He was teamed with another expert striker, Tommy Thompson, whose instinct for goals complemented Finney's. It was a telling partnership made complete by the support of little Jimmy Baxter, who had a passing flair of a Bobby Collins, a Johnny Giles, or a John White. Baxter floated the ball behind the defenders for Finney or Thompson to surge in on it. Right, left or centre, outside or inside, Finney was the complete forward.

Fourteen

Goal of a Lifetime

The sight of a goal satisfies some primitive instinct so that one never tires of watching the ball enter the net however devious the method. My son, a keen Leeds supporter, eagerly watched those endless television replays of Montgomery's remarkable reflex saves from Lorimer which won the 1973 Cup Final for Sunderland. 'Some day he is going to miss it,' he said wistfully as he saw for the fiftieth time Montgomery palm the ball on to the bar.

Fortunately each goal has its individual quality and the variety of ways of getting the ball into the net seem infinite. Of all those in games which I have taken part in, there are a few special ones so impressed on the mind that every detail is capable of instant recall. Inevitably the most memorable goal for me was my first in First Division football, the climactic experience of a strange sequence of events.

The year was 1951 and Charlton Athletic then used to spend one training day each season on the Aylesford Paper Mills Ground, near Maidstone. The attraction was a sauna bath, left to the Company by the Finnish Olympic team who had brought it with them to the London Games four years before. For the players light training followed by a sauna made a welcome change to normal routine. The connection with the paper mills was through the Glikstens, whose businesslike approach had taken Charlton straight from the Third Division to the First and whose timber interests extended into paper.

As I worked at Aylesford I was told to look after the team on its visit. Jimmy Seed, the Manager, asked over lunch if I would sign for Charlton. Thinking he might wish me to play the occasional Combination Game I made light of the request, saying I played for my amateur team, Pegasus, on Saturdays and was not free mid-week.

'However, I will be glad to sign if you give me a free ticket to watch your home game with Spurs at Christmas.'

Charlton's free-scoring Swedish centre-forward, Hans Jeppson, had just returned home and they were having a bad run. Spurs beat them easily enough at the Valley and my main interest was in seeing my England Amateur wing partner, George Robb, make a substantial contribution to Tottenham's 3–0 win. George had a left-foot shot as explosive as Bobby Charlton's and was to achieve the rare distinction of playing for England as an amateur and also as a professional. He chose an unfortunate match for his first and only full International. Robb was on the left wing when English invincibility at home was shattered by the Hungarians' 6–3 win at Wembley.

At the game's end Seed invited me in to sign. Immediately I had done so he said, 'Now you can play at White Hart Lane on Boxing Day. We meet Tottenham again and you might change our luck.' That ruined my Christmas dinner as I now had to train instead of eat. My main training in those days consisted of running up Tovil Hill just outside Maidstone. It was a steep little hill and if I was still running when I reached the top I reckoned to be fit. If I had to walk, then I had a rest and tried again until I could pass myself as in good condition. For the big match preparation I ran up it twice just to be sure.

Arriving early at White Hart Lane I waited expectantly for detailed tactical instruction that I presumed separated the professionals from the amateurs. Perhaps I missed the team briefing. My own was simple enough. 'What I want you to do,' said the Captain, Benny Fenton, 'is kick your corners to the far post.' 'And what I advise you,' said the Club doctor, 'is to have a tot of whisky for your nerves.' The second instruction was easy enough to carry out. There seemed no point in mentioning, however, that I found it hard to hit corners as far as the middle of the goal even on a dry ground, let alone on the muddy quagmire that the Tottenham pitch then used to become when it rained, as it did on this day.

As we went out my Kent cricketing colleague and inside partner for the day, Sid O'Linn, said, 'Seed has never seen you play and the scout who recommended you after one of your Amateur Cup games is in a bit of a state. He's told Kiernan and me to make sure you have a good game or Seed will have his head.' At least it was comforting to know one's inside was out to make life easy. For a quarter of an hour there was nothing remotely easy about it. Never had I run so far, or so fast – and yet made no contact at all with a ball that was forever spirited away from me. We were already two goals down and I felt out of breath and out of my depth. Then came the dreaded moment – a corner to take. The run-up was short and confined and in the extra effort to reach the far post my left foot slid away and my right sliced the ball diagonally backwards along the ground. It was not the type of corner to which First Division players were accustomed and twenty of them stared at it in contemptuous amazement. The twenty-first, Kiernan, ran on to the ball and swept it low inside the far post before anyone moved. I was in the game.

Just before half-time I shook off my back, Withers, at last and from the centre the invaluable Kiernan headed home to make me feel ten feet tall. 2–2 it remained until the closing minutes. Then Alf Ramsey, covering up on the goal line headed out a shot, but straight to me. From twelve yards out I hit the heavy ball as hard as I could and it flew over Ramsey's head into the roof of the net. That was the winner. It had been the dream debut, and the dream continued when reading the reports.

Rabbie Burns wished us the chance to see ourselves as others do. It's a doubtful privilege, the reflection through others' eyes is like looking in the distorting mirrors at a fun fair. Some parts seem instantly recognisable, some grotesque. That was my reaction to reading this description by Desmond Hackett, the old brown bowler himself, in the full flow of that confident, know-all, *Daily Express* style:

> Tony Pawson, a greying 31-year-old quiet-spoken little fellow ventured that 'I doubt if I am quite good enough' when Charlton chief Jimmy Seed invited him to play at Tottenham. It was the same Pawson with a soccer pedigree reading Winchester, Oxford University, Pegasus and England who scampered through the game yesterday to take part in two goals and score the winner four minutes from time.
>
> And when Charlton, rejoicing over their first goals and their first win after four games cheered amateur outside-right Pawson into the dressing-room, the man, who looks like a smaller edition of Raich Carter, murmured, 'Thanks, chaps. It was a great game, but jolly hard work, by gad!'

Such is the power of the press that my friends indeed believed Hackett had been hiding behind the dressing-room door and faithfully recorded those unlikely remarks. After the game Jimmy Seed invited me back to Charlton for drinks and then asked my expenses. 'Ten shillings and sixpence.' Seed ushered me to the safe with the Secretary, Jack Phillips, in attendance and said, 'I am very pleased with the way you played today. Here is ten guineas.' I would have been delighted to be paid for playing and was shortly, on the Wolfenden Committee, to recommend the abolition of the distinction between amateur and professional (a minority recommendation that took fifteen years to implement). But I had no intention of calling myself an amateur and taking money and made this clear to Seed. That led to a heated argument with Jack Phillips taking the money out, then putting it back, as one or other held the floor. Finally Seed laughed and gave me another drink instead.

In later seasons when I went back to Charlton he was to introduce me to visiting Directors as 'The amateur who asked for ten shillings expenses' as if I was a character in a Bateman cartoon. It was a strange end to an exciting day.

That goal gave me most pleasure to score. The one that gave me most pleasure to watch was scored not by a forward, but by that young giant among half-backs, Duncan Edwards. What might Duncan have achieved had he not been cut down before his prime by the Munich air crash? In a professional football career of only $4\frac{1}{2}$ years his burly frame became feared all across Europe where he was rated among the five best players of the day. At 16 Edwards stood 5 ft. $10\frac{1}{2}$ ins. and weighed $12\frac{1}{2}$ stone – and on the field he was never shy about using his weight or his height. That surging power made him a magnificent header of the ball and a formidable tackler, but despite his bulk he could dribble with easy assurance. As a 16-year-old Edwards forced himself into a Manchester United team with John Carey, Jack Rowley, Stan Pearson and the other headline names. Two years later he had shouldered his way into the National team, the youngest ever to play for England. In his first match at left-half he helped to send Wilshaw gliding in for his four goals as Scotland were destroyed 7–2. Thereafter he was hardly ever out of the side, despite having to battle for his place against such formidable rivals as Bill Slater and Jimmy Dickinson, the Billy Wright of Portsmouth.

Duncan never had a finer game than on 26 May 1956 in Berlin against the World Cup holders. I had a trainer's eye view of the match, having been asked to report it only the day before. That meant arriving in Berlin on the morning of an all-ticket match without a reporter's pass, or a ticket, and without much German to talk my way into the ground. The only solution was a dash to the hotel in which England's team were staying, where Walter Winterbottom kindly arranged to smuggle me into the ground in their coach and let me sit on the touchline bench. The one drawback was that the telephones were in the top tier of that vast stadium packed with 90,000 chanting, horn-blowing spectators and the phoning deadline for my 800 words was just two minutes after the final whistle. In the end I was fortunate to see the German's late consolation goal in their 3–1 defeat, as I was battling up to the booths when Fritz Walter scored. It was even more fortunate that I had anything recorded to telephone, for from the start I was caught up in the frenzied excitement, the Nationalist overtones of that memorable day. To the Germans we were still 'occupation' forces, not allies, and football was a continuation of war by more peaceful means. A win for them would be balm for wounded military pride. For us a win would be balm for wounded soccer pride, our prestige already lowered by two disappointing World Cup performances.

It was a cold, grey evening with the wind swirling the flags on the Stadium's rim. For twenty minutes Fritz Walter, the astute German captain, was the Torquemada of the mid-field, racking our defenders with the inquisition of those subtle passes which had so recently undone the Hungarians in that dramatic World Cup Final in Berne.

Then Duncan Edwards picked up a clearance inside his own half and swept upfield like some runaway tank. One tackle was slipped, another swept aside, another he crashed straight through and still the ball was at his toes, still he was accelerating. As he veered inwards towards the final defensive wall there was a sudden full swing of the right leg as thigh, body, and momentum merged in one explosive hammer blow. From twenty-five yards out his shot sped past Herkenrath, straining the net before he could move.

There was an inspirational quality in that goal which gave wings to his team and left the Germans drained in spirit. A nineteen-year-old lad had simply run straight through them, brushing aside the World Champions like some avenging Valkyrie.

Edwards' opposite number was the one-armed Schlienz, a clever, sophisticated user of the ball, but made to look frail and unbalanced by that short stump protruding from his vest. What a strange contrast he made to the robust dynamic Edwards, but suddenly it expressed the whole difference between the teams as Duncan's goal swept us on to comfortable victory.

The impulsive goal was not quite as spontaneous as it looked. Edwards had tended to be unselfish to a fault, as if not fully crediting his own matchless ability. Playing for the England under-23 side he would lay the ball off rather than shoot, particularly if he was playing behind a Manchester United club mate. In midfield too he was so clever and controlled in his play he rarely ventured on those surging, spectacular runs which transformed him from formidable player to irresistible force.

Against the Rumanian under-23 side England were still struggling to score when Edwards burst into a clear shooting position, checked, looked round and rolled the ball across to David Pegg, who was instantly tackled.

Afterwards the quiet and persuasive Winterbottom took him aside and asked, 'Why didn't you shoot yourself? You can clatter them in from two yards outside the area better than Pegg can from around the penalty spot. Trust your own power and work on it in practice.'

Before the Berlin game the Edwards run was still being worked on in the training sessions at Hanover. 'All the way, Duncan' had become the cry and as he set off the forwards would wheel aside, trying to take defenders with them out of his path. Johnny Haynes was the controlling influence, sometimes starting the runs with a wall pass then shouting to Edwards to go it alone without giving the return ball, while Haynes dropped in behind to cover.

And in the Berlin Olympic stadium the cry had been 'All the way, Dunc' as he set off on that awesome, cleaving run which cut so cleanly through the Germans.

That indeed was the goal of a lifetime. How tragic that Edwards' was to be so short. For in his own life there was to be no 'All the way, Duncan' as icing on the plane's wings in snow-swept Munich faded out the young giant of a footballer.

Fifteen

Goals Unusual,
Goals Memorable

Not all goals are so dramatic. Some come with a smile or a whimper, like three in my life which I recall with amusement.

Pegasus drew a quarter-final match in the Amateur Cup, a grim battle up at Crook Town. We had contrived the equalising goal from the wing, but the two of us were taken to task by the coach for not giving enough assistance to a hard-pressed defence. 'You may feel pleased with yourselves over the goal, but if you had worked hard enough they would not have scored. I don't want to see you loitering upfield in the replay.'

In that we not only gave gallant assistance to our defence, but helped in the one match-winning goal. Unfortunately it was into our own net. That was rather like breaking the plates when asked to assist with the washing-up. We were not asked again. 'We don't care what the coach says, you stay out of our area' was the defenders' reaction. I pass on the tip to any of those wingers worn down by work-rate requirements.

One worry I had always had when playing before a crowd – what happens if you have to leave the field for natural causes? At cricket you can always find an excuse, like getting another bat. But in soccer there are no natural breaks. The problem caught up with me when the England Amateur team were touring in Norway. We had just won one match 6–0 in Bergen, but were having a hard fight against the Stavanger districts combined team. With twenty minutes to go we were grimly hanging on to a 1–0 lead and for a quarter of an hour I had been in acute mental and physical pain from a stomach upset which could not be contained for long.

At that moment Jim Lewis, the centre-forward who was later to take Chelsea to their League Championship, gave me the perfect through pass. Seizing my chance I raced in to hit the ball high into the net – and kept on running. The mystified officials took some time to work out where I had gone and the attack proved so severe that I was unable to return to the field. But at least it was a spectacular exit.

In an amateur International against Ireland there was another goal that went to my head. It was the final thrust in a convincing win and made me light-hearted after a gruelling game in rain and mud. Aiming for the hot plunge as quickly as possible I had slipped off my wet kit just as the Chairman of Selectors arrived for his ritual presentation of caps. The Secretary put the boxes of caps beside him and he carefully placed his bowler hat on top before launching into his usual homily. 'Well played, boys, but . . .'

By the time he had finished his speech I was shivering cold with nothing on. So I tiptoed past him, picked up his bowler hat, and said, 'I presume this is my cap for the game?' as I continued towards the bath with it on my head. To 'get your bowler hat' is Army slang for dismissal and I was only too right. I did not get selected again for over a year!

Listening to Managers describing the meticulous planning that went into the goals their side scored there is always the question in the mind 'How much was planning? How much luck?' The Oxford University side was invited to take part in an Easter tournament in Amsterdam with a Swiss team, a Luxembourg team and our hosts, the now famous Ajax Club. For the opening match we were drawn against the Swiss First Division side. The Ajax professional coach was an Englishman who kindly advised us for the game. My instructions were that the left-half was a Swiss International who liked to move forward and must be chased wherever he went. The day was hot, the grass long and at half-time we were a goal down. So far I had hardly touched the ball and had spent all the time peering at the number on the left-half's back. This is my holiday, I thought, at least I can enjoy myself. I'm too tired to chase him any more, so let him go.

Our centre-half, Ken Shearwood, was given to massive soaring clearances and now that I loitered upfield this proved the ideal tactic. His lofted kicks left the half stranded and the left back had to come across to cover. At once we had the man over and won easily – a triumph of laziness over tactics. How many such haphazard goals are scored at higher level and looked on as brilliant tactical planning? Even Ramsey's Leadbetter ploy (the withdrawn left-winger gambit that took Ipswich from Third Division to First Division championship in three seasons) was just such an accident in its beginning.

The good Managers are the ones who, like the scientists, understand the significance of an accident when it happens. Let an apple fall on their head and they start thinking, instead of rubbing it.

The high scoring match that was most memorable for me was the Amateur Cup Final of 1953 when Pegasus beat Harwich and Parkeston 6–0, a record victory margin for any Wembley Final and the highest win we ever had in an Amateur Cup game. There was none of the nervousness of our first final two years before when we took the Cup for the first time.

But I had problems of my own before the start as I had developed a fever in the morning. It got worse as we neared the stadium and after changing I reported the fact to the Eminence of Pegasus, Professor Sir Harold Thompson. Tommy at once sent me up to the first-aid room high in the stands, followed by the curious glances of the spectators settling into their seats as I stumbled past in my playing kit and football studs. The verdict was a temperature of 102° and a recommendation not to play. To be fair to my team I reported it exactly, adding that I felt fit enough to have a go, but would stand down if the risk was not thought to be worth taking. The reserve fortunately had eaten a particularly heavy lunch and, in those days of no substitutes, was unprepared for battle. Since we neither seemed particularly fit it was decided to keep to the normal line-up. By half-time we were three up and the feverish hilarity in the dressing-room accorded well with my mood. There was plenty of good advice – whisky, brandy or champagne being the cure-alls suggested to keep me going in one second half. Having sampled each I went out again with my body swerve much improved. Wembley's wide spaces make it a wonderful hunting ground for wingers and I was kept busy as we piled on the goals. But when we went six up I still had not scored. Just before the close our powerful right-half, Reg Vowels, sent a shot skimming in from outside the area. Facing out towards him I felt it needed only a slight deflection as it passed to defeat the goalkeeper. My touch, however, sent the ball grazing over the bar and as I turned I found the goalkeeper unsighted and out of position. Had I only left it alone we would have scored seven – as Vowels is apt to remind me.

The goal rush caused an equal rush of words, but as usual Geoffrey Green caught the mood. This was his account in *The Times*:

Wembley in springtime is to Pegasus what Headingley and Worcester in summer once used to be to Sir Donald Bradman. The rich emerald surface, now sparkling once again under the proverbial Wembley sunshine, and the steep, packed curve of this amphitheatre seem to act as a stimulant on them. So it was on Saturday, when an all-ticket crowd of some 100,000 saw them carry off the F.A. Amateur Cup for the second time in three seasons. Theirs was a mature exhibition of pure football that cut poor Harwich and Parkeston to ribbons to the tune of six goals to none and reduced them to the status of a selling plater that has strayed by mischance into classic company.

Yet how little did the ending match the opening ten minutes when Harwich began so full of life and hope. There were the seeds of a surprise in that beginning, but a quick Pegasus counter at the eleventh minute destroyed the flower that might have been. A searing shot by Sutcliffe was turned past the bar by King at full stretch, and from the left-winger's measured corner kick Saunders glided unseen into the goalmouth to head past a goalkeeper going the wrong way. Three minutes later a glorious pass by Lunn sent Pawson tearing past Tyrell, and from his low centre, Sutcliffe forced the ball over the line with the support of Laybourne.

In a trice the match really was over. And shortly before half-time another fine move, one of many, but this time, as a contrast, conducted from head to head between Saunders, Lunn and Laybourne, saw Carr take the final nod in his stride and find the corner of the net with an angled left-foot shot.

For a moment at the change of ends the support of a swirling wind seemed to revive Harwich, but Cooper's shot on to the bar killed their last hope. Pegasus went smoothly on their way with Sutcliffe and Pawson, making light of a temperature, indulging in clever scissor movements with Lunn, Carr, and Laybourne. Soon Laybourne unleashed a left foot rocket into the roof of the net from Carr's pass to make it four up, then King fumbled a swift low cross from Carr on the right — part of another scissors movement — leaving Sutcliffe to pick his spot in an empty net.

The final touch came five minutes from the end. Pawson suddenly turned up on the left; Laybourne nodded down his centre and Carr stroked home the final goal to bring the widest victory ever achieved (war-time apart) by any side at Wembley.

A surfeit of goals is pleasant enough, but any game that is lacking in challenge is lacking in ultimate satisfaction for the players. Our Final of 1951 was a match with half the number of goals, but twice the impact on us.

Our opponents, Bishop Auckland, were the outstanding Amateur team of the day and none of us really expected to win. Just to have to got to Wembley was so improbable that we set out to enjoy the experience regardless of the result.

The mood was set by our 'coach' Vic Buckingham, the Tottenham player who was soon to take West Bromwich Albion so close to the Cup and League Double. He was the ideal mentor for us, a confident happy-go-lucky man with an uncomplicated view of life and football. His short pre-match talk is the only last-minute advice that has ever made any impact on me. 'Just remember four things. Don't worry about what Bishop Auckland will do. Make them worry about what you will do. Some of you may have an off day, but all of you must *want* the ball, all the time. If you can run off the field at the end you haven't given of your best. Win or lose *enjoy* the game.'

As we kicked in to goal before the start we took covert glances at the Bishop Auckland players. That is always a mistake. They looked so much stronger, so much more powerful in their shooting. Already there was a slight feeling of apprehension as the whistle blew, and my mind was preoccupied as I tried to kick one of the practice balls off the pitch.

Our centre-half, Ken Shearwood, similarly preoccupied, took a swing at the same ball just as I was kicking it. He caught me a crippling blow instead and for a moment my leg felt numbed. Wild thoughts ran through my mind. With no substitutes allowed should I hobble away before the kick-off and ask for the reserve to take over while he still could? And how silly would I look to the 100,000 spectators if I did? Fortunately the pain soon eased and the crowd was soon forgotten. They are far from the pitch at Wembley and once you start to concentrate on the game you are less aware of them than of the few hundreds standing close to the touchline and directly trans-mitting their hostility at some Northern ground, like Willington or Crook Town.

Bishop Auckland made all the early running and their left outside missed two early chances. I remained ill at ease until I had made some small contribution. Once I had headed down an awkwardly bouncing ball without checking my stride, and carried on to beat my back in a fast dribble, I was relaxed and happy, although the move ran to waste. Thereafter enjoy the game we did in a match that caught the public imagination in a way that is hard to credit now. This was Alan Ross' summary in the *Observer* of our 2–1 win.

Once more the sun shone all the afternoon and some hundred thousand people saw perhaps the most romantic victory yet in the history of the Amateur Cup. Pegasus, within three years of their formation, cantered away against Bishop Auckland, 7 times winners and 14 times finalists. The 'Bishops' were thus beaten in the final for the second year in succession.

No one could grudge the result. Pegasus, save for the opening ten minutes, when it looked as if they might well be overrun, displayed both more of the arts and graces of the game and greater determination. Their forwards, once they had found their touch, showed fine understanding, with Tanner at centre-forward holding the line together brilliantly.

Pawson, on the right wing, was precise and intelligent in everything he did. Carr fed Potts with neat, close passes, and Dutchman used the long cross pass with great effect. But it was eventually Tanner, fast, elusive and quick to seize every opening, who held the key to the match. Once he had shown that Davison held no terrors for him, the other forwards individually and together elaborated the pattern, based on the Tottenham Hotspur principle of doing the simple thing quickly, and made the ball do the work. It succeeded brilliantly.

That accorded with our own feelings. As we stood with the Cup in spring sunshine strong enough to dry the sweat on our shirts it was a moment of total fulfilment in which one hugged one's happiness to oneself.

Only twice before had I had that feeling of joy so overwhelming that it seemed impossible to contain. When the guns suddenly fell silent in North Africa and the surrendering columns of Von Sponek's men came down the craggy hills behind Enfidaville the heart lifted to the ending of the long pressures of battle. It was the same again on V.I. day in Italy as the fireworks flared instead of the tracer bullets and only the bells set the ears ringing. We had survived and we had won and just to be alive was indeed very heaven. On this Wembley afternoon there was again that feeling of pleasure so intense it was almost pain.

Six goals in a game is a remarkable achievement for any player in the top grades of modern football. Three outstanding forwards achieved this in unusual circumstances. Denis Law is the only man to score 7 goals in a Cup match and still finish on the losing side. His first 6 for Manchester City against Luton became the goals that never were. For the match on a waterlogged pitch was abandoned twenty minutes from the end of a typical English day for scorers, with the slush helping a powerful predator like Law. When the game was replayed it was Luton who won 3–1, Law who scored Manchester's only goal.

George Best's 6 in an afternoon in a fifth-round Cup match against Northampton in 1970 equalled the Cup record at the time. Three features made this a unique performance. It was in an away match in a late round, the goals were brilliantly taken, and this was Best's first game after a month's suspension, with whispers before the match that his career was finished. Best has retired as often as Melba, but this was his most dramatic return. Northampton had judged the conditions ideal for giant-killing with deep, clinging mud and pools of water glistening on the County ground, so sanded it looked like Blackpool beach. But this was also the very type of pitch on which British goalscorers flourish. And the day belonged to Best and United, even though Large and McNeil scored for Northampton, who also missed a penalty. Northampton had only conceded one goal in their last seven matches, but now they were beaten 8–2.

Best started it with a sure header after twenty-seven minutes. Eight minutes later he ran through the centre and left goalkeeper Book floundering as he slid the ball home. Book had as little chance of stopping the other four from Best or Kidd's two. Best's sixth goal a quarter of an hour before the end was the most impudently assured of them all as he snaked his way through and teased Book into diving the wrong way. It had been a masterly display of balance, acceleration and control as Best responded to the prompting of Charlton and Crerand.

Another six of the best gave Newcastle a record win in the Second Division and Len Shackleton a remarkable debut for them. He had just been sold by Bradford where his eccentric talents were not always to the liking of the no-nonsense Yorkshire crowd, who preferred crunching tackles and spirited, consistent endeavour without any of Shackleton's fancy tricks. The fancy tricks worked well enough in the 13–0 win over Newport County. Shackleton even received mild approval from his harshest critic, his father. When Shackleton had earlier scored 5 in a game his father's only comment had been, 'Your sister, Irene, could have backheeled another three.'

Six goals have been scored often enough in the League so that only special circumstances make them memorable. So why should 5 goals deserve a mention? John Summers' 5 for Charlton Athletic in December 1957 certainly do, for that was a unique game in modern times. Charlton lost their captain, Derek Ufton, after sixteen minutes when he dislocated a shoulder. With twenty-eight minutes left their ten men were losing 1–5. Then John Ryan scored to make it 2–5. Summers had been switched in from the left wing to attack down the centre and after sixty-four minutes he hit home his second goal of the game. Unbelievably he added another hat-trick in only eight minutes to make it 6–5 with nine minutes left. Just as the Valley crowd were roaring their appreciation of a miracle win John Hewie, who had played such an outstanding game as attacking centre-half in Ufton's place, tragically levelled the score with an own goal. Not even that could daunt Charlton, the happy ending coming in the final seconds as Ryan made it 7–6 for the most remarkable league win of all time.

Thirty-year-old Summers was a natural left-footer but scored all five with his 'swinger' right. He had only just held his place for that game. As manager Jimmy Trotter said, 'Things had not been coming off for Summers. So I moved him from inside-left to centre-forward. As a last resort I switched him to outside-left, his last chance to make good. How well he took it!'

Another unusual 5 was Jimmy Hill's for Fulham against Doncaster Rovers, for that was in an away game. That was indeed the match of his career as he bustled in, chin jutting forward, in his eager quest for goals.

Everton have been concerned in two of the more remarkable F.A. cup-ties, both high-scoring games. At Goodison Park on 7 January 1922 they welcomed Crystal Palace with all Merseyside looking on them as lambs for the slaughter rather than 'The Eagles'. Palace had been in the Southern League only eighteen months before but now they swooped in to prey on a team studded with Internationals.

On Everton's wings were Chedgzoy and Harrison, two England players. But the Eagles had wings of their own, and it was Bateman and Whibley who made the kill. Within four minutes Whibley had headed home Bateman's corner. The furious Everton counter-attacks were contained by Palace's only two Internationals, their half-backs Jones and McCracken. And in the twenty-first minute Jones' piercing pass sent centre-forward Menlove through to score the goal that had Palace two up at the interval. Again there were desperate Everton attacks to absorb, with goalkeeper Alderson making some stirring saves. Then in the last twenty minutes Whibley and Bateman unloosed the deluge, laying on two goals for Conner and one each for Menlove and Wood. To complete Everton's dejection Fazackerly, their best forward, missed a penalty.

A 6–0 defeat at home by a Second Division side is not a game Everton like to remember. But the one Joe Mercer recalls with relish is the fourth-round replay in 1934, the match against Sunderland which is rated the most perfect of all the pre-war Cup games.

Oddly it followed such a niggling 1–1 draw at Roker Park that the strictest referee of the day was summoned up for the Goodison match. He was kept busier whistling for goals than fouls in yet another wingers' spectacular. With Ireland's Coulter running riot for Everton and Scotland's Connor supreme on Sunderland's wing, one's goal was cancelled out by the other until Everton led 3–2 with only seconds remaining. Then Gurney somehow hooked in the equaliser for the goal-swapping to continue into extra time. Now it was 4–4 as Coulter and Connor completed their hat-tricks. And it was another winger, Everton's Albert Geldard – once, at $15\frac{1}{2}$, the youngest man to play League football – who brought his side home with two crushing goals. Eight of the ten had been scored by wingers in this classic contest.

The two goals which caused most flutter in English football were the two Walsall scored against Arsenal in the third round of the F.A. Cup in 1933. Arsenal, as usual then, were leading the First Division, Walsall an obscure Third Division side. For the public it was no match. And of all the giant-killing acts in the Cup none has caused more astonishment. It was no different in kind from Yeovil, with Alec Stock as player manager, beating Sunderland in 1949, or Ray Crawford inspiring Fourth Division Colchester to defeat the Leeds machine in 1971. But no other side has quite recaptured the Arsenal aura of invincibility, no other defeat sent out such shock waves of incredulity. Walsall played it rugged, but the man who started the Arsenal slide was skilful as well. Centre-forward Gilbert Alsop headed in Lee's corner to give Walsall the lead. And Gilbert Alsop scored 40 goals in the Third Division both that season and the next. For Arsenal's manager, Chapman, that was no mitigation. After Sheppard drove in the killer goal from a penalty, the man who gave it away was transferred without ever being allowed back into Highbury.

To the watchers one of the most momentous goals was Tommy Walker's penalty in 1936 which brought Scotland a draw with England. Twice the wind blew the ball off the spot and twice the 19-year-old Walker had to replace it before scoring the vital goal. Spectators' nerves were raw by the time the kick was taken and Scottish legend attributed the same agony to young Tommy Walker. That brilliant inside was in fact as phlegmatic as Bastin. Asked about it later he said, 'I vaguely remember the ball rolling off the spot. I just replaced it and hit it.'

Scoring is too important to be left to forwards, however expert. Bozsik at right-half was an integral part of the great Hungarian scoring machine. Billy Bremner has scored almost a hundred league goals and one memorable Cup Final goal for Leeds against Liverpool, the ball hit so hard and true that he had turned to salute his success before the ball reached the net. Another midfield man, slim Jim Baxter, is the Scottish ideal of the goalscorer. It points the contrast with the English game that their scoring half-backs should be best exemplified by the heavy gang, Ron Flowers and Jack Charlton. Flowers was often regarded as a forceful but clumsy player, lacking in skill. Yet he was precise enough in his shooting to be England's regular penalty taker and 6 of his 10 International goals were from the spot. That certainty, combined with the surging power which distinguished Duncan Edwards, put Flowers among the top twenty of England's scorers in the post-war period.

Jackie Charlton was himself a formidable and destructive defender yet that long giraffe-like neck and that power converted him into a dangerous striker at set pieces. With Leeds Charlton perfected the attacking gambit of standing on the goal line at corners. It drove defenders to distraction, sometimes creating goals for others, sometimes for himself as the goalkeeper found he could not reach the near-post ball. Against Portugal in 1969 Jack Charlton won the game by heading in the only goal from Bobby's corner. But he found, as forwards had long known, that referees tend to give the benefit of the doubt to defenders. Or, as Charlton put it more forcefully to Brian Glanville of the *Sunday Times*, 'Referees are 95% for the goalkeeper, 5% for me. They penalise me just for standing there. I've had fouls given against me as soon as the corner has been kicked. I've been pushed in the back, kicked in the back, climbed on top of by defenders, held by both arms, and I've never ever been given a foul.' But the big man still scored vital goals.

Television's action replays have shown how often referees are right when crowd and players dispute their decisions. Yet they are human and as capable of error as a player. Certainly there is no shortage of debatable goals given or disallowed.

The two most controversial goals which I have seen cost Leeds a championship and helped Huddersfield to relegation. Had Leeds not lost at home to Albion they might have won the League in 1971 to deprive Arsenal of the 'Double'. That looked an easy match in prospect for West Bromwich had not won an away game for sixteen months. Leeds, however, were uncharacteristically nervous in their early play to fall a goal behind. With twenty minutes left Hunter misplaced a pass. Tony Brown intercepted and went racing clear from his own half. Suggett was lying well ahead of him in the middle of the field some ten yards behind the nearest defender. With Leeds appealing for off-side even Brown was slowing to a halt. Then referee Ray Tinkler waved him to continue his long diagonal run to the left of the goal. There he drew the goalkeeper and slipped the ball across for Astle to score. That looked suspiciously like a forward pass and if so Astle was certainly off-side. But it was Tinkler's decision that Suggett had not been interfering with play which led to the ferment of controversy and an invasion of the pitch for which Leeds were fined £750 and had their ground closed for the first four games of the next season. Leeds were so thrown by the incident that they lost the match 1–2 and the title chance.

The off-side law still says, 'A player in an off-side position shall not be penalised unless, in the opinion of the Referee, he is interfering with the play or with an opponent, or is seeking to gain an advantage by being in an off-side position.' So Tinkler was perfectly entitled to take his view though it seemed incredible that Suggett in that menacing position could have been judged not to be interfering with play. But then I tend to go along with Danny Blanchflower's view. 'If you are on the field and not interfering with play what are you playing at?'

It was not the Referee but the law which was an ass. This provision is unnecessary and confusing, as is the first part of proviso (c) in Law II which says the player is not off-side if 'The ball last touched an opponent.'

The Huddersfield incident however was a straight case of a tragi-comic mistake with no awkward points of interpretation to cloud the issue.

On 2 April 1952 there was the strangest of conclusions to Tottenham's home game against Huddersfield. Charlie Buchan had this to say in the *News Chronicle*:

> The most amazing decision I have seen in more than 40 years experience gave Spurs victory over Huddersfield with a goal in the last minute.
>
> The two points give Spurs an outside chance of retaining the championship. The point that Huddersfield lost could put them into the Second Division.
>
> Extra time for stoppages was being played when Spurs forced a corner on the left-wing. Baily took it.
>
> His centre struck the referee, Mr. W. Barnes, of Birmingham and stopped. Baily walked up to the ball and passed it to Duquemin, who headed it neatly into the Huddersfield net.
>
> Mr. Barnes awarded a goal, but Huddersfield protested. He went across to the linesman, Mr. A. Cook (Sussex), and then pointed to the centre.

There is no shadow of doubt in my mind that the decision was wrong. Baily played the ball twice and Huddersfield should have been awarded an indirect free-kick.

There was no other player within fifteen yards of the ball when Baily played it the second time. The crowd broke into a roar and were still laughing about it as they left the ground.

Huddersfield refused to restart the game for at least a minute. As soon as the ball was in play the final whistle sounded.

When I spoke to the Huddersfield Chairman, Mr. H. Battye, he said 'We shall send a strong report to the League about it. But will that get us the point we have lost?'

He also said 'Mr. Barnes told me he did not think the same player had touched the ball twice.' Mr. J. Hirst-Wood, a Director, commented 'The law says a player may not play the ball twice from a corner kick. How can the referee award a goal?'

The 22,400 spectators might have seen Baily play the ball twice, but the referee was no doubt confused by being hit in the back by the ball – a penalty of the odd position he had taken up to watch the corner. Law 9 laid it down that the ball is in play if 'it rebounds off either the referee or linesman when they are in the field of play'. And Law 17, on corner kicks 'nor shall the kicker play the ball a second time until it has been touched or played by another *player*'.

There was no doubt Mr. Barnes erred, but it did not have the wide effects of that Leeds decision. Spurs did not win the title and Huddersfield were relegated – but by a three-point margin.

Players' own lack of knowledge of the rules has sometimes created entertaining situations. In the England *v* Scotland match of 1929 a freekick for 'steps' was awarded against the Scottish goalkeeper close to his line. Total confusion followed with the Scots under the mistaken impression they could not stand on the goal-line as they would not be ten yards away. So they lined up *behind* the Englishman taking the kick while the goalkeeper went to the far post to be ten yards distant. It should have been a gift goal. But instead of a gentle tap Wainscoat rolled the ball some yards to a colleague who was engulfed by the rush from behind. The Scots clearly beat the whistle in their dash, but that infringement of the rules saved them from the penalty of their ignorance of them.

A goal with far-reaching consequences was the one which got past Scotland's 'keeper in England's 1–0 win at Hampden Park in 1950. He had achieved so many fine saves that this was known as 'Cowan's match', even though Roy Bentley beat him at last with a flying header. That goal made England winners of the home championship. It also meant that Scotland declined to take part in the 1950 World Cup finals. They had been offered a place even as runners-up, but Scottish pride would only let them compete as champions. And not even Cowan could reach that killing thrust from the incisive Bentley which kept Scotland from their first venture into the World Cup. Perhaps they were better staying at home. At least they were spared England's humiliation of defeat by America.

It only took one goal too to bring Charles Williams an unusual distinction in 1901. He was the Manchester City goalkeeper whose lofty goalkick at Sunderland was helped on by a following wind, and the ball, touched by the other 'keeper, Doig, ended in the net. That was the first goal of its kind in League football. Recently Peter Shilton went one better, his massive clearance scoring direct against Southampton. And in a memorable Match of the Day commentary Ken Wolstenholme was busy explaining the new four-step rule interpretation with cameras focused on Pat Jennings, while his clearance scored unnoticed, bouncing over Stepney's head straight into Manchester United's goal. Perhaps the only goal which has not yet been scored is the one which would resolve the old conundrum: 'How do you score a goal in a League match and never go on the field of play?' Even this will happen some day. The traditional answer is that a man is substituted in the last few seconds with a corner due to be taken. He is told to take the kick and runs down outside the touchline to hit the corner left-footed from the right-hand side of the field, so his grounded foot stays out of play. The inswinger beats the goalkeeper and goes straight into the net. At once the whistle blows for full time. That sounded far-fetched until two International incidents brought it close to fulfilment. Kevin Hector came on in England's crucial World Cup game against Poland at Wembley with only seconds remaining, when Ramsey sent him out as substitute. In those seconds he was within an inch of scoring the goal which would have taken us to the Finals. And in April 1929 Scotland beat England when Cheyne of Aberdeen scored direct from a corner kick in the last two minutes – the only goal of the game. Some day the two incidents will happen together and the hypothetical puzzle become historic fact. At present it remains about the only way the goalscorers have not got the ball in the net.

Sixteen

Goalscoring Records

What is a goal worth? Herbert Chapman had a direct answer to that in 1925 when he bought Charles Buchan from Sunderland for Arsenal. Buchan was an outstanding inside forward, but to his sizeable fee Chapman added the bonus for Sunderland of £100 for every goal he scored during his first season. Fortunately for Arsenal's bank balance Buchan's goalscoring, 19 in League games and 3 in Cup matches, added only some two thousand pounds to the fee. Had he emulated Joe Payne of Luton he might have cost them £1,000 in an afternoon for Payne had a 10-goal tally against Bristol Rovers.

This is an account of that still unrivalled feat written in the less sensational style of 1936.

On April 14th Trevor Wignall of the *Daily Express* fixed his 'sportlight' on Luton's Joseph Payne. Yesterday's football man of the moment was Joseph Payne, deputy centre-forward of Luton Town. In a Third Division (South) match against Bristol Rovers he broke all records by scoring ten of his side's twelve goals.

The record was previously held by 'Bunny' Bell, now of Everton. Payne will probably not take it to heart if it is recorded that until Easter Monday 1936 he was one of the inconspicuous of Soccer. It is exactly two years since Payne became attached to the Luton Club. He started his football life as an amateur and it was when a junior with Bolsover Colliery that the eagle eye of a Luton scout fell on him. He was induced to turn professional and it was on Easter Monday 1934 that he had his first trial with the reserves. He was signed as a centre-forward, but it is a peculiarity that in his first four matches with the senior team he operated as a half-back.

Yesterday he made his fifth appearance with the first eleven and romance is added in that he gained his place as substitute for Boyd, who is on the injured list. Payne is not yet 22 years of age, stands 5 ft 10½ ins. in height and weighs over 12 stone. Which is the equivalent of pointing out that he is ideally moulded for a centre-forward.

Three of his goals were obtained in the first half and seven in the second – and nine were scored in succession.

The match report added further detail:

A referee's word, spoken after yesterday's game at Luton was over, meant a new name being stamped on soccer history. Joe Payne, deputy centre-forward of Luton Town, scored ten of his side's twelve goals against Bristol Rovers and set up the new individual record for the English League. But if referee T. J. Botham of Walsall had not been in such a good position to see Luton's seventh goal, Payne might not have broken the record. That vital goal came after 57 minutes. A centre from Rich was headed goalwards by Payne. The goalkeeper appeared to save with difficulty a split second before he was bundled into the net by another Luton forward.

When the game was ended it was thought that Payne had only equalled the record with nine goals. But the referee declared that for the seventh goal Payne's header had crossed the line before the goalkeeper stopped it.

Payne came into the side as a last minute change and in ninety historic minutes had helped Luton to their biggest win since the war. His goals came like this: 23 minutes – seized on long punt upfield that McArthur missed. Shot past advancing goalkeeper, Ellis. 40 minutes – Ellis pushed out a shot by Stephenson. Ball went to Payne. He tapped it in. 43 minutes – close range shot after Roberts had centred from the left. 49 minutes – Roberts–Stephenson run on the left wing. Payne met Stephenson's centre on the run and crashed it into the net. 55 minutes – centre from Rich. Payne headed the ball down to his feet and beat Ellis with snap shot. 57 minutes – that 'who scored it' scramble goal awarded to Payne after his header. 65 minutes – Godfrey passed to Stephenson. He cut through and his centre to Payne was perfectly made and perfectly taken. A hard-driven goal. 76 minutes – another Stephenson centre and another fine header that left Ellis helpless. 84 minutes – Stephenson forced a corner, took it himself and Payne headed his ninth. 86 minutes – scramble in the mud. Payne fell, but shot as he lay on the ground. Ball rolled in wide of the goalkeeper.

Roberts after thirty-two minutes and Martin after eighty-nine scored Luton's two remaining goals.

So in his first game as centre-forward for Luton Joe Payne achieved what now seems an untouchable record. An average player became suddenly unique. The bounce of the ball always has the last say over those who would forecast a logical result to a football match.

That record alone could not make Payne a great player, but a couple of seasons later he was to get a new total of 55 goals in a season in Third Division South. In the same season Ted Harston of Mansfield set an exactly similar record for the Third Division North, but Joe Payne is the only man who currently holds two major scoring records. And though he had little recognition he had a fine instinct for goals.

Payne did have one International for England. He scored twice in the 8–0 defeat of Finland in 1937, but was given no further chance. And though he was on Chelsea's staff at the end of the War they were aiming even higher with their sights on Lawton. So Payne has to be remembered by his records.

Christmas 1935 was a happy time for goalscorers with Ted Drake and Robert Bell setting records. Ted Drake had 7 in a First Division match at Villa Park on 14 December 1935. As Frank Coles wrote in the *Daily Telegraph*,

'How does it feel suddenly to be the hero of the whole world of football?' I asked Edward Drake an hour after he had equalled a 47-year-old football record by scoring seven goals in a First League match.

A very modest young man is Drake for all his forceful personality on the field. 'It just happened to be my day – and everything came off for me.' Certainly the ball ran kindly for Arsenal's leader in an astonishing game at Villa Park. At the same time I count myself extremely lucky to be one of the 60,000 witnesses of the finest centre-forward display seen for many years.

Drake was the complete footballer. Apart from deadly shooting, his ability to control the ball and beat an opponent when tackled – he mastered Griffiths many times – was quite exceptional.

He was also unorthodox. As long as he played the straightforward up-and-down game he knew he would be caught in Griffiths' stranglehold at third back. So Drake roamed from left-wing to right, waiting for the loose ball, which on this remarkable day seemed to be drawn to him like a needle to a magnet. Here is a brief catalogue of Drake's seven: 16 mins – Beasley passes forward to Drake, who,

from inside left, slips Griffiths and shoots through from 15 yards.
28 mins – a long upfield kick by Bastin. Drake races 20 yards with
Griffiths and Cummings challenging on each side. Just when the
centre-forward appears to be sandwiched he gets his right foot to the
ball which is in the net in a flash. A wonder goal. 33 mins – a Beasley
shot cannons off Blair's body and falls at Drake's feet 10 yards out.
An easy score. 46 mins – Drake nips between Griffiths and the goalkeeper when there seems to be no danger and flicks the ball into the
net from a fantastic angle. Goalkeeper Morton astonished. 50 mins –
Bowden rescues a ball from the side-line, passes back, and again all
is easy for Drake. 58 mins – Drake chases a loose-running ball at top
speed and crashes it into the net from 25 yards. 89 mins – Bastin
makes the opening and Drake completes it from 10 yards. In the
dressing-room afterwards the ball was presented to him by the Aston
Villa Directors.

The Villa, on the field and off, took their humiliating defeat with
fine sportsmanship. There was not one deliberate foul throughout
the match and no sign of ill-feeling.

It was the third time Villa had conceded 7 goals at home that season
and the defence had now given away 59 goals with eleven days still to go
to Christmas! Clearly, it was the kind of defence forwards would like to
find in their stocking, even though £25,000 had just been spent on five
new players who were indeed 'blooded' in their debut.

Ted Drake is as modest as ever – a lean and fit 12 stone, almost a
stone lighter than his best playing weight. The knees that took so many
knocks still pain him and he cannot sit for more than a few minutes
without restlessly moving his legs. That is the price that courageous
centre-forwards of his type had to pay for launching themselves so
bravely on goal.

'They were a reshuffled side which had not found its form. The backs
played so square, without the usual dog-leg cover, that Griffiths had no
support and there was always space to move into. I only had eight shots
at goal all afternoon and it was just one of those things that seven of
them went in. The eighth bounced down from the underside of the bar
and I was sure that was over the line too! The referee thought otherwise
and in those days that was good enough for us, so I had no complaint.'

Star players then were a part of the community, the folk heroes still in
close touch with their admirers. As Drake travelled happily home in the
Underground the fellow travellers crowded round to see the
autographed ball and congratulate him. Bold and clear is the signature

of the man he had made look foolish, the Villa centre-half. Griffiths was also the Welsh centre-half, a player who liked to attack. He was not given much chance to attack that day.

Those muddy winter grounds were ideal for the forceful goalscorers, with defenders finding it hard to run and goalkeepers grounded on their line or palming the heavy ball down into the forwards' path. And on Boxing Day Oldham Athletic's weak defence gave away 9 goals to Tranmere Rovers' dashing centre-forward, 'Bunny' Bell.

Tranmere were leading the Third Division North and the 12,000 crowd was by far the largest of the day for that Division. At the end the spectators rushed the pitch and carried Bell aloft on their shoulders in triumphal procession. They had reason to be happy. Seventeen goals were scored in that match, Woodward getting a couple and MacDonald and Urmson helping Tranmere's total to 13, equalling the record for the English League, with their 13–4 win.

Oldham can hardly have expected the deluge, for on Christmas Day they had just beaten Tranmere 4–1 at home. Bell had joined Tranmere five seasons before and was yet another centre-forward to be developed by the Club which had 'made' Dixie Dean for Everton and given 'Pongo' Waring to Aston Villa.

Oldham soon tired in the hard going and were no doubt a trifle dispirited to be 6 goals down after only twenty minutes.

The order of scoring was recorded as: Urmson 2 mins, Bell 7 mins, MacDonald 11 mins, Woodward 14 mins, Bell 16 mins, Bell 19 mins, Bell 33 mins, Brunskill (Oldham) 38 mins, Bell 40 mins. So it was 8–1 at half-time and poor Brunskill, who was injured early, saw five go in during the quarter of an hour it took to patch him up.

In aiming at a record score Tranmere became reckless in defence and the goals homed in at either end throughout the second half. Bell started as he left off, scoring again in the 46th minute. Thereafter it was Woodward 50 mins, Davis (Oldham) 53 mins, Bell 68 mins, Walsh (Oldham) 69 mins, Walsh (penalty) 71 mins. With two minutes to go Bell had only equalled the 7-goal record of Drake, of James Ross jnr of Preston in 1888 and of Whitehurst of Bradford City in a Third Northern match of 1929. But he ended with a flourish, scoring again in the 88th and 89th minutes, to hold the record until Payne took it from him. It was hardly surprising that the barrier in front of the dressing room broke under the surge of people as the final whistle went. There were a number of minor injuries as the joyous flood swept on to the pitch, but the reports of the day indicate that there would have been more serious accidents had the ground not been 'ankle-deep in mud'.

So Bell's day of triumph was a typically English football occasion with the centre-forward's strength and stamina as important as his skill. His qualities had attracted the scouts before, but the 9 goals hastened him on his way to Everton.

Joe Mercer played with him there and had this comment on his style. 'Bell was not a powerful shot and scored all his goals from close in. I cannot remember him scoring from more than twelve yards out. But he had a fine positional sense and was expert at glancing or side-footing the ball in.'

The Second Division's records are more recent.

In February 1955 all seemed well with our sport. On the first Wednesday of the month England's cricketers took the Ashes from Australia when Godfrey Evans thumped a ball from Keith Miller to Adelaide's distant square-leg boundary. Victory had been won by the tight bowling of Appleyard, Tyson, Statham, Bailey and Wardle, who so limited the scoring of the usually prolific Australians. But scoring was not similarly rationed over here. Three days later Tommy Briggs set a Second Division record with 7 goals in Blackburn's 8–3 win over Bristol Rovers. There had been little in the first half to prepare Ewood Park for such a one-sided finish. Indeed, Rovers had made most of the running, likely winners at half-time with a 3–2 lead. Briggs had scored only once, but he added 6 more in the second half as his forceful play found the gaps in a tiring defence.

Free scoring came naturally to Briggs and Blackburn that season, those goals already bringing his tally to 30, the Club's to 93, 30 more than any other in the Division. Eight goals was not out of the ordinary for them either, for they had taken 9 off Middlesbrough and had a 7 and three 5s in other matches.

And it was in February again two years later that the Second Division record was given another twist. Centre-forwards were expected to be the high scorers, but it was a winger who equalled Briggs' 7. Neville Coleman, Tim to his friends, had bought himself out of the R.A.F. three years earlier to play professional football. Now he joined the high-fliers of the game as Stoke beat Lincoln City 8–0. This was the day of the plunge with flooded grounds all over the country more like aquadromes than football pitches. A fast direct winger, the 25-year-old Coleman kept his head and his feet to take his League total for the season to 26 goals. It was another of those winter days when stamina is all important.

At International level only one British player has scored 6 goals, Joe Bambrick of Northern Ireland destroying Wales on a February day in

1930. Bambrick achieved this when marked by the Welsh captain, the legendary Fred Keenor of Cardiff. On 1 February Ireland beat Wales 7–0 and Bambrick turned the game into a wake for Finnigan, the Welsh goalkeeper. This Irish side had eight local players and only three 'Anglos' to add to the delight of the crowd and of the *Irish Daily Telegraph*, which exulted:

> Not since the International tournament was resumed after the war has Ireland achieved such a resounding victory. Phenomenal is the only way to describe the double hat-trick of Joe Bambrick, the Linfield centre. He left the opposing defence standing on occasion after occasion and was robbed of even greater harvest by the narrowest of margins. If he never came off in a Representative match before, this magical goal-getter – the most successful scoring opportunist who ever donned an Irish jersey – more than pulled up the arrears.
>
> He rose to the occasion and delighted the Irish crowd by the wizardry with which he hoodwinked the backs and made the Welsh goalkeeper with the Irish name a figure to excite sympathy, for it certainly was not Finnigan's fault that he was beaten so often.
>
> Bambrick, we are afraid, will have to suffer more than ever the penalty of fame and 'slip it to Joe' as a popular by-word will receive new impetus. The match has confirmed what has been confirmed more than once in Ireland's International story – that a team which failed in advance to arouse popular enthusiasm and at whose expense indeed some could not restrain cheap jibes, confounds the pessimists (and some official critics) and brings off a glorious, decisive and memorable victory.

Bambrick roved so successfully that it was the backs Hugh and Jones who came in for most criticism for failing to contain him, while Keenor, the centre-half who 'lost' Bambrick, was praised for his endeavours to get his own forwards moving.

Bambrick scored all the first 6, 2 in the first half and 4 in the second, despite the handicap of a leg injury to their Irish captain, M'Cluggage, of Burnley. But it was M'Cluggage who scored the last goal, beating the disheartened Finnigan with a 30-yard free-kick in the final minute. One of the other 'Anglos', Chambers of Bury, was the main provider for Bambrick, the tireless little right-winger making most of the openings. But at the end they were all 'slipping it to Joe'. As the paper recorded, 'Bambrick, now irrepressible, registered his fifth goal. As an opportunist he was in a class by himself and his colleagues played to him most unselfishly, imbued only with the idea of finding the surest method of scoring – by passing to Joe.'

The one time Keenor got in the game was in capturing the ball at the finish and getting it autographed by his team. Handing it over at the dinner that night he commented that he had played football for twenty years and been in twenty-five Internationals, but no one he marked had ever scored 6 against him before. He ended, 'I wish you the best of luck, Joe. You deserve it. I only wish that the goals may not go to your head, boy, and that you continue to score well for your team and country.' Bambrick – more or less embarrassed, as the account has it – stuttered his thanks, adding, 'If my head gets any bigger I will need to prick it with a pin to let the air out.' The likely size of Bambrick's head did not worry the League Managers and that record 6 goals soon had him playing English League football as well as increasing his goal tally for Ireland to 11, only 2 behind their outstanding goalscorer, Billy Gillespie of Sheffield United. And the Welsh team he had massacred held Scotland to a 1–1 draw at Hampden Park in their next match to prove they were no push-overs – nor even 'Keenor and ten others' as the Scots expected.

No player has matched Bambrick's effort but Willie Hall, the Tottenham inside forward, scored 5 goals in a home International. His day of triumph was 16 November 1938. That morning he read the papers giving his return to the side a lukewarm reception. 'Inside right must also have caused the selectors some hard thinking, although many had disagreed with the dropping of Hall after the Scottish League match. Hall had previously given a polished display against the Rest of Europe and Matthews for one must welcome his return.' He did indeed. So well did the two combine that they shared the honours of England's 7–0 win.

Ireland's captain, Cook of Everton, was the unfortunate left-back continually bemused by the Matthews double shuffle – deceived by the inward sway, then beaten by the dart past on the outside. Poor Cook never recovered from the bluff of Matthews' first move. After only five minutes he swayed as if to go inside Cook – and did so. The instant through pass left Lawton running unchallenged through the middle to rifle a spectacular shot into Twoomey's net.

Between the thirty-fourth and thirty-eighth minute Hall had the fastest hat-trick in International football. The first was made for him by Matthews' trickery and McMillen's miskick, the second driven home from Lawton's pass, the third slid in with the desperate Twoomey far off his line.

There was laughter mingled with the applause as Old Trafford saluted Hall's fourth goal, an overhead bicycle kick like that with which Denis Tueart was to win a Cup Final for Manchester City in 1976. It was Matthews who left Hall to tap in his fifth and Matthews whose sinuous dribble ended with a precise angled shot to give England a 7–0 victory. The game was won for England by the dominance of Willingham, Cullis and Mercer in mid-field, the combination of Hall and Matthews on the right.

'We have known Matthews as a fine player, sure in his control of the ball and beautifully balanced on his feet. This afternoon he reached the pinnacle, and at the close the crowd rose to him as one man to salute the player whose wizardry had them fascinated', was the *Daily Telegraph* comment.

Matthews had tested Ireland to destruction, but it was Hall, neat and sure in all he did, whose sharp responses put him in the record books.

Joe Mercer was making his England debut that day and his comment on Hall's performance is typically modest. 'That was the finest match I have *watched*. Willingham, Hall, and Matthews won it on their own. Stanley was at his peak then and when he was in form he was dazzling. He made the openings and Hall's finishing was crisp and assured.' Hall's skill won him some rough attention over the seasons; during the war he suffered thrombosis of the legs and both of them had to be amputated.

In 1973 Malcolm Macdonald, then of Newcastle, previously of Fulham and Luton, latterly of Arsenal, equalled Hall's 5 goals. The match was at Wembley and a World Cup qualifier. But in another sense the record rated with the 5s of Vaughton and Heggie in the nineteenth century. For the opponents, Cyprus, were almost as unsophisticated at World level as were Ireland when they first started to compete in the 1880s. Yet a Cup game is always demanding and no one other than 'SuperMac' was able to score that day in England's 5–0 win.

H. A. Vaughton of Aston Villa scored 5 against Ireland in the heaviest ever defeat of a British team. That 13–0 win was put in its proper perspective by Charles Alcock, F.A. Secretary and also a leading forward of the time. In his summary of the season in the *Football Annual* of 1883 he mentions neither score nor scorers, saying only 'The Irishmen are comparative novices at the game and have only this season had the courage to compete for international honours.'

Vaughton was one of the two left-wingers in the customary 6-man forward line of the day. Usually he was one of the right-wing pair and the *Football Annual's* comment on his ability underlines that the Irish were very unsophisticated to let him get 5. 'Plays on the right with Holden. Very unselfish and plays well for his side. Not a good shot at goal.'

His opposite winger was opposite also in character and a much more formidable player who scored regularly. Charlie 'Bam' (E. C. Bambridge) was the outstanding player of a footballing family and had 12 goals for England. Of him the *Annual* commented, 'Keeps up his reputation as one of the most brilliant forwards: Plays on the left; Very fast and a very sure shot at goal; Less selfish than he used to be.'

Charles Heggie's 5 against Ireland was scarcely more remarkable than Vaughton's. Up to February 1891, when they beat Wales 7–2 in Belfast, Ireland had conceded 157 goals in 25 Internationals against England, Scotland, and Wales. Over the whole period from 1882 their goalkeepers had let in more than 6 goals a match, while the Irish learnt the game. In 1886 Heggie did at least have a good goalkeeper to beat as Gillespie was rated 'brilliant', and had clearly had plenty of opportunity to show his skill. The *Football Annual* recorded, 'The meeting with Ireland was chiefly remarkable for the success of the Scotch centre, Heggie, who scored the majority of the goals which fell to his side.' The F.A. Cup has provided the most recent record of them all, the more surprising in a goal-starved decade. Ted MacDougall, the Scot whom Liverpool let go at nineteen, and who was then sold by York for only £10,000, made Cup history with 9 goals in Bournemouth's 11–0 defeat of Margate. That took him past 100 goals for Bournemouth in 122 matches and also gave him the individual goalscoring record in the Cup's long history.

A scoring record as late as 1971 is something of a freak and that November day was certainly an unhappy one for goalkeepers. In the League Everton put 8 past Southampton's Eric Martin, while Arsenal's Bob Wilson let in 5 at Wolverhampton where he had once played as an amateur.

So Margate's Chic Brodie had some to sympathise with him – but not Ted MacDougall: 'Manager John Bond has made me professional enough to want to score goals all the time. Margate may only be Southern League, but so far as I was concerned they were Cup opponents to be crushed – and the more I could score against them the better.' And score he did at regular intervals, stabbing the first one home after only two minutes when Brodie dropped the ball. After twenty minutes Mel Machin's searching cross was headed confidently home. Seven minutes later MacDougall's left-foot shot just bobbled over the line and he scored again as he headed in Scott's cross two minutes before the interval. The shaken Brodie dropped the ball once more in the fifty-seventh minute and once more MacDougall was loitering with intent to snatch a simple goal. The robbery continued with 4 in the last quarter of an hour taken from a tired and dispirited team. The sixth was a trifle fortunate, with Brodie parrying the shot but the ball still screwing over the line. The next was MacDougall's best as he outjumped everyone to glance in a corner. To complete his harvest festival there was a penalty, after Boyer had been brought down, and another close header from Machin's cross.

The record gave him helpful fame but it was another three and a half years before he took the field for his country against Sweden and scored Scotland's only goal of that drawn match.

Scotsman Jimmy McGrory had no rival as a goalscorer. Arthur Rowley took 619 matches to score his 434, but McGrory's League goals were at the rate of more than one a match, 410 in 408 games. His 8 against Dunfermline Athletic remain the highest individual score in a Scottish Division I game.

A mere 4,000 crowd watched Jimmy McGrory establish the Scottish First Division scoring record on 4 January 1928. Celtic beat Dunfermline Athletic, bottom of the table with only 8 points from 25 games, by 9–0 and McGrory scored 4 in each half.

The *Glasgow Herald* match report was as brief as goalkeeper Harris' glimpses of McGrory's shots. 'A very one-sided game was witnessed, Celtic having much the better of the exchanges all through. McGrory, their centre-forward, created a record for the Scottish First Division by scoring eight goals, four in each half, the other marksman being Thomson, who scored the fifth.'

Dunfermline had just been beaten 7–0 at home by Partick Thistle in their previous match so the margin of Celtic's victory was no surprise. But, as the newspaper commented, 'The match will become historic for the fact that their centre-forward McGrory by scoring eight goals made a new individual record for the Scottish Senior League, the previous best being six goals. In achieving this McGrory was assiduously served by his colleagues, but nevertheless showed skill and marksmanship that further confirmed his title as the most dangerous and successful leader of attack in the country.'

For McGrory there was one unique feature about it. His reputation was as an outstanding header of the ball. But all those eight were scored with his feet. For him that was a record indeed.

Seventeen

The Penalty Takers

Some players prefer to blast their penalties, some to stroke them. The best, like Houghton or Ramsey, combined firmness with accuracy. Whatever the method there is a compelling fascination in the kick. Basil Easterbrook looks at some of the stranger penalties and some of the most crucial.

It was a June Saturday and perfect weather for watching cricket. Normally at this time of year I would have been doing exactly that, but 1947 was no normal year. Winter waited until February before it struck, then it bit hard and it lingered. For something like two months Britain was in the grip of a miniature ice age and sporting activity was virtually at a standstill. Football fixtures piled up and with a Government ban on mid-week soccer still in force as the economy tried to recover from the Second World War the league programme was extended to 14 June.

On reflection it was perhaps a suitable day for a hat-trick of penalties to be scored for league football has never before been played in mid-June and thankfully never since. The match was a Second Division local 'Derby' at Saltergate between Chesterfield and Sheffield Wednesday. The Owls had had the worst season in their history up to this point, mercifully having no knowledge of the humiliation which was to come to Hillsborough just over a quarter of a century later. In 1947 they missed relegation to the Third Division (North) by 3 points. Chesterfield, on the other hand, needed 2 points from this final fixture to have a chance of finishing fourth and beating their previous best of fifth in 1904–5. Chesterfield's prospects did not look good. Newcastle United, their rivals for the talent money which fourth place carried in those days, were away to Newport County, who had conceded 131 goals in 41 matches. The previous September Newcastle had beaten Newport 13–0 at St. James's Park and but for a missed penalty United would have set a League record for a winning margin.

Now the penalty spot was to play a far more dramatic role in deciding fourth position in Chesterfield's favour. The score from Somerton Park was a real coupon smudger: Newport County 4, Newcastle United 2. Chesterfield beat Wednesday by an identical score. In the fifty-sixth, sixty-fourth and seventy-seventh minutes Wednesday incredibly conceded three penalties and Chesterfield went from 1–2 down to 4–2 up in twenty-one minutes. Full-back George Milburn, completing his nineteenth League season, did not give Wednesday goalkeeper Roy Smith a chance with any of the three penalties.

Milburn's favourite expression when addressing someone else was: 'kid'. After the match he said to an understandably po-faced Smith, 'Well, kid, I guess you know now that lightning never strikes in the same place twice.' Milburn, uncle of the even more famous 'wor Jackie' of Newcastle United and England fame, hit the first penalty high to the right of Smith; the second was also to his right but along the ground; the third was to his left into the other corner. Milburn had become only the third player to score a hat-trick of penalties in a League match. The late Billy Walker, one of the truly great inside forwards, first did it for Aston Villa against Bradford City in 1921. Alf Horne of Lincoln City was next when he successfully tucked away three spot kicks against Stockport County in 1935. Since Milburn the penalty hat-trick has certainly been achieved three times – by Charlie Mitten for Manchester United against Aston Villa at Old Trafford in March 1950, by Ken Barnes for Manchester City against Everton at Maine Road in December 1957 and by Trevor Anderson for Swindon Town against Walsall at the County Ground, Swindon, on 24 April 1976.

In October 1949, only two years after the Chesterfield affair, Sheffield Wednesday gave away three penalties in a match against Grimsby Town. Stan Lloyd, the Mariners' outside right, scored from the first and third, but McIntosh, Wednesday's goalkeeper, managed to push the second against a post.

Even rarer than a penalty hat-trick is a hat-trick of penalty misses, but it has happened. The first time was at Turf Moor on 13 February 1909, when Burnley were awarded four penalties in a Second Division match. Walter Scott, Grimsby's goalkeeper, was beaten by the third but saved the first, second and fourth. The next instance was a First Division game on 27 January 1912 when Eli Fletcher twice and James

Thornley failed from the spot for Manchester City against Newcastle United. It happened again on 6 March 1924 when Crewe Alexandra registered nought out of three in a Third North match against Bradford Park Avenue.

The hush that settles over a crowd whenever a spot kick is about to be taken indicates how charged with drama is the penalty. It is precisely the same emotion as when two men, hands hovering over their gun belts, face one another in the deserted street of a Western horse opera. It is the ultimate one-to-one confrontation.

Few people realise that the first three seasons of the Football League were played with no such thing as a penalty kick. Nor indeed was there a penalty area marked on the pitch. For any foul committed in front of goal the referee simply awarded a free kick. Oddly enough, or perhaps understandably in a period when 'hacking' was considered to be the norm, it was not the tripping or bringing down near goal in good positions of the man in possession which really incensed clubs robbed of vital points. It was when a player other than the goalkeeper palmed or punched the ball off the line or over the bar that brought an increasing flow of written protest to the offices of the Football Association. It was the secretary of the Irish Football Association who came up with the solution. Infringements in front of goal should be punished by the awarding of a penalty kick. What, he was asked, did he mean exactly by the term penalty kick? He replied, 'A free shot at goal with only the goalkeeper allowed to defend.' And so in 1891 the first penalty area made its appearance, extending right across the width of the field, marked by a line twelve yards from the goal line. Any offence within that area brought the award of a penalty kick, but there was no penalty spot. The kick could be taken on the actual line and anywhere along that line with the opposing players obliged to stand six yards back. Another important difference to the penalty kick as we know it was an absence of limitation on the goalkeeper's movement until after the ball had been kicked. He could move about or advance towards the penalty-taker to try to upset his concentration and his aim.

Although evolution swiftly and smoothly changed the pitch markings until they became familiar to contemporary eyes nothing could change the tension and impact of shock at the awarding of a spot kick. Penalty! Is there a more emotive word in the game?

Only the fact that it was war-time prevented a match at Selhurst Park in 1941 developing into a major soccer sensation after the referee awarded Crystal Palace a penalty which Brentford refused to accept. They walked off the field and after a moment's hesitation the Palace players and the referee followed them. As it was war-time the referee did not abandon the match as he certainly would today. He decided on diplomacy and after talking to both teams the game was restarted fifteen minutes later. In the early 1930s Craig, the Plymouth goalkeeper, was frequently called on to take spot kicks for Argyle. The same thing happened at Birmingham in February 1946 when Don Welsh, Charlton's captain, called up 'keeper Sam Bartram to take a spot kick. Bartram had taken three penalties while guesting for York City and scored each time in war-time matches. This one he sent against the bar and was then obliged to make a mad dash the length of the pitch to get back on his own line before Birmingham could put the ball between the posts!

There was an odd penalty incident at White Hart Lane in September 1958 when Spurs beat Wolves 2–1. In the thirty-sixth minute Broadbent was brought down by Hopkins and a penalty awarded. Slater beat Hollowbread with a low shot from the spot but the referee noticed that two or three over-eager Wolves players had moved forward before the kick was taken. Slater was ordered to take it again but this time he shot high and Hollowbread brought down the 48,000 house by tipping the ball over the bar. This time a Spurs player moved too soon and the referee demanded the kick be taken a third time. Billy Wright wisely replaced Slater and gave the job to Clamp, and though Hollowbread got his fingertips to the ball he could not keep it out.

This was nothing compared to two amazing stories from the Eastern Counties League within two months of each other. In November 1950 at Clacton's Old Road Ground referee E. H. Morrison gave Spurs 'A' a penalty. The kick was taken five times before Morrison was satisfied the goalkeeper had not moved. This is what happened:

1. George Ludford shoots but goalkeeper Ken Starling punches out; 2. Ludford shoots over the bar; 3. Ludford shoots, Starling punches away. Exit Ludford, enter E. Higgins of the Spurs ground staff; 4. Higgins shoots, scores but is made to take the kick yet again; 5. Higgins scores again. 'Goal' said the referee.

After all that the game was abandoned owing to fog with Spurs 'A' leading 4–1! Seven weeks later in Jaunuary 1951 Lowestoft's right-half Peter Moody made five attempts to score from a penalty against Newmarket Town. Three times the referee ordered the spot kick to be retaken because Lowestoft players moved. The fourth time a Newmarket player offended. And the fifth? Moody's shot was saved by goalkeeper Bloomfield.

There may well exist more bizarre penalty situations in more minor competitions but the point has been well enough made.

There was a unique happening in a Scottish League match in 1910 between Motherwell and the now defunct Third Lanark, whose home, Cathkin Park, Glasgow was almost in the shadow of world-famous Hampden Park. The goalkeepers of both teams scored from penalties – an incredible 'double' which has never been repeated in any British competition of senior standing.

On Boxing Day 1935 Tranmere Rovers defeated Oldham Athletic in a Third North match at Prenton Park by 13–4. Seventeen goals represents the highest aggregate score in any Football League fixture since the competition began in 1888 but Tranmere forfeited the distinction of being the only club to reach 14 because their No. 9, 'Bunny' Bell, missed a penalty, despite scoring 9 times himself.

A penalty is always a moment of high drama whenever it happens but it tends to be rather a case of heaping Pelion upon Ossa when it decides the destination of the F.A. Cup in the dying seconds of the Cup Final. It happened at Stamford Bridge in 1922, the last Final to be played at a venue other than Wembley Stadium. After 89 minutes the battle of Huddersfield Town and Preston North End was without a goal. Town made the last attack of the match and their No. 11, W. H. Smith, was tripped as he cut into the box. Billy Smith took the kick himself, scored, and the match was over.

Sixteen years later there was an amazing reversal of fortune when the same two teams met at Wembley in 1938. The game was already assured of a line in the record books as the first of Wembley's sixteen Finals to go to extra time. All but 30 seconds of this had been used up and nothing seemed more certain than that a replay would be needed for the first time in the Cup Final since 1912. As at Chelsea's ground in 1922 neither team had been able to score. The last attack was mounted, but this time it was Preston who came surging forward. As Mutch, North End's stocky little inside forward, moved into the area George Young, the Huddersfield centre-half, brought him down. Ever after Young insisted that Mutch, a considerably smaller man than himself, had fallen over his thigh but his protestations of innocence are purely academic for the referee awarded a penalty. As at Stamford Bridge in 1922, so at Wembley in 1938 – the man who was fouled was entrusted with the job of converting the spot kick. George Mutch hit a rising drive and for a fraction of a second it looked as if he had either aimed in the reach of Hesford or too high. In the event the ball just scraped past Hesford's groping fingers and under the bar. Preston had gained a revenge that was so historic and so apt it could hardly have been more satisfying.

The concession of penalties has cost teams much, but the missing of penalties has more than once affected the long-term future of a club. At the end of the 1923–4 season it appeared Cardiff City were going to take the Football League Championship out of England only fourteen years after becoming a professional organisation. Their only rivals were Huddersfield Town and it was all to play for on the last day of the season. Town won their fixture but Cardiff only drew theirs after missing a penalty. That meant the title had gone to Yorkshire by the merest fraction of decimals. The final records of the clubs were: Huddersfield Town Played 42 Won 23 Drawn 11 Lost 8 Goals For 60 Against 33 Points 57. Cardiff City Played 42 Won 22 Drawn 13 Lost 7 Goals For 61 Against 34 Points 57. It was the start of Huddersfield's great hat-trick of championships. Ten years later Huddersfield were runners-up to Arsenal but Cardiff City, bottom of the Third Division South, had to go cap in hand to the League and seek re-election – a bitter moment for a club that had won the Cup only seven years before.

In the spring of 1955 'Nobby' Noble of Rotherham United missed a penalty at Port Vale and that single kick cost his side not only promotion to Division One but the Second Division championship! This was how the table looked at the end of the season:

		P	W	D	L	For	Agst	Pts
1	Birmingham City	42	22	10	10	92	47	54
2	Luton Town	42	23	8	11	88	53	54
3	Rotherham United	42	25	4	13	94	64	54

Birmingham and Luton were promoted, Rotherham stayed down and never again did they look remotely capable of bringing First Division football to homespun Millmoor.

Might Cardiff have dominated the Football League scene for many years if they had scored that solitary spot kick? Could Rotherham be justifying their nickname 'The Merry Millers' and making life awkward at the top for the more fashionable, wealthier clubs to this very day? Probably not, for as Voltaire observed, 'God is always on the side of the big battalions', but down in the valleys and among the depressing heavy industrial complex that is the heart of Rotherham you will still find a grey head or two shaking in regret and discussing with anyone prepared to listen the might-have-beens. As Harold Macmillan said with equal truth and an absence of Voltaire's cynicism 'Old men do *not* forget'.

Eighteen

Top of the World

In Helsinki before the 1952 Olympics when we went out for our first training session all eyes kept straying to the next pitch. There the Hungarians were practising, and such was their control, their tricks with the ball, that it seemed to be a different game they were playing. So it was no great surprise when they won that competition, or when they beat England a year later. Yet for others it was difficult to believe that English football might have been overtaken. This was Frank Coles' comment in the *Daily Telegraph*: 'The Hungarians are nimble of foot and mind. They will win the Olympic title if they can overcome the winners of the 5–5 drawn game between Russia and Yugoslavia. How would this copy-book team fare against, say, an English First Division side fighting for points for weeks on end? My answer is they would be left struggling hopelessly.'

The entertaining part of that misappreciation is the thought that the Hungarians had no hard grind, no lengthy programme of matches. Of that team Puskas played in 84 Internationals for Hungary and scored 85 goals, almost double the English record.

Even the Final did not impress Frank Coles. 'There was so much hand-wringing and hair-tearing as Hungary beat Yugoslavia in the Final. There was so much aimless dashing and pointless kicking that the match in British eyes was a joke and in poor taste at that.'

The joke was on us when both Hungary and Yugoslavia had beaten England within two years, with almost the same teams as played in the Olympics.

Even in 1952 Olympic soccer had no relation to 'amateurism' or 'taking part'. It was a mini World Cup with all the East European teams putting out their full national sides, which had trained together far more intensively than any England teams.

In the same Olympics the Russian team was their full-strength side and that 5–5 draw in Tampere one of the most unusual games. Yugoslavia were leading 5–1 with only thirteen minutes to go in a match refereed by one of the best English officials, Arthur Ellis. In those final minutes the Russian centre-forward, Bobrov, completed a brilliant hat-trick which earned a replay, won 3–1 by Yugoslavia. When the Yugoslavs scored their 5, joy was unconfined with the hugging holding up the play. Despite their remarkable recovery the Russians were quite impassive, giving no sign of elation even when they scored their fifth and equalising goal with a bare two minutes left.

Bobrov had been one of the stars in the Moscow Dynamo team which played four matches in England at the war's end.

That 1945 team had as high a work rate as Ramsey's men and the speed with which they shuttled from defence to attack so unnerved Cardiff that Dynamo won 10–1. They also drew 3–3 with Chelsea and then beat an Arsenal side with some impressive guest players, such as Stanley Matthews, by 4–3. At once the Russians issued a communiqué claiming victory over England – which was not far wrong. The game, however, was played in thick fog which also seemed to envelop the Russian referee Latychev, so the result, like the communiqué, was not to be taken too seriously.

The Olympics still seems a fruitful source of misunderstanding. Poland were Olympic champions when they knocked England out of the World Cup in 1973. Many writers therefore kept referring to them as 'amateurs', as if they were handicapped part-timers. Nothing could have been more misleading about the team which finished third in the World Cup, even though their best forward, Lubanski, was injured in the game with England, and took no part in the Finals. In preparation the Polish team had training programmes which started in 1971 and involved 150 days' training and 39 matches. Some part-timers! And it is meaningless to call a team which has such outstanding forwards as Lato, and Gadocha, and Deyna 'amateurs'.

A quarter of a century ago soccer in the Olympics was already what the rest of it is fast becoming – a showpiece of national chauvinism, an extension of politics by other means. The sooner the hypocrisy is ended and the Olympic Games are recognised as a contest between the best in the world the better.

The Hungarian team made the deepest impression on me of any national forward line, with Puskas, and the 'golden head' Kocsis, the outstanding scorers. No other national forward line has matched their three-year brilliance. The only better line was that expensive merging of all the talents at Real Madrid. There were forwards of such individual skill that tactics hardly mattered. The likes of Di Stefano, Puskas, Gento and Kopa had to be left free to do their own thing. And never did they do it better than at Hampden on 8 May 1960. Canario by then had succeeded Kopa on the right wing and that fine inside forward, Del Sol, completed an outstanding attack.

This was the day Real beat Eintracht 7–3 to win their fifth successive European Cup Final, having monopolised the competition since its start in 1955. And such was the manner of their victory that it has a place in the *Official History of Scottish Football*. Scotland had cause to know just how good was Real's play, for in the two legs of the semi-final Eintracht had beaten Rangers 12–4, scoring six times in each leg. And Real put Eintracht to the sword, as John Rafferty records in that history.

> There were 127,621 at the Final, the biggest crowd ever at a European Cup tie. They saw what was the best game of football played until then and there will never be many better. They were moved to ecstatic appreciation. Never in Hampden's history have there been more emotional scenes than when Real Madrid, in their white, cavorted round Hampden's field in their lap of honour. All the desirable football skills had been on view and those legendary characters, Di Stefano, Puskas, and Gento, whom they had known about from television and newspapers, came to life before them and larger than life.
>
> During a game which beat out a steady rhythm of satisfaction for the full ninety minutes they thrilled to the haughty generalship of Di Stefano, to the technical magnificence, cool ingenuity, and precise shooting of Puskas, to the flashing speed of Gento.
>
> Around them were the other great craftsmen, Del Sol, Canario, Santamaria, and the rest. Real were no ordinary team. They were a collector's team with treasures gathered from all the football world. Their problem was to select the best of the best.

To win the European Cup five times in succession was a true measure of Real's supremacy. No other club side has been so far beyond the reach of chance or the ball's bad bounce.

Not even Hungary's master side could match that sustained and effortless superiority. As with the Austrian 'Wunderteam' of the thirties, Hungary's run of success ended prematurely in the World Cup. It is one of football's ironies that perhaps the greatest of all national teams failed to take the Jules Rimet Trophy. And that they lost the final to the team they had beaten 8–3 in their group. Germany were no doubt taking that preliminary game at a training canter as they were certain to qualify. But no side can accept such a drubbing without some fight and in truth they were merely bemused by the Hungarians' brilliance, baffled by their tactics. At least they fought hard enough to cripple the central figure in Hungary's attack, forcing Puskas off the field with an ankle injury. Puskas later claimed that Liebrich's tackle was a deliberate foul. Certainly it benefited Germany, for when they met again in the final Puskas was still not fully fit.

At first that seemed hardly to matter for Hungary had scored twice in the first eight minutes with Puskas and Czibor slipping their shots past Turek. But very little else was to pass the German goalkeeper and when he was beaten the shots slapped against the post or were cleared off the line by Kohlmeyer. And as the German defence steadied, Fritz Walter organised the quick counter-attack. From his pass Morlock slid home the first German goal and before half-time left-winger Rahn, a player much like Billy Liddell, had forced in the equaliser from a corner.

There was mounting desperation now among the Hungarians as Turek frustrated them time and again with acrobatic saves. With just five minutes left Bozsik made one of his rare errors. Schaeffer seized on the misplaced pass and sent an instant ball to his target man, Fritz Walter, available in space as ever. Walter's centre was pushed out but there was Rahn to shoot home. It was not like the Hungarians to go quietly. As they raged back at the German goal Puskas reasserted himself at last and seemed to have shot home a magnificent goal. But a controversial off-side signal from the Welsh linesman, Mervyn Griffiths, ruled it out.

Still Turek had to make another dramatic save from Czibor before the band could play *Deutschland über Alles* as German spirit finally triumphed over Hungarian skill. The Germans were rated lucky, but they had found a method that was to keep them at the top and win the Cup again for them twenty years later. It was based on strong wing play, a goal poacher in the middle, constructive intelligence in the centre of the field and disciplined strength in defence.

Hungary's great team was an accidental growth of great talents flowering together, but it was carefully nurtured by the State with the players being developed together in the Army team, Honved. There has been no similar burgeoning of ability since and it was politics which finally dissipated that team. At the Olympic Games in Helsinki there was a separate village built for the Iron-Curtain countries, since Russia did not want their athletes sullied by contact with the West. Among the usual crop of world records in the games was one by a Hungarian hammer-thrower, Czermath. In our village the story went that he received a telegram from fellow workers on his collective which read, 'Congratulations on throwing the hammer further than it has ever been thrown before, now throw the sickle after it.'

The Hungarians had a gallant try before the next World Cup and the failure left Puskas and others to seek their fortune elsewhere in Europe, while their countrymen were beaten back into obedience to the imperial Soviet.

Politics also deprived Hungary of the enjoyment of at least one trophy despite the defeat by Germany. That remarkable header of a ball, Sandor Kocsis, set a record for the finals with 11 goals in all and qualified to be first holder of the special cup presented by Mexico for the leading scorer in the competition. The Hungarians objected to Kocsis accepting it as it was contrary to team spirit and smacked of the 'Cult of the individual' which was currently under attack in Russia's political doctrine.

It was a pity there wasn't a team-scoring cup. Hungary had averaged almost $5\frac{1}{2}$ goals a game compared to the 2 of the other fifteen countries. They had the misfortune to miss the trophy that mattered and yet they still proved themselves the greatest scoring machine put together by any nation.

Brazil was to put that claim to the test four years later when they won the Cup in Sweden. A front four of Garrincha, Vava, Pelé and Zagalo, backed by Didi, is as near the perfect forward line as one can hope and runs the Hungarians close. It was good enough to beat the host country 5–2 in another classic final, which lacked only the close challenge of Germany's win. Yet like the Germans the Brazilians had to fight back against adversity. Before the game most of us critics had forecast a Brazilian win, *unless* the Swedes had the luck to play in the rain or the skill to score the first goal, shattering the confidence of their flamboyant opponents. It rained and Brazil had to cope with a slippery surface to which they were little accustomed. And it was the tall, elegant Liedholm who scored the first goal, with Stockholm reverberating to the applause. But at the end the Brazilian commentator behind me was making as much noise on his own. Throughout the afternoon his high-pitched voice came ever closer to hysteria as Garrincha, Vava, and Pelé twisted the Swedish defence to destruction. And with Brazil leading 4–2 the torrent of words had become a single exultant chant '*Bra*-zil, *Bra*-zil,' shouted so loud he seemed to have no need of wireless to be heard back home. The final goal left even him stunned to momentary silence by its breathtaking brilliance, as Pelé outwitted and outjumped the outnumbering defenders to steer home Zagalo's deep centre. The 17-year-old prodigy had scored already, a goal that even better demonstrated the full range of his skill. On the edge of the area he called imperiously for the ball from left-back Nilton Santos, chested down the pass, bounced it on his thigh to lob it over a challenger, then slid his shot inches inside the post.

The signs of greatness were clear enough, but Pelé was not the central figure in Brazil's win. After that first goal it was Garrincha who drove them to take charge. His dazzling dribbles had defeated France in the semi-final and there were two men now detailed to watch him. That made no difference to the 'little bird' who hummed past as if they weren't there. And as he jinked clear of the two of them, that sure finisher, Vava, came sliding in to sweep the crosses home.

Garrincha's misshapen legs, one bowed, one bent, carried him past tacklers with bewildering ease and his finishing could be as deadly as his dribbling. When Brazil knocked England out in the quarter-final in Chile in 1962, Greaves, scorer of his side's goal, in the 3–1 defeat, felt that he would have been on the winning side but for the power of Garrincha's shooting. And in Sweden he was the destructive force, the whirlwind spirit of Brazil's victory against a team described by their manager George Raynor as a little slow. Certainly they were not fast enough to keep up with him, and Garrincha certainly was in the class of Matthews and Finney, or even of the two combined.

Pelé was not yet the star of Brazil, nor of the competition. Kopa and Fontaine of France were the strikers who kept scoring the goals. Clever little Raymond Kopa worked the openings and the long-striding, hard-hitting Juste Fontaine gathered the goals – 13 of them, more even than Kocsis, and still a record.

The tired Irish side were beaten 4–0 in the quarter-finals and Fontaine had 2 of the goals. Scotland earlier felt the power of his boot, as his and Kopa's goals finally dismissed their chance of qualifying from their group. They lost 1–2 with John Hewie slamming a late penalty against the post. But twice Fontaine had sent the orange ball slapping against their bar and Scotland were fortunate to stay in with a chance so late in the game. Fontaine had come from Morocco to take Kopa's place in the Rheims club. And there was little to choose between the two.

South American football was now in the ascendancy. Uruguay had won the competitions of 1930 and 1950, but Brazil was to go one better.

There had been exciting South American forwards before. The 'Black Diamond', Leonidas da Silva, was the leading goalscorer of the 1938 World Cup and the hero of a remarkable 6–5 win over Poland in that competition. Leonidas, with his blazing pace and supreme confidence, had scored four times and four times Willimowski had answered with goals, the Polish inside a striking contrast with his blond hair and elegant style. As Leonidas warmed to his game he had thrown away his boots for greater freedom, but with the laws then specific about footwear the referee had ordered him to put them on again.

There had been Brazil's fine inside trio of Zinzinho, Ademir and Jair who came so close to winning in 1950. There had been Uruguay's tall, gangling Schiaffino, the pale, melancholy inside-left with his telepathic passing, his close control. And it was Uruguay who had a winger better even than Sweden's deadly pair of Kurt Hamrin and 'Nacka' Skoglund. Little Alcide Ghiggia was in Garrincha's class and as oddly shaped. There was no sign of the athlete in his frail, thin limbs or his hunched shoulders. Yet he was a master of the change of pace that catches defenders flat-footed. One moment he would be brooding over the ball, the next he would have darted clear with explosive speed. His skill helped Uruguay to the 1950 Final, and his power of shot then won the World Cup from Brazil in their own capital. It was Ghiggia who helped Uruguay back into that game, his pass letting Schiaffino cancel out Friaca's goal. And it was Ghiggia who sent the winner searing past Barbosa's fingertips to win a Final refereed by Mr George Reader of Southampton, who had been taken off the League list as too old, but whose schoolmaster's authority and good humour kept this passionate game under tight control.

These were great players all, like Kubala of Spain, Sweden's Gunnar Nordhal, and Italy's Boniperti, who nearly tested England to destruction in that 8–goal draw which preceded Hungary's famous victory. But now came the unique player. In Leonidas Brazil had produced the forward with the clean cutting edge, the 'Black Diamond' who sliced through the hardest defence. Now they had the player without price, the 'Black Pearl', Edson Arantes do Nascimento. Fortunately for writers and commentators the world over he preferred a shorter title. 'I am Pelé' identifies him wherever football is played, even if they call him 'Pellay' in America in the twilight of his career, or 'Pelly' in Liverpool, where they watched him hacked out of the 1966 World Cup. But everywhere the name is spoken with affection, except by those who had to mark him. Inevitably Pelé was paid the supreme tribute of the great forward – World Cup managers marked him for destruction. He was cut down in Chile in 1962 and the hatchet men were as ruthlessly efficient in England four years later. There the contract went to Zhechev of Bulgaria and Vicente and Morais of Portugal. The killer thrust came from Morais, who missed with one scything kick, but flailed again to have Pelé carried off to sit disconsolate, a red blanket draped round him, as the doctor patched him up. He had the spirit to limp back, but for Brazil it was now a losing battle with Pelé crippled.

The agony should be remembered along with the ecstasy, for a forward like Pelé is going to have much to endure. After 1966 he did indeed contemplate refusing to play again in the harsh competition of the World Cup. Fortunately he underwent instead the hard physical training which prepared Brazil to match the strongest physical sides in winning the World Cup yet again in Mexico in 1970. There he was still the king, the man around whom Brazilian plans still centred. Because he was not at ease with Manager Saldanha, Pelé's team mate of 1958, Mario Zagalo, was given the job. And before the finals the Brazilian officials were saying 'Pelé has set his mood. Everything has been timed to come to its peak at the right moment. We are ready to explode.'

And explode they did with Pelé as their atomic power. He had always hankered for a unique goal, one no one else could match – ever. He was to miss it by inches against Czechoslovakia and to inspire from England's Gordon Banks the save which cannot be matched – ever. Banks, caught covering the near post, hurled himself across goal and in a blur of action scooped out Pelé's forceful, downward header, which seemed yards beyond his reach.

Against Czechoslovakia Pelé, well inside his own half, glimpsed goalkeeper Viktor standing nonchalantly on the edge of his area. With a short backlift and no hint of warning Pelé sent a 50-yard shot effortlessly over Viktor's head as he backed desperately for his goal, then spun anxiously to see the ball graze past the post. That indeed would have been the most memorable of the 1,216 goals he had scored before coming back from retirement to join New York Cosmos in June 1975, to help promote football in America.

The thousandth goal in top-class football was a memorable occasion for Pelé, even though match and goal were undistinguished by his standards. Playing for Santos against Vasco da Gama on 19 November 1969 he kept the 75,000 spectators in suspense until eleven minutes from the end. In the first half Pelé hit a post and missed a clear chance. In the second the score was 1–1 when he made a typical burst into the penalty area and was as typically tripped. Referee Amaro de Lima gave the penalty and Rildo, the Santos captain, stepped up to take it. He soon changed his mind as the crowd chanted 'Pelé, Pelé'. Under the floodlights Pelé drove his shot low past Andreade and the Stadium was aglow with emotion. Andreade stripped off his jersey to reveal a silver shirt with 1,000 emblazoned across it. He was as well prepared for defeat as Ma Lizzie Carter for victory, when she pulled back her long coat to show the world a shirt inscribed 'Jimmy's Won' as her son's American Presidential victory was confirmed.

Brazil's President received Pelé as part of his triumphal celebratory tour. Four days after his feat Pelé's State Governor unveiled a monument to him, an imprint of that lethal right foot. Only a hard-hearted referee spoilt that day, marring the Governor's tribute by sending Pelé off for 'disrespect' after twenty minutes of the match which followed. To the local crowd the referee was the man guilty of disrespect, for Pelé was their idol 'without fear and without reproach'.

Pelé had surprising speed and elasticity for one who is so thickset, with neck, body and thighs swelling with muscle. In 1970 he was put at the 'fat man's' table to watch his weight in training. But it is his combination of strength, speed, and athleticism which made him so formidable. There was also the intuition. A religious man who was upset when the more extravagant christened him 'God', he genuinely felt, like boxer Rocky Marciano, that 'someone up there loves me'. He said, 'God has given some extra instinct for the game. Sometimes I can take the ball and no one can foresee any danger. Then in two or three seconds there is a goal.'

When I heard that, my mind went back to watching Matthews create a goal against Scotland in two or three seconds when, with the field spread before me, I could see no danger. Both had this seventh sense. 'Sometimes I can make goals happen out of nothing. It makes me humble because this is a talent God gave me. He made me a footballer, and he keeps me a footballer.' That is the greatest scorer of them all's own epitaph on himself. There was indeed something of the missionary about Pelé who, with his Santos club, had helped popularise the game in so many developing countries. And he still had one giant task to perform. Zeal for football, and the need for money after business ventures turned sour, brought him back from his first retirement to accept an offer by Cosmos of New York. Pelé was to do more for stimulating soccer in the United States in a couple of seasons than others had done in two decades. His attraction was universal and he charmed Americans as he had charmed so many others. The final farewell to this modest superstar, who had scored some 1,300 goals at about a goal a game, was an emotional occasion in New York with Pelé playing one half for Cosmos and one for Santos. The world-wide tributes acclaimed his status.

When Pelé was eliminated from the 1966 World Cup, Portugal's Eusebio, the competition's leading scorer, was hailed as a new and perhaps greater successor. Certainly he had the same remarkable range of ability and an even more spectacular shot. The master was not unduly impressed, however. Pelé's comment was, 'Eusebio is a great player, but he needs others to make things happen for him.'

That was fair comment, but it was really Eusebio's love of the spectacular which prevented him rivalling Pelé. When Pelé sought a great goal he tried to manufacture it out of the impossible, like that fantastic thrust at Viktor. For Eusebio every goal had to be dramatic and that led him to squander some simple ones. Manchester United should be grateful for that weakness. When he was through with only Stepney to beat to bring Benfica the Cup he had to risk a great booming, triumphal shot. It was not enough to win the game. It had to be won with a style that would identify the victory as Eusebio's. So that flourish, that drawn-back leg, gave Stepney the chance to set himself for a remarkable save, leaving United to heave themselves back off the floor. None of the cool killers like Pelé, Law or Greaves would have missed that chance. They would have gone gliding round Stepney, or slid the ball quietly and accurately past him before he was ready. A simple goal, the press would have called it, but the match would have been won. Instead there was the spectacular near-miss – and that sums up Eusebio against the world's best.

Yet what thrilling goals he did score; how impertinent it seems to criticise a man who brought such excitement into the game. I first saw him at Wembley in October 1961. He had won his first cap for Portugal a few days earlier, aged nineteen, and had scored with one of those stinging shots which were to be his speciality.

At Wembley he twice erupted from midfield with a smooth surge of pace, then left the bar above Springett's head vibrating from the force of the driven ball. England won the game safely enough with two simple goals from John Connelly and Ray Pointer, but it was those two ringing shots of Eusebio's which caught the imagination of press and public.

Eusebio came from abject poverty in Mozambique to wealth and adulation with Benfica. So it was natural he should enjoy the limelight, should push away congratulating team-mates, to acknowledge on his own the plaudits of the crowd rising to one of his masterstrokes.

When he came to Portugal from the Lourenço Marques Sporting Club there were seven months of legal wrangles before he could play for

Benfica, with Sporting Club of Lisbon claiming a prior right. A short time later he came on as substitute in a match against Pelé's Santos in the Paris Final of an annual International tournament. There was half an hour left and Santos were leading 5–0, but there was still time for Eusebio to score a hat-trick, and steal attention from Pelé.

The World Cup 1966 was the showpiece of his talent and of the slight flaw in his genius. He was the leading scorer in the competition with 9 goals. Papers hailed his 'pure, instinctive genius', and rated him the most spectacular player in the competition. This was how I saw him as Hungary were beaten 3–1 at Old Trafford. 'Eusebio, challenging the goalkeeper for a high ball, was cut across the forehead, but his play never suffered. Indeed the white bandage round his head was a convenient marker for the passes which streamed to him. All great players have their own distinctive tricks and there were two he used to great effect. The first was to stab his toe at a pass, flicking the ball up and behind the man moving in to tackle. The other was to turn deliberately into the circle of defenders, slipping the ball one side of a player, then brushing past on the other.'

The great goals came later. Against Bulgaria his presence alone frightened Naidenov into heading into his own net, before Eusebio's lethal shot sent Portugal further towards easy victory. Then came the confrontation with Brazil, the challenge to Pelé. Pelé was crippled too early for that contest to develop, but it was a master's thrust with which Eusebio finally dismissed Brazil from the competition they had won twice in succession. As a corner was cleared the ball came out to Eusebio bouncing high and awkward. He still hit it down, flat and hard into the net before anyone could move to challenge. That made it 3–1 and left Pelé to hobble away defeated, a raincoat draped over his dark shoulders. The 'Black Panther', Eusebio, strode on to win a remarkable quarter-final game against the North Koreans at Goodison Park, Liverpool. These small agile men had been the toast of Middlesbrough in their group, but still no one took them too seriously, even though they had eliminated Italy. Yet within twenty minutes they were 3 up on Portugal as Goodison giggled in disbelief, and incredulity echoed from every radio and television set.

That was just the setting to spur Eusebio. He became a team in himself, doing the fetching and the finishing. Running at the Korean defence he jinked through them and drove home a fierce shot. When Torres was tripped Eusebio swept home the penalty with that sure right foot. The score was 2–3 at half-time and Portugal were back in the game.

Soon Eusebio had sent Simoes free down the right and, as the cross came over, hard and low, he was there to meet it, and lance it home in mid-leap. At once Eusebio went racing again down the left, leaving three opponents trailing. As he cut in he was tripped by a despairing tackle. Eusebio limped over to take the kick, but it still arrowed into the net. And it was Eusebio who made the final goal. It was the standard move for the Portuguese as he crossed from the left, the tall Torres nodded it back and Augusto headed home.

It was a short step from the exhilaration of that victory to defeat and dejection against England. Nobby Stiles, that snapping terrier of a player, seemed to subdue him by reputation alone. Eusebio made little positive contribution, hovering uncertainly on the edge of the area until Coluna shook his fist to drive him on and Stiles' surveillance was almost contemptuously confident. With Portugal fighting back against Charlton's two goals Torres won a penalty off big Jack, and Eusebio hit home the precise penalty, the first time Banks had been beaten in the competition. Even that failed to lift him. It was lucky Stiles could ignore him for three minutes from the end he had to come catapulting in to block Simoes' close shot, wheeling instantly to rebuke those who had nearly let Portugal back into the game. For Eusebio there were now only the tears of frustration, and the play-off for third place.

Eusebio's rivals as best forward in the 1966 World Cup games were Bobby Charlton and Florian Albert of Hungary. Like Eusebio Albert lacked consistency, but could play with dazzling brilliance. After their defeat by Portugal Ferenc Puskas spent time with the team, joking and persuading, as he tried to renew the Hungarians' belief in themselves. The confidence certainly returned for one of the great matches of the competition as Brazil was destroyed by Albert's arrogant mastery and a goal of flawless beauty. The Goodison crowd chanted 'Albert, Albert', revelling in the imperious gestures, the ease with which he glided past the despairing tackles, the menace of his swooping runs. And Albert, having scored himself, started the goal which completed the 3–1 win. His elegant first-time pass caught the defence off balance to send Bene running free down the right. As they raced back to cover Bene curled the ball behind them, and there was Farkas, socks round his ankles, racing in to volley. Farkas standing tall, hit the shot in full stride, meeting it a foot behind his body to keep it so low that it flew past Gylmar at knee height.

In a 'goal-of-the-month' competition Shankly selected as best Bettega's goal, which gave Italy their 2–0 World Cup win over England in Rome in 1976. There were no Liverpool goals on show so perhaps

Shankly reasoned that any goal which beat Clemence, Liverpool's agile 'keeper, must be the winner. But with this chance so beautifully fashioned by Causio's back heel he labelled it the goal of the century. Perhaps he did not see the one Albert fashioned for Farkas.

The great goalscorer must have the nose for the easy goal and certainly in taking it, as well as the ability to score the occasional impossible one. That makes Puskas the only real rival to Pelé. Even when he looked tubby and unathletic in his later days with Real he never lost that swift acceleration, that certainty in finishing, that lethal left foot shot from unexpected angles and distances.

Compare his 85 goals in 84 internationals for Hungary with England's best finisher's record, Greaves' 44 in 57 games. That is a measure of the talent of the man who kept his family nickname 'Ocsi', or 'Kid-brother' when he was world famous. At seventeen he came into Hungary's side against Austria and scored a goal. That was in 1945 and for the next eleven years only the rare injury ever kept him out of the National side at a period when Hungary went thirteen years without a home defeat – from losing 7–2 to Sweden in 1943 to Czechoslovakia's 4–2 win in 1956. With Nandor Hidegkuti, and Sandor Kocsis he formed the sharpest spearhead any country has ever fielded. Inevitably he was moved from his home club Kispest to Honved, the side of 'The People's Army' where the 'galloping major' was left free to concentrate on his football. And he was touring with the Honved side when the Hungarian revolution erupted in 1956. He was reported as killed in the battles as Russia beat them back into line, but in fact he had settled in Vienna, as it was too dangerous to return to the country where he had been treated as a king, made wealthy by gifts of goods to preserve the 'equal pay' fiction of Communism.

Puskas was now thirty and overweight, but his friend Oestereicher worked an improbable package deal which took them to Real. Oestereicher was indeed a fine coach, but had difficulty at first in communicating with players of many tongues. But if your forward line includes Kopa, Di Stefano, Puskas and Gento what words do you need to know except 'go out and play'? There was no need of complicated coaching or tactics to keep Real ahead as Puskas was once more part of a remarkable winning run. From February 1957, when they lost 3–2 to Atletico Madrid, Real were unbeaten at home for another 122 matches spread over eight years, with 114 won outright.

With Pelé and Puskas you can take your choice of which is the best scorer of them all, but it has to be one of them. If you look for the most complete and commanding forward then it has to be Di Stefano. This hard, dour Argentinian was undisputed boss of Real's team. Those he did not like soon disappeared. Waldyr Pereira, or Didi, had been the star of the 1958 World Cup, with Sweden's Simonnson an outstanding forward in it. Their style and manner did not suit 'Stef.' – so they went. Puskas, who had had to object to the 'Cult of Personality', when Kocsis won that individual trophy, now found himself teamed with the greatest cult figure of them all.

In their first season together with both sharing the lead in the Spanish League with 26 goals apiece Puskas had an easy scoring chance late in the final game. Instead of shooting he rolled the ball back for Di Stefano to score. That was the way to his heart and the two became magically linked on the field, friends off it. The reserved autocrat and the carefree extrovert ideally complemented each other. That Eintracht game summed up Di Stefano's ability to organise and dominate his team from midfield, then come striding up on cue to score with arrogant disdain. Like Greaves he had the gift of moving in late and unnoticed. In midfield he had the tight control, the passing skills which prevented him being effectively screened out of the game however close marked. He was a poor header of the ball, but with the football world at his feet what did that matter? If you did not give Stef. the ball where he wanted it you did not last long at Real.

Are there any present-day players to compare with those two? For goalscoring Gerhard Muller is close to the Puskas class and for all-round skill some take Cruyff as Di Stefano's equal.

Against today's hard defences Muller scored 54 goals in his first 40 Internationals and it was typical that he should end his career for Germany with a goal which won the 1974 World Cup Final. It was characteristic too that this individualist should decline to play again for his country as he disliked the extra travelling and the disruption of home life when added to his club football. Muller was always one to make his own rules. However closely defenders marked him he had the ability to get the killing touch to a ball they thought was screened from him.

Three goals illustrate his special skill. In Mexico in 1970 those two late goals forced England into extra time in the quarter-final. Then as Lohr headed back across goal Labone tried to intercept, stretching for a ball he could not reach. But Muller, whom he was marking, had wheeled silently away to the spot where the ball would drop. Bobby Moore's leg was only inches off the ground to challenge for the ball when Muller was striking his waist-high volley past Bonetti. Once more the king of the penalty box had found space and struck too fast for anyone to follow. It was the same sharpness that sent him in to win the World Cup Final against Holland in 1974. And when Leeds challenged strongly for the European Cup it was Muller who killed them off – waiting until the last second before moving in to flick home a delayed centre.

When Muller first joined Bayern they were in the Regional League South and the Yugoslav coach objected. 'Will you have me put a bear among my racehorses?' The bear with the stocky legs and thick body scored 35 goals to lift them at once to the main Bundesliga. His special characteristics are fast muscle, fast starting and the instinct for goals. A powerful left foot and perfect balance in awkward positions are ancillary aids. But he is the natural scorer and sensible coaches have left him to loiter with intent round the penalty area and get on with the stealing of goals.

There was an appropriateness in West Germany and Holland meeting in the 1974 World Cup Final with Cruyff and Muller in opposition. Cup games do not so often work out according to form. For Walter Winterbottom, who has seen all the great players of the post-war era, Cruyff is the best of them all, even allowing for relative failure in that game. 'He has better all-round skills than Pelé' is his analysis. Joe Mercer's instinct says 'Don't rate him so high. In that final he had a flying start, but Bertie Vogts then played him out of the game. That does not happen to the really great in so vital a match.'

There are always two views of a player. This was the view of the F.I.F.A. Committee of experts, chaired by Walter Winterbottom, in their analysis of the best in the world in those finals.

Great footballing teams are built around inspirational players. They stride the game with confident authority. Their performance and their manner stimulates their colleagues. They, more than others, seem able to rise to the occasion, to respond to challenge and opportunity. They are leaders, as well as being good players with special technical talent.

No one will question the enormous value of the leadership qualities and personal example of Franz Beckenbauer and Johan Cruyff to their teams. There were some games in this competition when Beckenbauer seemed content to play an inconspicuous overseer's role, allowing other key players to 'drive' the midfield action, but at other times, particularly against Sweden, Poland and the Netherlands, he exerted himself to the full as a 'libero' in supporting the attacks of his forwards or covering the gaps in defence.

Johan Cruyff has unique physical attributes: a lean powerful frame with long legs. Like all elusive forward players, he possesses fast muscle, capable of quick reaction and contraction. He can start more quickly than opponents which gives him scope to avoid a tackle, dodge past a player and race or outjump him to the ball. His endurance enables him to work incessantly throughout the game, moving first in attack then in defence, dribbling to create an opening or running off the ball to help a colleague. Then he is gifted with high skill in techniques, deft in his ball control and sensitively accurate in his passing. He is everywhere getting involved in the play, taking corners and free-kicks, and then positioning himself well away from the ball to create a diversion as a start to a new phase of play. His example of unsparing use of energy is copied by his colleagues. Everyone seems determined to play with great zest and courage.

Johan Cruyff is more than a world class player. If there is a rebirth of attacking, adventurous play, then he has been its symbol in the World Cup of 1974. What better way of writing your name in the annals of football could there be?

For the greatest goalscorer it is a toss-up between Pelé and Puskas, with Dean, Greaves, Law and Muller also challenging. For the all-round forward Cruyff is in contention with Finney and Di Stefano and Pelé, and Alfredo Di Stefano will demand selection as imperiously as he demanded the ball. In my book he gets it.

Nineteen

These We Have Feared

How do goalkeepers react to the menace of the goalscorers? Goalkeeper Bob Wilson, who played such an important part in Arsenal's double of 1970–71, is a man of unusual composure. Yet there is a handful of forwards whose presence on the field was enough to weaken his knees.

It's not the ones who boom it in like Bobby Charlton or Peter Lorimer, who worry a goalkeeper. When they shoot you know the ball may end in the fiftieth row of the terraces or bulging the net or stretching you to a spectacular save. If it goes in there won't be any criticism, and if you save their shots you win the applause and look good. Nothing they do can undermine your confidence.

Yet there are just a few players of exceptional talent who can make you look and feel foolish. You are never sure how they will try to beat you, only that they will do the thing for which you are least prepared.

Jimmy Greaves, George Best and Johan Cruyff were the three who caused me that uneasy apprehension. However a goalkeeper covers the angles there is always some small gap he must leave. These three could sense it and put the ball there with unerring accuracy.

George Best was as deceptive and accurate with his head as with his foot and that made him a special problem. Jimmy Greaves, however, had developed to an exceptional degree the art of sudden shooting, when you were least prepared.

That was the other ability which made all three so difficult to deal with. As a goalkeeper you can sense when a forward, who has broken through, momentarily loses control of the ball. That is when you dive in to challenge. These exceptional forwards had the reverse perception and seemed always to anticipate the moment when you were getting set for the save. As you started to gather yourself you found they had already shot and the ball was speeding past before you could spring. If you tried to anticipate them and dived early, then they sensed that too and held the ball. That left you stranded and looking even more foolish.

Greaves always seemed to catch you off balance. In the 1968 season we played against him four times in League and Cup matches between Arsenal and Tottenham. Each time we marked him so closely he hardly had a kick. In the four games combined he had just four half chances, yet he beat me three times. That is an unbelievable ratio and with anyone but Greaves you would regard it as a freak. Yet he was doing that all through his career. Greaves deceived you because he was always so well balanced he could shoot without warning, often flicking the ball past you with no more movement than if continuing his dribble.

With Cruyff it was the changes of pace that surprised you. He has such sudden and fierce acceleration he comes on you quicker than you expect, or reaches balls that seem beyond him.

Goalkeepers are often blamed, when such forwards should be congratulated. Peter Shilton was criticised for being slow in getting down to the shot from Domarski which gave Poland a 1–1 draw at Wembley in 1974 and put England out of the World Cup. In fact it was the surprise of the shot which beat him, with Domarski hitting the ball before he was set. All credit to the forward and no blame to Peter.

Sam Bartram had the same feelings when he faced Lawton from Charlton Athletic's goal. 'His heading was so good he could make you look foolish. He had a fine understanding with Goulden at Chelsea and once as Len was about to take a free-kick against us Tom pointed at the corner of my goal and said, "That's where I will head his kick, Sam." And that was just where his header went. He hit it so accurately I could not reach it even though I knew where he was aiming.'

The German goalkeeper, Herkenrath, who played brilliantly at Wembley in 1954 even though England won 5–4, had the same feeling about Len Shackleton. 'Twice he made me look foolish. That trickster Shackleton waits until I dive at his feet, then flicks the ball over my head.'

No matter how good a goalkeeper may be, sure shooting can leave him stranded. In the thirties England's outstanding goalkeeper, Harry Hibbs of Birmingham, had 9 put past him by Sheffield Wednesday.

Catton commented, 'That Wednesday could beat such a 'keeper nine times only shows how much the man in goal depends on those in front of him. One remembers James Lawrence of Newcastle being defeated by eight shots in twenty-eight minutes from Sunderland's forwards and he had no chance of even touching one of the balls driven goalwards.' Hibbs was humiliated by another small man with the Greaves touch for making goalkeepers look silly. 'Hooper scored three of Wednesday's nine and created most of the chances. This little man has a ball control only equalled by his self-control. As a player he is a will-o'-the-wisp.' That's the type goalkeepers fear.

Centre-halves had their jinxes too. Bernard Joy, of Arsenal, the last man to play as an amateur in the full England side – against Belgium in 1936 – was one of many to find Lawton a problem.

His main strength was in the air. He would stand well out at corners, beyond the far post, towards the angle of the area. Then he would come in with a diagonal run, soar up to meet the ball and hover there to head home. As a big man myself I found how to counter that, but then he proved almost as dangerous on the ground. Tom was fast and beautifully balanced and there was no weakness in his game. You could not let him have a sight of goal, because he had the scorer's instinct. Whatever gap the goalkeeper left he found it. Playing behind him in a war-time game I watched him run through, and the moment the goalkeeper set himself for a shot to his left he hit it past his right hand. And he hit the shot with the outside of his foot to curl it well inside the post. He did the same against me at Goodison, turning clear, seeing the goalkeeper at the near post and swerving the shot inside the far post.

'Jock' Ephraim Dodds of Sheffield United and Scotland was another like Lawton, who was always difficult to mark. He had the same style and build, the same all-round skill. I never played against Dean, missing the privilege by one match, but I watched him make it hard even for Herbie Roberts. Lawton tended to meet the ball square on, heading hard and straight. Dean was more subtle in his heading, glancing the ball down, now left, now right, without the goalkeeper being able to guess where he would put it. Wherever it went it was headed down and in.'

Walter Winterbottom, later the England team manager, says he found Freddy Steele a hard man to mark. 'He was a good all-round centre-forward with the skills which allowed him to average a goal and a half a game in his six Internationals for England in 1937. A quick, elegant footballer, good with his head, a little like Alan Gilzean. Playing centre-half for Manchester United against Stoke I had problems enough coping with him. Then there was a moment of panic as Steele had to go off and Matthews was moved into the centre. I was in awe of his dribbling skill so I concentrated on screening him, keeping always in front of him, and holding off the tackle as long as possible. Perhaps because he was out of position this seemed to unsettle Stanley. He never ran at me as I feared, but always laid the ball off.'

That experience no doubt encouraged Winterbottom to dissuade England players from rushing into the tackle against the skilled continental ball players when he was managing the national team.

Andy Nelson was the strong man of the defence in the team which Ramsey took straight from Third Division to First Division championship. In his long career with Ipswich, and as manager of Charlton, he has had to work out how to play some of the most menacing of recent goalscorers. Only two worried him.

Greaves and Law were always a threat. You were never sure what they would do even when they seemed subdued. Greaves's timing was so good and if he got in behind you his finishing was uncanny. Denis was very hard and fast, at you all the time, and difficult to head off. Their styles were poles apart, but they both had this instinct for goals, this feel for an opening and for the moment to strike, never going too early so that you could easily pick them up.

However good a forward is it is essential not to try and change your style because you are frightened of him. If you do he's won before the ball is kicked. Football at the top level is a game of instinct, not intelligence. Over the years you build up habits which come naturally to you and you react automatically to situations. Your colleagues come to expect you to do certain things and rely on you behaving that way. If your habits are not good enough to cope with the great players, that's your bad luck. Try and adjust for one game, one player, and it will be twice as bad. Greaves and Law will go on doing the things they have instinctively done right for years and the defender's best hope is to do the same.

Nelson has also had close experience of two formidable scorers whom he was only too glad to see keep up their flow of goals. Ray Crawford had 289 league goals and was essential to Ipswich's success. 'Ray was slow and never a strong shot. He looked languid and cumbersome, but he was deadly accurate close to goal and had a marvellous positional sense. In the area the chances just seemed to home to him and he kept knocking them in. It looked simple, but like the Ipswich style it was not quite as simple as it looked. He was well paired with Ted Phillips who was such a strong shot. They complemented each other. Derek Hales has this same feel for a goal, but he is much faster and more incisive. At Charlton we expected him to make his impact in the penalty area, where he is quicksilver and hits the ball much harder than Ray could. He is a penalty-area shark and does not link as well as Ray used to in midfield.'

Derek Ufton has had complementary experience to Nelson. He was England's centre-half in 1953 and played with Charlton in First and Second Division, before turning to management.

As a big man myself I was never put off by the physical centre-forwards. Nat Lofthouse and Cliff Holton were very good of their type, but they were too straight-forward to bother me, even though they were powerful and with an explosive shot. Cliff Holton was always among the goals with Arsenal, and then scored a record 42 in a season with Watford. He had 295 in his career and clearly he could be a handful for centre-halves. But the big, the strong, and the fast rarely bothered me. Trevor Ford was the only one of the 'hammerheads' to give me a battering. He was so powerful and well balanced, very hard, very quick and a courageous header, who challenged for everything. He had a fierce shot in either foot too and was the most complete centre-forward I played against.

Normally speed did not worry me as I was fast myself and swift enough in the turn. Milburn was the one who was too quick for me up at Newcastle, where the 'Geordie' crowd set his pulses and his feet really racing. When he played away at the Valley he was a yard slower and easy to contain.

I don't forget those who scored a hat-trick against me, so I don't forget Milburn or Brian Clough either. It was easier for me to face Ford than to face Clough. 'Face' is the wrong word, because it was when Clough got behind you that he was so dangerous. He had his eye on goal all the time and was always hovering around the area. If you lost sight of him for a moment he would dart in behind your back and then you had no hope of catching him. Give him a chance and he took it with the cold precision of Jimmy Greaves.

Don Revie was a difficult man to mark, when he started the 'Revie' plan and lay deep. But he tended to go *too* deep. We soon found the wing-half could pick him up and I did not need to follow. After that it was not difficult to beat his system. Certainly he was nothing like the problem set by the one centre I really feared – Ronnie Allen. Allen was so intelligent in his positioning he was always in that no-man's land where I was not quite sure whether to leave him or pick him up. And while I hesitated he would send Johnny Nicholls racing in to score or come gliding up to take the return pass and score himself.

For Gordon Jago, the travelled manager who was once Charlton's centre-half, Brian Clough was the most difficult man to mark. 'He was so quick and so sure. And though he looked slim, he was very strong and quite able to hold you off. Strength alone does not get you far at the top. A striker needs great acceleration or great skill to be outstanding. Clough had both.

'I've always looked for the same qualities in my forwards, not tough tearaways. That was why I brought Bowles and Givens to Queen's Park. I watched Don a lot at Luton where he played in many positions. Wherever he played there as no mistaking his speed or his skill with the ball. He is the type good defenders fear, even if he isn't very forceful.'

For Billy Wright the two British centre-forwards who gave him most problems were a contrasting pair, John Charles and Lawrie Reilly.

Standing 5 ft. 8 in. I appeared to have a problem whenever a big centre-forward came on the field. But in fact my ability to jump high more than made up for the few inches' height advantage of the player I was marking. Most big men have little spring in their calves and their gain on the ground becomes a loss in the air. Nat Lofthouse could climb well, but he was not really tall, only a few inches higher than me. So it was an even competition with him. Our duels were the most entertaining of my playing career. Nat was a whole-hearted trier who went in hard, but without malice and was always cheerfully competitive. 'Come on, Wrighty,' he would say. 'You are not up to form today. I will score five.' Yet we always seemed to beat Bolton by a wide margin. He would get the best of me on occasions in the air, but then Bert Williams would make a remarkable save. 'It's always one or other of you damned pair getting in my way' was the Lofthouse lament.

But John Charles was not only six inches taller than me he was that unique person, a large man who could jump his height. When I first marked him at Ninian Park he was always up there above me. And when I looked at the pictures in the *South Wales Echo* there we were at the top of our jump and still that six-inch difference. He was the only large man I ever marked who could match my spring.

Normally I had no fears of the small fast men, since I could match them in speed of running and turning. But Reilly was always a worry because he had such a fine positional sense. As long as he was in front of me he could be controlled. Let him get behind my back and there was no way of catching him.

At the time I first played against him I still had the special English failing of ball watching. All our concentration was on the play, not on the men moving off the ball. Lawrie was adept at stealing into dangerous positions and he was the one who forced me to adjust my game and widen my range of perception. I still kept watching the ball, but tried always to be aware of the movement of the man I was marking – particularly if it was Reilly.

There were a lot of jocular remarks when Walter Winterbottom talked of 'peripheral vision', but that's what English players lacked.

Reilly taught me exactly what it meant – it meant you had to have eyes in the back of your head to watch the likes of him and to be aware all the time of the play being shaped around you.

And it had to be all the time with Lawrie. He was known as 'last minute Reilly' for his habit of getting the late decisive goal, as at Wembley in 1953. We were leading 2–1 with a few seconds to go and then Reilly nips in behind Ramsey to score from an acute angle. You could not take your eye off him for a second.

Among overseas players, Alfredo di Stefano was incomparable. He had all the skills except heading – and he didn't need that because he played with forwards who gave him sufficient openings on the ground. Anyway he was adept at making his own. He was always given freedom to play deep and use his intelligence and anticipation to decide when to strike. The best individual goal I've seen was his for Real against Eintracht in the final of the European Cup as he weaved through from the half-way line, beating player after player before shooting the ball home. For me he is the incomparable footballer, better than Pelé, or Puskas, or Finney.

Jimmy Greaves had this ability to surprise you however well you knew his play. He seemed able to reach the ball you thought was unreachable. You had him screened but suddenly his toe would dart out and flick home a ball you were sure was yours. And always he seemed to flick it just inside the post, not just outside.

We had a splendid defence at Wolverhampton, but he once put five past us in a game we could have won on balance of play. We were left arguing and reproaching ourselves until we realised most forwards would not have scored from one of those half-chances.

That game when Greaves scored 5 for Chelsea in a 6–2 win had its amusing side. In 1958 in Sweden we staged a journalists' 'World Cup' against other nations' football writers. In our drawn game with Sweden we had the pleasure of watching one of their great forwards of the past, Sven Riddell, and in our match with Brazil the horror of being watched by the whole England team. They enjoyed their chance to be making the derisive comment, and left before, for the only time in my life, I scored 4 goals. Before they went Billy Wright had formed a very poor opinion of our right back, Tony Stratton Smith. Tony went to this match against Chelsea on the Wolves' coach and Billy told him, 'I have never seen a more inept defensive display than yours against the Brazilian writers. So now watch closely how it should be done and you may learn a trick or two.' Six goals for Chelsea gave Stratton Smith the chance for some equally pointed comment on Wright's play!

'Pure magic' is the usual comment on any goal that is out of the ordinary. There are a few that deserve the title, the ones created by the magician's art of illusion. While the eye is drawn to his right hand, the trick is performed with the left. And it is so often the great goalscorers who turn arch-illusionists, fixing on themselves the anxious concentration of their opponents, while others steal in to score.

When England played Brazil in the 1958 World Cup Didi was looked on as the man to watch. His speciality was the 'banana' kick, bending the ball outrageously past goalkeepers unused to seeing it swerve. Coming deep from the wing-half position, as Beckenbauer was to do later, he was thought to be the main goalscoring danger. Bill Slater was given the task of neutralising him.

I understood that I must not let Didi past me to give him the chance of that lethal shot. So in the first half I stood right off him, waiting for him to come at me, determined never to sell myself. In fact Didi's role in the Brazilian team had changed and he was now the link man setting up their dangerous forwards like Garrincha or Vava. Holding off was playing into his hands, giving him time to make his precision passes. We had a harrowing first half with only some brilliant goalkeeping by Macdonald keeping them out. At half-time we talked it over with Walter Winterbottom and Bill Nicholson and it was agreed I could close mark him to cut him off from the ball or hustle him into a hurried, misplaced pass.

The danger of his scoring was much less than the danger of his making goals for others. I had been misled by his reputation. Once I went with him and disrupted his distribution, we had disrupted their attacking efficiency. In the second half they were rarely a threat and we should have won had Derek Kevan not been pushed as he was poised to score.

Bill Slater moved from wing-half to centre-half late in his career with Wolves and England, just like Billy Wright.

It's an easier place to play as you slow up. But the forwards who worry you tend to be the ones who have the particular skills you lack. I preferred taking on these physical centre-forwards such as Nat Lofthouse because I had the build to withstand their aggression and there was nothing subtle about their attack. The one who always troubled me was Ray Pointer, who was so quick, so elusive in his dribbling. He did not often play for England because he did not fit the 'English' style, but I always hated playing against Burnley while he was in the side. I knew he was going to test me on the turn. For Scotland and Liverpool Ian St John had some of the same attributes. He lacked the skilful control of Pointer, but he was always putting you under pressure with his hard, wholehearted effort.

The great players will always trouble you, even if they are the type you normally take in your stride. John Charles, for instance, was someone very special. He had the strength all right, but he had all the other skills too. In Italy he had learnt how to screen the ball and for all his bulk he was a light as a dancer on his feet, delicately precise in his control.

In the International against Wales at Wembley in 1954 I left the field with the impression that we had only been playing John Charles. We had a narrow 3–2 win and he got both of their goals. Only a hat-trick by that underrated goalscorer Roy Bentley saw us home. Charles seemed to be playing centre-half as well.

Whenever I had to mark Charles I adjusted my style so that I *never* challenged for the ball in midfield unless I was *certain* of getting it first, or of winning it in the air. I would put him under enough pressure so that he had to lay off a pass, but I would never commit myself, because he was so likely to win the ball that *you* expected to get. Then he would leave you trailing.

From an earlier period Joe Mercer had to contend with many of the great players of the time, whether as ordinary wing-half or virtually as 'sweeper' in his late period with Arsenal, when he tucked in behind the centre-half and saved his legs.

The best of them all fortunately was on my side. I have never seen anyone to better Bill Dean as a goalscorer. But the ones that worry you are not always the best players. Charlie Vaughan of Charlton was not a great centre-forward in anyone's book. But he gave me the shivers. I had a bad game against him to start with and that gave him confidence and undermined mine. After that he could usually do what he liked with me. I worried for a time. Then I thought there is always someone who plays in a way that probes your particular weakness. Everyone has his Achilles heel and you have to recognise that some player is going to find it. The important thing is not to be disturbed and to recognise that this is just one game of many. And to be honest about it and warn the others they may have a bit more covering to do for you in that game.

As a youngster Alex James was the man who turned me inside out. We were not tactically sophisticated then and he would draw me in midfield then chip the ball over my head to Bastin. If I chased Bastin he would flick it back to James, so that I spent the afternoon travelling fast and never arriving.

Raich Carter was another who was difficult to mark. He and Doherty were a fine pair, but Raich was the more complete player. He was good in midfield and a strong and accurate shot with either foot.

As a manager I enjoyed developing players who were not too gifted naturally. Gerry Hitchens was one. We called him 'Champion the Wonder Horse' because of his high, prancing action as he ran. At first he was very awkward in the turn and very slow to use the ball. He would work out to the left wing and get stuck there with everyone waiting for the cross. But he was strong and a real trier and we made a good footballer of him in the end – good enough to be very success-ful in the hard, defensive game in Italy.

There are some promising players now like Trevor Francis, who has this ability to run through a defence without checking and turning as so many modern players do. Then I have a high regard for Steve Coppell. He and Hill had great success when their style was new and sides were not used to being attacked by old-fashioned wingers.

Manchester United stole a march with their changed tactics, but it does not take long for other sides to catch on. Tommy Docherty found the going harder in 1976/7 and so did his wingers, who were better marked. This was the test for them. But Coppell seemed to go on doing everything right. He does not turn into trouble. Does not waste balls and works at high intensity throughout a match. He should prove one of the good ones. But you can never be sure. I once said to that shrewdest of football managers, Arthur Rowe, 'Do you agree with me that George Best is the finest player there has been with that wonderful elasticity, those extraordinary all-round skills?' As usual Arthur answered a question with a question. 'But will he last like Tom Finney?'

He didn't, did he? He's lost his pace and his superstar quality. Finney kept his to the end. How can you tell which of today's prospects will make it like Finney and last like Finney?

How indeed? There is no certainty who will be giving the centre-backs nightmares in the 1980s. Will it be young Peter Ward, looking as slight as Greaves and with some of his finishing flair? His 32 goals in his first full season helped Brighton to the Second Division and Ward into the England Squad. But can he sustain his scoring at the higher level, as Mariner did on transfer to Ipswich? Or will the goals dry up as they did for Derek Hales when he went from Charlton to Derby? Today's goalscorer is tomorrow's marked man and only the exceptionally talented shrug off the shackles season after season. And many, like Latchford or Withe, need the skills of wingers such as Thomas and Robertson to make them again a plague to goalkeepers.

Twenty

Get Ahead, Get a Goal

We talk of this as the permissive age, but for sportsmen the training discipline is stricter, the pressure to conform greater than ever before. The East Germans now produce their Gold Olympians like battery hens, the specially reared products of a political system in which human individuality counts for little. And these are the 'amateur' sportsmen who still take the Olympic oath proclaiming that it is not the winning, but the taking part that matters!

Professional football fortunately does not lend itself to such stereotyped development. The moving ball and the changing mosaic of the field put too high a premium on quickness of thought and adjustment, on certainty of instinct. That may explain why Russia has never reached a World Cup Final despite the intensive disciplined effort.

Highly ordered patterns of play have helped mould better defences, but not improved that supreme individualist, the goalscorer. Perhaps the discipline starts too early now and accounts in part for scorers becoming a vanishing species in need of protection by the Wild Life Fund.

When cricket took itself too seriously it temporarily lost grip of its following. Football has been in danger of the same mistake – of communicating that it is about fear rather than fun, hard labour rather than happy spontaneity.

At least the pace and passion have survived in soccer, together with the total commitment. It is up to the goalscorers to keep a little wit, humour and invention alive in the game.

We must not too early discipline the play or stress the conformity if football is to stay healthy and goalscorers flourish. Later by all means add the defensive sophistication, but give them their years of free invention before the wall of systems closes around them.

In the last quarter of a century there have been great advances in technique, especially in the instant control of the high ball on chest or thigh. Yet it is mainly the defenders who have benefited from improved coaching which has helped eliminate the errors on which forwards thrived. It is the defenders who have increased their skills and their numbers. 'Keep it on the Island' was the standard exhortation of the crowd in my young days as backs with legs like tree trunks sent their clearances soaring to the sky. Now their passing is as precise and orderly as their covering and they are chosen for their speed as much as for their strength. So the forward has to be ever more inventive, since it needs the unexpected to beat the well drilled. And, except at free-kicks or other dead ball plays, the unexpected comes from the forward's imagination, not the coach's plan.

Jock Stein, the great Celtic Manager, labels football a simple game with a simple requirement. 'All I need is four at the back who can tackle, three in the middle who can pass, and three up front who can run, dribble and shoot.'

Run, dribble, and shoot are natural skills and the coach's job is to improve on nature, not change it. It is usually the simple advice which makes the most impact even on good players. 'Heel up, head and toe down' was Bloomer's advice to those about to shoot. As in game after game you see English League players loft the ball over from a few yards out you wonder if such simple advice might not be more valuable than the complex tactical instructions. For wingers the near post centre and the far post shot are other simple skills too often ignored.

Jimmy Hill was our coach before the 1952 Olympics. He had been no mean scorer himself, his eager quest for goals once bringing him those 5 in a match for Fulham. After watching me in a practice game he commented, 'It took me fifteen years to realise football is a passing, not a dribbling game. How much longer is it going to take you?'

That made an instant impact on me, as did his Preston coach's remark on Tom Finney, 'Shall I buy you your own ball?' The passing skill could be easily grafted on, but it would have been too late to learn the intuitive art of the dribbler. Matthews knew instinctively that the man coming in to tackle right footed is off balance if you pass him on his left. But few backs of his day were taught that if you go in with one foot and scythe the other round a fraction of a second later you should catch a man whichever way he goes.

There are plenty of good habits which can be shown to the young player without drilling him to respond to situations with the unthinking reaction of a Pavlovian dog.

When that outstanding sports administrator, Sir Stanley Rous, started teaching at Watford Grammar School he found the gym plastered with notices of instruction. Every one was a 'don't'. In clearing them out he commented, 'Even the Ten Commandments have one "Thou shalt" amid the "shalt nots".'

The goalscorer more than most needs the encouragement of the 'do' rather than the inhibition of the 'don't'. Happily the last World Cup in 1974 gave a push towards acceptance that attacking flair is as important as defensive sweat even though English teams still took a couple of seasons to recognise this. They might earlier have paid some heed to this report by the FIFA technical committee studying that World Cup.

The records show that, leaving aside corners and free-kicks, a huge majority of the attempts to score result from flank attack moves. Those tacticians who press for a return to the use of fast, elusive wing-forwards must have been encouraged by the overwhelming evidence that flank attacks still provide by far the most opportunities to score goals.

These facts must also encourage those who believe in the strategy that attacking players should try to 'empty' the space in front of goal so that when a centre is made from the flank they can run in to meet the ball and shoot or head for goal.

It became fashionable to believe that once the back four became an integral part of the game the winger was dead, since he could always be close marked. The leading teams, however, kept their faith in the winger. Liverpool always have a Callaghan or a Heighway, Leeds a Gray or a Lorimer. Manchester United regained a little of their former glory with the cocky Hill and the busy Coppell. Clive Woods has been integral to Ipswich success, Tueart to Manchester City's, while Brian Clough, uncharacteristically letting someone else speak for him, used attacking wingers to bring back goals and First Division football to Nottingham Forest. If you wait, old ideas come back in fashion. It's those who chase blindly after today's winners who end as tomorrow's losers.

'Copy the Hungarians' was the cry. Then 'Copy the Italians', or the Brazilians or the Dutch. By the time we tried to copy them they were losers too just as we became while some other countries were busy imitating our 1966 winning method. Slavish imitation never works, because it is usually at the expense of your own natural strengths. The secret of success is grafting the best of another's game to the best of one's own as the West Germans have done with such fine and consistent results.

Pace and passion have been the best of the English method – allied in earlier days to destructive finishing. We have allowed a situation in which the continentals say of us as we once said of them, 'Their approach play is good, but they don't know how to score.'

The one country which does not seem to excite the copyists is the one that has steered a middle course with consistent success. West Germany won the World Cup in 1954 and 1974, was beaten finalist in 1966 and semi-finalist in 1958 and 1970. Their two imperturbable managers, Herberger and Schoen, have built on the German ability to marry the strength of the English game and the trickery of the continental, their gift for discipline put to good use in defence, but the front runners allowed freedom of expression.

This is how the FIFA technical committee analysed their style in 1974. 'Germany base their play on intelligent shrouding and interception in defence and two main types of attack: the frontal "basketball" type of play using the shortish double passing movement at quick tempo and the fast raids on the flank using the speed of a strong running forward or overlapping full-back.'

Germany have always played to their own strength and ignored the extremes of current theory. So they have never been out of fashion or honours. Always there have been raiding wingers and a striker of the calibre of Morlock, Seeler or Muller hovering on the edge of the area unburdened by defensive duties.

When the Brazilians first introduced a version of the back four system for the World Cup in 1958 they had no doubt that wingers were still vital to the scoring of goals. This was how their method impressed Blanchflower when he wrote about them before their Final victory over Sweden.

Coalblack 'Didi' of the lightning reflexes and swerving shot is the recognised master of the team. Seventeen-year-old Pelé had a wonder game against France and right-winger Garrincha, with animal-like speed and instinct, is a bewildering player whose shadow must lead a frustrating existence trying to keep up with him.

Tactically they employ a system which best suits their character. The two full-backs play very wide and the left-half drops back to play a dual role with the stopper. In simple terms it is a line of four full-backs. The two wingers and twin centre-forwards operate as a front-line attacking force of four. Between these lines of attack and defence Didi and Zozimo supply a wandering half-back service.

One lesson the English League has passed on is the need for fitness as well as cleverness. Almost a century ago John Goodall, outstanding forward of the Preston Invincibles and later Bloomer's inside partner at Derby, had this to say about the growing emphasis on speed. 'The footballers of today cannot control the ball and go the pace they do. Football is not a foot-race and should be judged so as to show the art of being master of the ball.' That is no longer true. In the modern work-rate football it has proved possible to combine speed and control. That was the feature of Ramsey's successful team, which other countries adapted, as the FIFA report noted.

A team can easily delude itself into thinking it has mastery over its opponent because of superior skill and speed in playing the ball, but pressure of work-rate and aggression by opposing teams can whittle away the edge of supremacy in technique until interpassing skill and ball control begin to fail.

The ability to run almost continuously without discomfort is achieved by anaerobic and aerobic endurance training. Most coaches now push their players in training sessions to achieve high standards in endurance tests.

In preparation for the World Cup in 1970 for Mexico, Brazil was conscious of the higher work-rate of European teams and, therefore, emphasised endurance running in the fitness preparation of their players. By regular application of the Cooper run (distance covered in 12 minutes) players achieved a high level of endurance fitness and this was felt to be a major contributing factor in winning the trophy for the third time. Not surprisingly, the Cooper method of achieving fitness has spread throughout all levels of football in Brazil.

Fitness in terms of strength, speed and endurance is measurable. Sweden, renowned in many sports for a high quality of fitness, concentrated in their training sessions on relating speed and endurance to interpassing skill. A notable feature of Sweden's tactics in matches of the final competition was the use of the long forward pass into an open space, with a player running at speed to break through the opposing defence. Yet as soon as possession of the ball was lost the player raced back to help in defence.

The Cooper run was devised by an American major and accepted by the

Brazilian trainer as being the best method of improving cardiovascular performances. The principle was simple: run for 12 minutes regularly on the same course or track, but cover a greater distance every time you run.

For Brazil's clever ball players that seemed a boring exercise. Pelé in particular felt that he had the flair and fitness which made it unnecessary. But the interest of the Cooper run is in the challenge it generates against oneself as well as others. In the first test, Pelé came last. With his pride challenged he outstripped all others in his percentage improvement. That was reflected in his performance on the field in the Mexico World Cup. Films were used to prove to his own satisfaction that he was a more complete forward than ever, getting through his midfield and defensive work as well as scoring or making goals.

The Cooper run is now rated even more effective than circuit training in improving stamina. It adds a little, but not much, to the old routine of lapping and roadwork to which earlier generations of footballers were subjected. The old ways are now laughed off as madness but clearly there was *some* method in them. They played their part in the days when greater stamina and better finishing gave Britain the edge on overseas sides. The Cooper run is just a more scientific and sophisticated version of a gut-feeling about fitness which obsessed the old coaches.

But the Cooper run cannot give the fitness for the explosive bursts that are demanded of the forward against today's tight defences. That is the aim of the 'anaerobic' training. You can run 100 metres almost without taking breath but without oxygen the muscles soon become inert, clogged by lactic acid. England players used to be asked by Winterbottom, 'How long do you think it will take me to leave you totally exhausted by pressure training?' Ten or twenty minutes was the usual response. 'Will you bet I cannot do it in ninety seconds?' always got a taker. The player was then put through a combination of exhausting exercises to be done at maximum exertion – squat jump, crawl round a bench, jump backwards and forwards across it. Those who have watched the 'Superstars' seizing up in the squat jumps during their televised competitions will not be surprised that the player never lasted the ninety seconds. Well within that time the oxygen was exhausted, the muscles accepting no more messages from the brain.

That demonstration was to impress how quickly a player can spend himself – 43 seconds should be the time for total exhaustion at maximum pressure – and the need to cultivate quick recuperation. Exercises based on a 45-second cycle of intense activity using the ball to add stimulus and concentration, and aiming at ever shorter recovery periods, improves the sharpness as the Cooper run improves the stamina. Maintaining the keen edge of fitness is still essential to the goalscorer – if he is ten per cent under he's just an ordinary player again. But however successful the anaerobic training is in improving performance you still cannot beat the simple laws of nature. Deprive the muscles of oxygen and you stop them functioning. Demand too much running of a goalscorer, however fit, and you reduce the chance of his taking the scoring opportunity, as his muscles and reflexes slow. Strength, speed and stamina are fundamental aspects of the British game and have to be nurtured along with ball skills. But the goalscorer needs a little nurturing too.

You may have difficulty in instant recall of England's right back when we won the World Cup Final, for George Cohen would not expect to figure in anyone's list of all-time greats. You will never forget Jimmy Greaves's name and he would be in everyone's list. Yet for the match that mattered most in our football's history he was left out. When goalscoring was really vital, it was too serious to entrust to the best of them all.

We are not the only ones to demand the impossible – to want the specialist to be also an all-rounder. Anderlecht paid £210,000 for Duncan McKenzie, that tricky, selfish forward absorbed in his own skills, which managers do not always enjoy as much as he does. Despite scoring 75 goals in 175 games McKenzie was always in and out of League sides, his precocious talent not always fitting the accepted team pattern. Managers looking for mistakes had no trouble noticing them and in their depressed periods that was all they saw – peering at the specks of error and ignoring the great beam of talent.

So Anderlecht appreciated his clever dribbling, his private play, as McKenzie aimed at the impossible and occasionally hit his target? Not at all! 'We wanted the English *drive*' was Manager Raymond Goethals' reason for laying out all that money on the transfer and paying McKenzie some £50,000 a year. Naturally it was not long before Goethals had dropped him, just as Notts Forest, Mansfield and Leeds were wont to do. This was 'for a necessary period of re-adjustment', the managerial euphemism for 'stop playing your game and start playing mine'. And he was soon up for sale again, back home with Everton.

Pace and passion are indeed the best characteristics of the English game, but you have to change Duncan McKenzie to get them. If you accept him as he is you get a very exciting, but very different package.

Looking at us through foreigners' eyes McKenzie made this revealing comment to Brian James of the *Daily Mail*. 'In England I never had freedom. Managers over there tell the Press: "Stan Bowles, Rodney Marsh, George Best . . . I'd never have anyone like that in *my* team."

'Then what do they do? Spend the week drilling their teams to stop Stan, Rod and George. If they are not good enough to play for you, why be scared of playing against them? It's illogical. The other players are often just as bad. When you slide past three blokes and stick one in the net they love it. Try it – and fail – and they go spare.'

That is the attitude which has left our game short on goals and flair. Managers cannot help looking at the errors and concentrating on eliminating them. That is so much easier than being creative. Danny Blanchflower watching Best and Cruyff battle it out in a World Cup game had to check the same instinctive feeling.

'I found myself looking at George's mistakes and saying, "Why cannot you do the simple thing, George?" Then I realised Cruyff was making more mistakes than George. What mattered were the things they were doing gloriously right. They were forwards, they could make mistakes, 99% of which would not matter. But either might win the match with a couple of brilliant touches beyond the vision of the good competent player. In fact their flights of fancy cancelled out but it made compulsive viewing.'

After Holland had walked over England to win 2–0 at Wembley a few months later, a senior F.A. official said to Revie, 'What was Madeley doing wandering aimlessly around in midfield?'

'He was meant to be marking Cruyff out of the game, but he couldn't find him' was the sad response. We don't seem able to find any Cruyffs ourselves now and if we do, in England at least, there is a danger that the flair will be ironed out of them. Ron Greenwood may change that.

However much the game develops there are some unchanging truths. One we seem to forget is Steve Bloomer's dry comment, 'A forward needs his energy for scoring goals.' Cooper runs and anaerobic training cannot invalidate that advice. Ask too much of strikers and the expense of effort leads only to a waste of goals.

Our Pegasus team of the first Final had a reunion match many years later at Malvern College where the captain, Dennis Saunders, was in charge of football. As we middle-aged gathered in the dressing room our centre-forward, John Tanner, was the last to arrive. John had been a remarkable goalscorer, an amateur international who never seemed to miss the possible chance as long as the ball was on the ground. He was another G. O. Smith, slight and elusive, and I share with him the experience of being the only two amateurs since the war to score in both

First Division football and first-class cricket. Tanner's runs were for Oxford University Cricket Club, his goal for Huddersfield in the First Division, which dates him. He was smoking a cigar as we changed and we chided him, 'You won't last ninety minutes.'

'Don't worry about me. You have to do the work. I earn my keep taking the chances.' In fact he missed the only 3 that came his way, but his point was valid. Six seconds of effective effort from a scoring expert can be worth more than ninety minutes puffing by an average work-rate forward in today's 'total' football.

That great devotee of toil and sweat, Stan Cullis, said of Greaves, 'They say Jimmy does not run around enough. He wouldn't have to for me. I'd tell him to stand around and wait. That would be enough.'

Those whom Cullis tongue-lashed to greater effort might wonder if he could have kept to that, but the thought was right. If a manager has one player with the knack of scoring his instruction to him should be, 'You are only here for the goals.'

Six of the Best

Career Records of Six Outstanding League and International Goalscorers

Season	Club	League		Internationals	
		Goals	Matches	Goals	Matches
Steve BLOOMER					
1892–3	Derby County	*	28		
1893–4		*	25		
1894–5		*	29	3	2
1895–6		*	25	6	2
1896–7		*	29	4	3
1897–8		*	24	2	1
1898–9		*	28	4	3
1899–1900		*	28	1	1
1900–1		24	27	5	2
1901–2		15	29	–	3
1902–3		12	24		
1903–4		20	29	1	1
1904–5		13	29	1	3
1905–6		12	23		
1906–7		6	9		
1906–7	Middlesbrough	18	34	1	2
1907–8		13	34		
1908–9		16	28		
1909–10		8	20		
1910–11	Derby County	19	28		
1911–12		18	36		
1912–13		13	29		
1913–14		2	5		
		352	600	28	23

* Figures are unreliable for these years but Bloomer's total is recorded as 297 goals with Derby, 55 with Middlesbrough.

| Season | Club | League | | Internationals | |
		Goals	Matches	Goals	Matches

George CAMSELL

Season	Club	Goals	Matches	Goals	Matches
1924–5	Durham City	8	12		
1925–6		12	10		
1925–6	Middlesbrough	3	4		
1926–7		59	37		
1927–8		33	40		
1928–9		31	40	6	2
1929–30		28	34	5	2
1930–1		32	37		
1931–2		19	37		
1932–3		17	33		
1933–4		23	36	2	1
1934–5		15	26		
1935–6		29	38	5	4
1936–7		18	22		
1937–8		9	23		
1938–9		12	11		
1939–40		–	1		
		348	441	18	9

20 of Camsell's goals were scored in Third Division North, 93 in the Second Division, 235 in the First Division.

His 18 International Goals in 9 games were: *1929* May 9th 2 v France (4–1), May 11th 4 v Belgium (5–1), October 19th 2 v Ireland (3–0), November 20th 3 v Wales (6–0); *1933* December 6th 2 v France (4–1); *1935* December 4th 2 v Germany (3–0); *1936* April 4th 1 v Scotland (1–1), May 6th 1 v Austria (1–2), May 9th 1 v Belgium (2–3).

William Ralph DEAN

Season	Club	Goals	Matches	Goals	Matches
1923–4	Tranmere Rovers	–	2		
1924–5		27	27		
1924–5	Everton	2	7		
1925–6		32	38		
1926–7		21	27	12	5
1927–8		60	39	4	5
1928–9		26	29	1	3
1929–30		23	25		
1930–1		39	37	–	1
1931–2		45	38	1	1
1932–3		24	39	–	1
1933–4		9	12		
1934–5		26	38		
1935–6		17	29		

| Season | Club | League | | Internationals | |
| | | Goals | Matches | Goals | Matches |

William Ralph DEAN—*cont.*

Season	Club	Goals	Matches	Goals	Matches
1936–7	Everton	24	36		
1937–8		1	5		
1937–8	Notts County	–	3		
1938–9		3	6		
		379	437	18	16

Hughie GALLACHER

Season	Club	Goals	Matches	Goals	Matches
1921–2	Airdrieonians	7	11		
1922–3		10	18		
1923–4		33	34	–	1
1924–5		32	32	5	3
1925–6		9	16	–	1
1925–6	Newcastle United	23	19	3	2
1926–7		36	38	1	3
1927–8		21	32	1	2
1928–9		24	33	8	3
1929–30		29	38	4	2
1930–1	Chelsea	14	30		
1931–2		24	36		
1932–3		19	36		
1933–4		13	23	–	1
1934–5		2	7		
1934–5	Derby County	23	27	–	1
1935–6		15	24		
1936–7	Notts County	25	32		
1937–8		7	13		
1937–8	Grimsby Town	3	11		
1938–9	Gateshead	18	31		
		387*	541*	22	19

* includes Scottish League matches

Jimmy GREAVES

Season	Club	Goals	Matches	Goals	Matches
1957–8	Chelsea	22	35		
1958–9		32	42	1	3
1959–60		*29	40	2	4
1960–1		41	40	13	8
1961–2	A.C. Milan*	9	10		
1961–2	Tottenham Hotspur	21	22	4	7

* Italian League games omitted from final totals

Season	Club	League		Internationals	
		Goals	*Matches*	*Goals*	*Matches*
1962–3	Tottenham Hotspur	37	41	4	8
1963–4		35	41	8	9
1964–5		29	41	6	6
1965–6		15	29	5	9
1966–7		25	38	1	3
1967–8		23	39		
1968–9		27	42		
1969–70		8	29		
1969–70	West Ham	4	6		
1971–2		9	32		
		357	527	44	57

Nat LOFTHOUSE

Season	Club	League		Internationals	
1946–7	Bolton Wanderers	18	40		
1947–8		18	34		
1948–9		7	22		
1949–50		10	35		
1950–1		21	38	2	1
1951–2		18	38	7	7
1952–3		22	36	8	8
1953–4		17	32	6	5
1954–5		15	31	2	5
1955–6		32	36	4	5
1956–7		29	36		
1957–8		17	31		
1958–9		29	37	1	2
1959–60					
1960–1		3	6		
		256	452	30	33

Top Scorer in League Football – Arthur Rowley

The career record of Arthur Rowley gives him the highest total of goals in peacetime League matches in England

Season	Club	Goals	Games
1946–7	West Bromwich Albion	0	2
1947–8	West Bromwich Albion	4	21
1948–9	West Bromwich Albion	0	1
1948–9	Fulham	19	22
1949–50	Fulham	8	34
1950–1	Leicester City	28	39
1951–2	Leicester City	38	42
1952–3	Leicester City	39	41
1953–4	Leicester City	30	42
1954–5	Leicester City	23	36
1955–6	Leicester City	29	36
1956–7	Leicester City	44	42
1957–8	Leicester City	20	25
1958–9	Shrewsbury Town	38	43
1959–60	Shrewsbury Town	32	41
1960–1	Shrewsbury Town	28	40
1961–2	Shrewsbury Town	23	41
1962–3	Shrewsbury Town	24	40
1963–4	Shrewsbury Town	5	19
1964–5	Shrewsbury Town	2	12
		434	619

The Price of a Forward

Of thirty-six British transfers which set new records starting with the first £1,000 transfer, all except six involved forwards.

Year	Name	Position, if not a forward	From	To	Cost
1905	Alf Common		Sunderland	Middlesbrough	£1,000
1907	George Wilson		Everton	Newcastle U.	£1,600
1911	Jock Simpson		Falkirk	Blackburn R.	£1,800
1911	Billy Hibbert		Bury	Newcastle U.	£1,950
1912	Danny Shea		West Ham	Blackburn R.	£2,000
1914	Horace Barnes		Derby County	Manchester C.	£2,500
1919	Frank Barson	Centre-half	Barnsley	Aston Villa	£2,750
1920	Joe Lane		Blackpool	Birmingham	£3,650
1920	Stan Fazackerley		Sheffield United	Everton	£3,750
1920	David Mercer		Hull City	Sheffield U.	£4,500
1921	Tom Hamilton	Right-back	Kilmarnock	Preston N. E.	£4,750
1922	Sidney Puddefoot		West Ham	Falkirk	£5,000
1922	Warney Cresswell	Right-back	South Shields	Sunderland	£5,500
1923	Jack Hill	Centre-half	Plymouth Argyle	Burnley	£6,000
1925	Bob Kelly		Burnley	Sunderland	£6,550
1927	Jimmy Gibson	Left-half	Partick T.	Aston Villa	£7,500
1928	David Jack		Bolton W.	Arsenal	£10,890
1938	Bryn Jones		Wolves	Arsenal	£14,000
1947	Billy Steel		Morton	Derby County	£15,500
1947	Tommy Lawton		Chelsea	Notts County	£20,000
1948	Len Shackleton		Newcastle U.	Sunderland	£20,050
1949	Johnny Morris		Manchester U.	Derby County	£23,850
1949	Eddie Quigley		Sheffield W.	Preston N. E.	£26,500
1950	Trevor Ford		Aston Villa	Sunderland	£30,000
1951	Jackie Sewell		Notts County	Sheffield W.	£34,500
1957	John Charles		Swansea Town	Juventus	£35,000
1958	Cliff Jones		Sheffield W.	Tottenham H.	£45,000
1958	Albert Quixall		Leeds United	Manchester U.	£65,000
1961	Jimmy Greaves		Milan	Tottenham H.	£98,000
1962	Denis Law		Turin	Manchester U.	£115,000
1968	Allan Clarke		Fulham	Leicester C.	£150,000
1970	Martin Peters		West Ham	Tottenham H.	£200,000*
1971	Alan Ball		Everton	Arsenal	£220,000
1972	David Nish	Back	Leicester C.	Derby County	£250,000
1974	Bob Latchford		Birmingham	Everton	£350,000*
1977	Kenny Dalglish		Celtic	Liverpool	£440,000

* one or more players included in fee

David Nish is the only player since 1927 who has set a British record transfer fee without being a forward. Major transfers in 1976 also centred on forwards with over a quarter of a million pounds being paid for Mariner, Hales and Macdonald, with Macdonald's £330,000 the highest.

Scorers of 250 Goals in English Football League Peacetime Matches (to start of 1977–8 season)

	Goals	*Int'l Caps*
G. A. Rowley 1946–1965 (WBA, Fulham, Leicester, Shrewsbury)	434	Nil
W. R. Dean 1923–1939 (Tranmere, Everton, Notts Co.)	379	16
J. Greaves 1957–1971 (Chelsea, Spurs, West Ham)	356	57
S. Bloomer 1892–1914 (Derby, Middlesbrough)	352	23
G. H. Camsell 1924–1939 (Durham, Middlesbrough)	348	9
V. M. Watson 1920–1936 (West Ham, Southampton)	317	5
P. J. W. Atyeo 1951–1966 (Bristol City)	315	6
Joe Smith 1908–1929 (Bolton, Stockport)	315	5
H. Johnson 1919–1936 (Sheffield United, Mansfield)	309	Nil
H. Bedford 1919–1934 (Nottingham Forest, Blackpool, Derby, Newcastle, Sunderland, Bradford, Chesterfield)	306	2
H. K. Gallacher 1921–1939 (Newcastle, Chelsea, Derby, Notts Co., Grimsby, Gateshead)	296	20 Sc.
G. Hodgson 1925–1939 (Liverpool, Aston Villa, Leeds)	296	3
C. Holton 1950–1968 (Arsenal, Watford, Northampton, Crystal Palace, Charlton, Orient)	295	Nil
D. H. Morris 1920–1934 (Fulham, Brentford, Millwall, Swansea, Swindon, Clapton Orient)	291	Nil
J. Hampson 1925–1938 (Nelson, Blackpool)	290	3
R. Crawford 1957–1971 (Portsmouth, Ipswich, Wolves, WBA, Charlton, Colchester, Brighton)	289	2
E. W. Hine 1921–1938 (Barnsley, Leicester, Huddersfield, Manchester Utd.)	286	6
A. Chandler 1920–1936 (QPR, Leicester, Notts Co.)	282	Nil
T. E. Keetley 1919–1934 (Bradford, Notts Co., Doncaster, Lincoln)	278	Nil
G. Brown 1921–1938 (Huddersfield, Aston Villa, Burnley, Leeds, Darlington)	276	6
R. T. Davies 1959–1973 (Chester, Luton, Norwich, Southampton)	276	29 Wa.

	Goals	Int'l Caps
R. Allen 1946–1965 (Port Vale, WBA, Crystal Palace)	274	5
C. M. Buchan 1910–1928 (Sunderland, Arsenal)	272	6
K. Wagstaff 1960–1976 (Mansfield, Hull)	271	Nil
R. Hunt 1959–1972 (Liverpool, Bolton)	268	34
D. B. N. Jack 1919–1934 (Bolton, Arsenal)	266	9
E. C. Harper 1923–1935 (Blackburn, Sheffield Wed., Spurs, Preston North End)	260	1
K. Hector 1962– (Bradford, Derby)	257	2 as sub
N. Lofthouse 1946–1961 (Bolton)	256	33
T. Briggs 1947–1959 (Grimsby, Coventry, Birmingham, Blackburn)	255	Nil
J. Cookson 1925–1938 (Chesterfield, WBA, Plymouth, Swindon)	255	Nil
C. Wayman 1946–1958 (Newcastle, Southampton, Preston North End, Middlesbrough, Darlington)	254	Nil
B. H. Clough 1955–1964 (Middlesbrough, Sunderland)	252	2
I. J. Allchurch 1949–1968 (Swansea, Shrewsbury, Newcastle, Cardiff)	250	68 Wa.
J. Bradford 1920–1936 (Birmingham, Bristol City)	250	12

(Sc. = Scotland, Wa. = Wales)

British Internationals Scoring Ten or More Goals by June 1977

	Main Club	*Goals*		*Matches*	*Dates*
ENGLAND					
Bobby Charlton	Manchester United	49	in	106	1958–1970
Jimmy Greaves	Tottenham Hotspur	44	in	57	1959–1967
Nat Lofthouse	Bolton Wanderers	30	in	33	1950–1958
Tom Finney	Preston North End	30	in	76	1946–1959
Vivian Woodward	Chelsea	29	in	23	1903–1911
Steve Bloomer	Derby County	28	in	23	1895–1907
Geoff Hurst	West Ham	24	in	49	1966–1972
Stan Mortensen	Blackpool	23	in	25	1947–1953
Tommy Lawton	Everton	22	in	23	1938–1948
Mike Channon	Southampton	21	in	45	1972–
Martin Peters	West Ham	21	in	67	1966–1974
George Camsell	Middlesbrough	18	in	9	1929–1936
William Dean	Everton	18	in	16	1927–1932
Roger Hunt	Liverpool	18	in	34	1962–1969
Johnny Haynes	Fulham	18	in	56	1955–1962
Tommy Taylor	Manchester United	16	in	19	1953–1957
Bobby Smith	Tottenham Hotspur	13	in	15	1960–1963
Martin Chivers	Tottenham Hotspur	13	in	24	1971–1973
Wilf Mannion	Middlesbrough	13	in	26	1946–1951
Bryan Douglas	Blackburn Rovers	13	in	36	1957–1963
Charlie Bambridge	Swifts	12	in	18	1879–1887
Gilbert O. Smith	Corinthians	12	in	20	1893–1901
F. Dewhurst	Preston North End	11	in	9	1886–1889
Cliff Bastin	Arsenal	11	in	21	1931–1938
Stanley Matthews	Blackpool	11	in	54	1934–1957
Dennis Wilshaw	Wolverhampton Wanderers	10	in	12	1953–1957
Jackie Milburn	Newcastle United	10	in	13	1948–1955
Allan Clarke	Leeds United	10	in	16	1970–1975
Eric Brook	Manchester City	10	in	18	1929–1937
Francis Lee	Manchester City	10	in	27	1968–1972
Ron Flowers	Wolverhampton Wanderers	10	in	49	1955–1966

In 1936–37 Freddy Steele of Stoke City scored 9 in 6 Internationals

	Main Club	Goals		Matches	Dates
SCOTLAND					
Denis Law	Manchester United	30	in	55	1958–1974
Hughie Gallacher	Newcastle United	24	in	20	1924–1935
Lawrie Reilly	Hibernian	22	in	38	1948–1957
Kenny Dalglish	Celtic	16	in	47	1971–
R. C. Hamilton	Rangers	13	in	11	1899–1904
R. S. McColl	Queen's Park	13	in	13	1896–1908
Billy Steel	Derby County	13	in	30	1947–1953
Alan Gilzean	Tottenham Hotspur	12	in	22	1963–1971
George Ker	Queen's Park	10	in	5	1880–1882
Colin Stein	Rangers	10	in	21	1968–1973
Bobby Johnstone	Hibernian	10	in	17	1951–1956
Bobby Collins	Celtic	10	in	31	1950–1965
WALES					
Trevor Ford	Aston Villa	23	in	38	1946–1956
Ivor Allchurch	Swansea Town	22	in	68	1950–1966
Cliff Jones	Tottenham Hotspur	16	in	59	1954–1969
John Charles	Leeds United	15	in	38	1950–1965
Dai Astley	Aston Villa	12	in	13	1931–1939
Billy Meredith	Manchester United	10	in	48	1895–1920

John Toshack had scored 9 after 29 matches.

NORTHERN IRELAND					
Billy Gillespie	Sheffield United	13	in	25	1913–1930
Joe Bambrick	Linfield	11	in	11	1928–1938
Johnny Crossan	Sunderland	10	in	23	1959–1967
Jimmy McIlroy	Burnley	10	in	55	1951–1965

THE REPUBLIC OF IRELAND'S scorers of ten or more

Don Givens	Queen's Park Rangers	15	in	32	1969–
Jimmy Dunne	Sheffield United	14	in	15	1930–1939
Noel Cantwell	Manchester United	14	in	36	1954–1967

Main Individual Scoring Records

Most Goals in a Game

Scottish Cup	John Petrie (Arbroath) 13 goals v Bon Accord 5.9.1885
FOOTBALL LEAGUE	
Third Division S.	Joe Payne (Luton Town) 10 goals v Bristol Rovers 13.4.1936
Third Division N.	Robert Bell (Tranmere Rovers) 9 goals v Oldham Athletic 26.12.1935
F.A. Challenge Cup	Ted MacDougall (Bournemouth) 9 goals v Margate 20.11.1971
SCOTTISH LEAGUE	
Division 1	Jimmy McGrory (Celtic) 8 goals v Dunfermline Athletic 14.1.1928
Division 2	Owen McNally (Arturlie) 8 goals v Armadale 1.10.1927 Jim Dyet (King's Park) 8 goals v Forfar Athletic 2.1.1930 John Calder (Morton) 8 goals v Raith Rovers 18.4.1936
FOOTBALL LEAGUE	
Division 1	Jimmy Ross jnr. (Preston North End) 7 goals v Stoke City 6.10.1888 Ted Drake (Arsenal) 7 goals v Aston Villa 14.12.1935
Division 2	Tommy Briggs (Blackburn Rovers) 7 goals v Bristol Rovers 5.2.1955 Neville Coleman (Stoke City) 7 goals v Lincoln City 23.2.1957

Most Goals in a Season

FOOTBALL LEAGUE
Division 1	William Dean (Everton)
	60 goals in 39 games 1927–8
Division 2	George Camsell (Middlesbrough)
	59 goals in 37 games 1926/7
Division 3 S.	Joe Payne (Luton)
	55 goals in 39 games 1936–7
Division 3 N.	Ted Harston (Mansfield Town)
	55 goals in 41 games 1936–7
Division 3	Derek Reeves (Southampton)
	39 goals in 46 games 1959–60
Division 4	Terry Bly (Peterborough)
	52 goals in 46 games 1960–1

SCOTTISH LEAGUE
Division 1	William McFadyen (Motherwell)
	52 goals in 34 games 1931–2
Division 2	Jim Smith (Ayr United)
	66 goals in 38 games 1927–8

British International Scorers of 5 or more Goals in a Match

Joe Bambrick (Northern Ireland)
6 goals v Wales at Belfast   1.2.1930
Malcolm Macdonald (England)
5 goals v Cyprus at Wembley   16.4.1974
Willie Hall (England)
5 goals v Northern Ireland at Old Trafford   16.11.1938
Steve Bloomer (England)
5 goals v Wales at Cardiff   16.3.1896
Charles Heggie (Scotland)
5 goals v Ireland at Belfast   20.3.1886
H. A. Vaughton (England)
5 goals v Ireland at Belfast   18.2.1882

World Cup Final Individual Records

Highest scorer in a Final
   Geoff Hurst (England)   3 goals v West Germany in 1966 at Wembley
Highest scorer in Tournament Finals
   Juste Fontaine (France)   13 goals in 1958 in Sweden

Index

© Copyright Cassell & Co. Ltd., 1978